'Culturally, the most dangerous people in the country.'
**Tony Wilson's In the City Music Festival brochure, 1997**

'Full of wild tales from the highest of times, this is the story of an intrepid crew of idealistic hedonists whose quest for freedom and joy created some of the peak moments of Britain's rave counterculture.'
**Matthew Collin, author of *Altered State* and *Rave On***

'Harry's hysterical tale of the adventures of anarchist pranksters DiY takes us on a sharp-witted, semi-mystical trip through the urban party dives of the north and the ancient pathways and sites of the south-west. Embracing the misfits and freaks it meets along the way with a massive hug, *Dreaming in Yellow* bounces somewhere between a magical memoir, acerbic cultural commentary and a rollicking rave story. It slaps us right back to a time of utopian and hedonistic countercultural exploration which, despite the acid spectacles of nostalgia, might just help us to reimagine the shitstorm we're living through now. A riot, a scream, a fucking amazing party!'
**Aaron Trinder, director of *Free Party: A Folk History***

'They had the longest guest list in history and were the only outfit to be thrown out of the Haçienda on their own night. Twice. They were home to the lost and found, the travellers, the groovers, the lovers and the ravers. They put the "E" in Free and the "Ooooo" in Groove, and, sailing under the banner of the Love Cabbage, spread beautiful chaos wherever they landed. DiY – the true Robin Hood pirates of the underground scene.'
**DJ Vertigo**

'If ever a name encapsulated an ethos, it was DiY. Set against swallowing the prêt-à-porter pleasures of consumer society – clubbers too militant about what they want, what they've paid for, their consumer "rights" – they set out on an adventure that was simultaneously musical, psychic and social. An experiment in conviviality. No master plan or manifesto, other than: Do it yer'sen.'

**Scott Oliver, *VICE* magazine**

In 1986, already a veteran of both the Haçienda and numerous festivals, Mark Harrison moved from his hometown of Bolton to Nottingham, intending to become a human rights lawyer.

Instead, he became Harry Harrison and a founding member of DiY, an ever-expanding collective of DJs, party organisers, clubbers, travellers, visionaries and degenerates who achieved international notoriety in the early nineties following their involvement in seminal outlaw events such as the Castlemorton free festival, legendary club nights and music production including an album for Warp Records.

In addition to steering DiY through the debauchery and hedonism of the era, Harry also championed their political and social significance, and that of the wider free party movement, writing numerous articles for magazines such as *i-D*, *The Face*, *Mixmag*, *DJ Mag* and XLR8R. He has been a regular on various discussion panels, including with Howard Marks at the Ministry of Sound, the Salon team at Festival 6 discussing acid house, and the infamous panel on Superclubs at Glasgow's 'In the City' Music Festival.

As the rave generation burned out at the end of the nineties, Harry continued his research whilst living in London and San Francisco, eventually landing in rural Wales where he lives a relatively quiet life and finally wrote this book after twenty years of talking about it.

First published by Velocity Press 2022

velocitypress.uk

Copyright © Harry Harrison 2022

Printed and bound in Great Britain by Clays Ltd, Elcograf S.p.A.

Cover design
Steven Leech

Typesetting
Paul Baillie-Lane
pblpublishing.co.uk

ISBN: 9781913231149

# Dreaming in Yellow

The Story of the DiY Sound System

## Harry
## Harrison

'As far as we can discern, the sole purpose of human existence is to kindle a light in the darkness of mere being.'
**Carl Jung**


'The pursuit of pleasure must be the goal of every rational person.'
**Voltaire**

Dedicated to Pete and the other comrades
who didn't make it through…

# SPECIAL THANKS TO:

Dilys and our children, Iris and Albion, for their patience (kids, please don't read this book until you are at least eighteen); Colin Steven at Velocity Press; Matthew Collin; Aaron Trinder; Steven Leech; Peter Birch; Simon Smith; Grace Sands and Rick Down; Matt Anniss; Adrian 'Pezz' Perry; Kate Martin; David Brooks; Andrew Brooks; Jackie Norbury; Chilly Phil; all the travellers who did so much (too many to list); Jack Harlow; Scott Oliver; Laurence Ritchie; Emma Kirby; Boysie Bawden; Mark Darby; Dave Langford; Andrew Riley; Juliet Russell; Diccon, Helen and Also Festival, Smokescreen; New Order; Neil Tolliday; Richie Jones; Tim Holmes; Pod; Miles Halpin; Doug Gilbert; John Stripey; John Ousey; Jean Harry; Jane and Tony Harrison; Judy and Gordon; David and Amanda; George, Albert, Rob and Sam; Hector Caton; Soma and Jelly; William Blake; Tim Wilderspin; Aberytswyth; Sad Dad's Club; Joy Divison; Barbara Lyons; Cath Cave; Emma Goldsmith; Emma Goldman; Jane Bromley; Noel Kilbride and Carmel; Devon Jevons; Sheena; Becki Pate; David Kerslake; George Miles; Brenda Harrington; Steve Ingram; Daniel Bennett; Joseph Savage; Dave Green; Matthew Twigger; Richard Bland; Helen Wilcoxson; Helen Waddingham; Nikki Lee; Jason Cook; Lee Simpson; Brett Slater; Drew Hemment; Mel Woods; Peter Swift; Gaynor Pearce; Angus Finlayson; Dickie and Jane; Becky Seagere; Dave Mooring; Julie Hood; Clifford; Helen Jayne; Quadrant; Ged Day: Damian Stanley; Moffball; Rob Lights; Nicki Wells; Lucy Fleming-White; Adey Barsby |; Marcus Woody; Damian O'Grady; Charles Webster; Andrew Weatherall; Lee Etherington; Noel Bowden; Sally Morris; Al Royale; Giddy Fruit; Simon Thomas;

John Callow; Lisa Jones (x2); Elizabeth Drake; Tony Davis; Matt Smith; Nick Clague; Alan Lodge; David Bowen; Sharon Storer; Julian Hicks; Stroudos; Debbie and Ross; Richard Burton (not that one); Mark Wightman; David Hayes; Darren Murphy; Sarah Halliwell; Steve Cobby; James Baillie; Dave Beer, Ralph Lawson; Huggy; Justin Robertson; Otto and Jake; Darren Davies; Derrick Carter; Luke Solomon; Mark Farina; Jared Wilson; Carl Loben; Lily Moayeri; Sally Curls; Pete One; Rory Colquhoun: Scotty Clarke; Steve Grey; Bill Drummond; Jimmy Cauty; Julian Cope; Culam Nelson; Rebecca Cheetham; Nancie Davison; Amber and Neil; Callum Wordsworth; Nicki Jane; Molly Ward; Jonny Lee; Neil Macey; Shaun Ryder; Bez; Tony Wilson; Robin Banks; Ken Kesey; Andrea and Barry; Mad Mandy from Preston; Jonny Dangerous; Charlie Bucket; Lisa Bailey; Joanne Wain; Mandy Molyneux; Mark and Rose; Mick Leivers; Mark Blissenden; Andy Compton; Jon Kosecki; Steve Bryant; Steve Wilson; Rob Crook; Phineas Watson; Mark Johnson; Gary Johnson and the Earthtone posse; Wicked Crew; Hardkiss; Alvaro; Alex Fabregas; Charles MacNulty; Adrienne Chang; Leslee Cross; Freddie; Tee Cardaci: Ursula and Tom…

And all the other dancers, chancers and romancers everywhere.
Apologies if I forgot anyone, tricky list . . .
Big Love
Harry

# FOREWORD

## The Long Night's Journey into Day

Sitting round a living room in the rundown New Basford area
of Nottingham, Simon, Harry, Pete, Rick and Jack from the
DiY sound system are planning their next big party, swapping gossip and deciding who's going to drive to Manchester,
Liverpool, Birmingham and Sheffield to distribute tickets. On
the walls, rave flyers compete for space with anarchist posters. A
mongrel dog sprawls in front of the fire. The phone rings and
the stereo plays constantly; Pete gets up every five minutes to
mix in the next record. An anarcho-hippy-punk in oily overalls
drops by to tape a house track.

This all seems like it was a long time ago now – sometime towards
the end of 1990, back when people still phoned each other on
landlines and taped records onto cassettes. It's an extract from an
article I wrote for *i-D* magazine – an early attempt to explain how
DiY and sound systems like them were creating something genuinely new and vital.

'House music anarchists' is how the article somewhat mischie-
vously called them, describing how this intrepid crew of idealistic
hedonists was part of a new generation of sound systems that had
evolved out of the rave scene of 1989. They had been inspired by
the euphoric liberties of illegal parties in fields, warehouses and
aircraft hangers but had become disillusioned with exploitative
promoters, rip-off ticket prices and dodgy parties that got busted

before they even got going. Charged up with the daredevil spirit of the time, they decided they could do better and set out on a madcap quest for freedom and joy that would take them across countries and continents over the years that followed, inspiring many others along the way.

DiY were a somewhat motley crew of nonconformists and misfits, and its members were already veterans of various subsects of British youth culture at the time – the post-punk movement around Manchester and the north-west, Factory Records and the Haçienda; the free festival circuit, where Hawkwind's psychoactive space-rock surged out over the wide-open spaces of the English countryside; the hippie-punk squat scene in Nottingham's Hyson Green and Forest Fields; the city centre funk, soul and hip-hop clubs; and early house music nights where the sounds of Chicago, Detroit and New York felt so shockingly new. All these inputs and influences came together, intermingled and mutated to make DiY unique.

From reggae sound system crews onwards, collectives of like-minded souls have always played a crucial role in developing dance music culture. The alliances of dancefloor comrades that coalesced out of the chaos of the rave scene to form sound system collectives in Britain in the early 1990s were also inspired by punk rock's emancipatory ideas of self-sustaining, autonomous sonic activism. The free party philosophy that they developed offered an alternative to conventionally transactional economic relationships within dance music culture and showed how an idealistic collective could exert a transformative influence on those who gathered around it.

The idea of the dancefloor as a nocturnal zone of liberty in an iniquitous society goes back to the early days of disco in the United States, when nightclubs were refuges for the marginalised and oppressed. From the disco era onwards, dance music culture has continued to play a vital role in creating environments in which people can celebrate in freedom. In Britain, the rise of acid house and the rave scene represented a reassertion of communal and egalitarian values in reaction to the individualistic free market doctrine of right-wing prime minister Margaret Thatcher's Conservative government, setting the scene for DiY to thrive.

But it was their chance meeting with some convivial travellers at Glastonbury Festival in 1990 that opened up the way forward. The cultural synergy of travellers and ravers was crucial to some of the most important developments that followed amid the kaleidoscopic whirl of sound and motion that was the 1990s. The travellers had the sites and the outlaw wisdom; the ravers had the new sounds of house and techno, and, of course, the vital chemical accelerator, the drug that subverted preconceptions and broke down cultural barriers – MDMA. Links with the travellers also connected DiY and other sound systems to British utopian traditions dating back to the seventeenth century and radical pre-socialist movements like the Diggers and the Levellers, who believed that the land should belong to all and that no lord had the right to stand above any commoner.

The travellers had bitter personal experience of the abuse of state power to crush cultural dissent. At the Windsor Free Festival in 1974 and the 'Battle of the Beanfield' near Stonehenge in 1985, they had been subjected to violent assaults by police whose aversion to 'alternative lifestyles' was demonstrated with disproportionate force. Soon enough, the free parties came under attack too. As far back as 1990, Simon DK described a raid on one event where DiY were playing, as police officers stormed the place and trashed the speakers: 'They were smashing the decks, confiscating records. There was a guy standing on the roof of this van filming it and the police were trying to truncheon his legs.'

The idea that no one was making a pile of money out of these events sometimes bemused the authorities. Rick from DiY, then known as Digs and now as Grace Sands, once told me about a raid on a party in the south-west of England when the police were completely perplexed because they didn't find bundles of banknotes after nabbing the instigators: 'They couldn't believe it was free. They couldn't understand why we would want to come down from Nottingham to do something for nothing. They were convinced there was a Mr Big behind it, making millions. We only had three quid between the four of us. They told us we were too scruffy to be acid house promoters.'

The energies of the free party generation reached an ecstatic peak at the legendary week-long festival-rave that drew some 30,000 revellers to Castlemorton Common in 1992. Castlemorton sparked a tabloid moral panic that caused the Conservative government to bring in the Criminal Justice and Public Order Bill in an attempt to shut down such unlicensed events forever, particularly if the DJs were playing 'sounds wholly or predominantly characterised by the emission of a succession of repetitive beats', as the legislation memorably put it. The law didn't kill off free parties completely, but there hasn't been an event on the scale of Castlemorton since then.

For a few glorious but intense years, the DiY crew were part of a network of free-thinkers and bliss-seekers that stretched across the country, skipping from club night to free party, licensed rave to illegal festival. 'We spent our time in the pursuit of life, liberty and happiness,' as Harry writes in this book. Musically, DiY's DJs followed their own path, and their reputations grew as a result: Digs and Woosh, Emma, Jack, Pezz, Pip and the inimitable Simon DK; Tim and Max, Cookie, Little Lee, Dick, Osborne, Nail, Ged and Damian, Stoney, Jules . . . the creative community around the crew expanded as their renown spread.

Of course, it wasn't all glittering nights and blissful dawns; there were some calamitous misadventures and harsh comedowns too. As Pete Woosh once eloquently put it: 'Many of us flew close to the sun and got burned.'

Pete passed away in 2020, a year after DiY celebrated their 30th anniversary with a soul-stirring series of parties and social events in Nottingham. For those of us who were fortunate enough to be there, it was clear that three decades after it all began, what had endured through all those years was music, friendship, a collective sense of idealism and an irrepressible appetite for joy that continues to bind people together.

DiY's escapades on the outlaw frontiers of the rave scene have already established their place in British countercultural history. But the deeper, more personal story of how it all happened, and how it was lived by the people who were involved, hasn't really been set down in detail – until now, anyway. So read on, and let Harry tell you all about it.

**Matthew Collin**

# PROLOGUE

Late evening, Friday 22nd May 1992. My oldest friend and I had walked slowly, disbelievingly, up the small hill and were now sitting on the grass, pleasingly cool after the heat of the gloriously radiant spring day. Silently we looked out across at what had been, until a few short hours ago, a peaceful and forgotten corner of Middle England. Now, in the settling, liminal dusk, it resembled some giant military operation, or perhaps a huge, dark creature with endless rows of bright white eyes.

In every direction, visible from our vantage point, luminous streams of headlights flowed along the entry tracks and the roads stretching into the distance. Several thousand cars, vans, trucks, buses and horseboxes containing unknown numbers of ebullient revellers were pouring onto the enormous common laid out below us. Twenty-four hours earlier, we had never heard of this place. Castlemorton Common had just been another name on the map, another quintessentially sleepy English shire; it was certainly not the sort of place where history is made.

On that portentous night, Pete was two days shy of his twenty-seventh birthday; I was eighteen months to the day younger. It had been ten or so years since we had met at an underage drinking establishment in Bolton, and we had been through innumerable existential rites of passage together during the intervening, tumultuous decade. We had been founder members of a music collective that had grown exponentially in tandem with the explosion of dance music and had, beyond our wildest expectations, succeeded in uniting our twin passions of music and protest into a remarkable, cohesive alliance.

Pete had introduced me to Crass, the seminal anarcho-punk band, and in their brilliant pamphlet 'A Series of Shock Slogans and Mindless Token Tantrums', they quoted Wally Hope as declaring: 'Our temple is sound, we fight our battles with music, drums like thunder, cymbals like lightning, banks of electronic equipment like nuclear missiles of sound. We have guitars instead of Tommy Guns.'

Only we had replaced guitars with acid house. Seemingly out of nowhere, house music had shown every possibility of providing the perfect weapon with which to dismantle, in some small but meaningful way, the anodyne and monotonous world which we had grown up in and largely rejected. From small parties around inner-city Nottingham in the summer of 1989 onwards, our collective, known as DiY, had tried to use the irresistible power of these new electronic sounds as a musical weapon to challenge convention, to attempt to unite people beneath a banner of liberation and pleasure. And now here we were, witnessing the effects that the actions of our group, and those of many more, had catalysed into this huge free festival.

Various sound systems, including our own, were transmitting their rhythmic pulses across the darkening common, mingling with shouts of joy, recognition and exhilaration. This looked, smelled and sounded like revolution: a righteous revolution against the entrenched and heartless establishment which had been quietly and ruthlessly running England for centuries. We had intended to shock and to challenge, and now the sheer scale of this revolution had become clear; ranged endlessly below us, magnificent yet terrifying, and for once it looked like we were winning.

The first free festivals we had attended many years before had been small, myopic and backward-looking affairs, culturally and

musically outdated. But now we had arrived at this, a whole generation seemingly drawn to these relentless beats and their concomitant
clarion call to social action.

I turned to Pete and voiced my fears: 'You know what, I think we
might have pushed this too far.'

Pete, looking out over the great chaos below, just replied quietly:
'It's never too far.'

1

Nottingham's Lace Market is an ancient cluster of thoroughfares, which, according to the city's website, was once home to troglodyte settlers many millennia ago. It has retained its labyrinthine jumble of small, narrow streets, which for decades contained factories involved in the production of lace. It now hosts many boutique shops, bars and small businesses. And nightclubs.

Located at 41–43 St Mary's Gate and opened in 1983, the Garage was the most renowned. Formerly the Ad-Lib club, this dark, confined rabbit warren of a space was arranged over three floors, black-walled and claustrophobic. There was a dancefloor in the cellar, a café on the top floor and a courtyard outside where the clubbers could cool off and talk. Located on the middle floor was a split area, with a bar at the top of the winding stairs and a sweatbox of a dance-floor – high-walled, black, windowless, sticky.

At some point during 1986, Graeme Park played house music in this room, probably becoming the first person to do so publicly anywhere in the United Kingdom. This statement might be contested, however, and there are some who would claim that DJs at venues in Manchester or London were playing house just as early. But whatever the chronology, Nottingham could count itself lucky. Within these dark walls, Graeme would continue to play to a small but prescient dancefloor every week for the next three years, establishing himself and the club as the first epicentre of this new music in the Midlands.

By 1989, among those who had begun to congregate every Saturday during those halcyon days at what would later become the Kool Kat were a dissolute group, noticeably different to the fashion-orientated regulars. Although equally as seduced by the twin synthetic temptations of house music and ecstasy, this loosely organised and growing gang had emerged from different cultural origins. This grouping of punks, squatters, ex-students, anarchists, vegans and other nonconformists, with a smattering of football lads and wannabe fashionistas thrown in, celebrated shared values coming not from fashion but from politics. Their politics, however, were based on hedonism as much as protest, dancing as much as discussion.

For several months in 1989, after a summer drenched in the music of Soul II Soul, Happy Mondays and the Stone Roses, these friends had been organising parties amid the large Victorian houses and squats around Forest Fields, Hyson Green and Mapperley Park in Nottingham's NG7 postcode. Based on the blues parties so prevalent in those areas back then, these events were ramshackle, with music usually provided by cassettes and small rented sound systems or loud stereos, combined with smoke machines and strobes. Drawing increasing numbers of partygoers to their all-night sessions, and the first stirrings of interest from the local police force, these could unquestionably be labelled acid house parties. Do-it-yourself acid house parties, suffused with the music of Detroit, Chicago and London, of Phuture, Renegade Soundwave, MESH, Mr Fingers, Rhythim is Rhythim. House music, ecstasy, friends, flashing lights, smoke machines, lack of sleep, chaos, the police. The basics.

Later that year, the time came to experiment with these ingredients in a proper venue. On a bitterly cold Thursday night, 23rd November 1989, something unforeseen was happening within the confines of that legendary nightclub. Outside, the streets were empty and quiet; inside, an eclectic mix of those drawn from the fringes of the city's alternative crowd was dancing to house music. As the biggest revolution in musical culture since punk was beginning to sweep all before it, it was no longer considered the private preserve of hip Londoners and clubbers; this was, in hindsight, a very early genesis of the counterculture adopting house as its soundtrack. This dynamic, unbeknown to all that time, would lead to the near-complete domination of youth culture by electronic dance music, and eventually to the insurrection at Castlemorton and beyond.

But back in the inky black box of the Garage, no one knew or cared about the future. This was still just some friends having fun. That a temporary autonomous zone had been created in a public place and the ingredients mixed together effortlessly that night was not the immediate concern; right now, there was a large vegan birthday cake to be eaten. In the DJ booth was one of the music obsessives within this nascent crew, Simon Smith. Wrestling with the Technics 1200 record decks, which were new to us all, he played one of his epic sets that were to become ubiquitous over the next few years, and although the mixing was occasionally off, the musical choices were transcendent. Simon had arrived at house musically via punk and its antecedents, just one of the myriad roots that would collide and synthesise into the early acid house movement.

One of these roots would come from the On-U Sound label, through the genius production of Adrian Sherwood, arriving via the electronic warpings of Tackhead, Gary Clail and Mark Stewart. Another was through the punk-influenced twelve-inch singles of World Domination Enterprises and Renegade Soundwave, and another, the purer house and techno, imported from the States and available in one small section of Nottingham's Selectadisc and Arcade Records. Simon managed to weave all these disparate elements together that night, topped only by a new track, representing another piece in the house jigsaw, 808 State's 'Pacific State' – this was a new creature, sophisticated house music, relaxed and made in Manchester.

As the dancing continued, with constant sprayings of the smoke machine and people face to face with the strobe, in the bar there were other conversations taking place. It was my twenty-third birthday and we were intoxicated on many different levels, not just the obvious intoxication of drugs and alcohol but also the intoxication of possibility presented by all these different types of people, this variety of youth cults and subcults dancing together to this new music. At the dread hour of two, as we spilt out raucously into the deserted streets of St Mary's Gate, and in the days and weeks to come, this night would be discussed endlessly. What had worked and what hadn't? Did we need a regular venue? Did we need more DJs and lights, more records and a more reliable source of pills?

And, with greater imperative, we needed a name to unite behind to proclaim ourselves as an actual entity. As we threw more house parties around Nottingham's less salubrious quarters, obtained decks and bought records, someone must have commented that, as an outfit, we were very 'do it yourself'. This reflected not only the punk ethos of our approach to parties but also our opposition to the commercialisation that had already begun to creep into the pay party scene and our determination to proceed as a collective with no individuals making a quick buck from the hard work of others. A few weeks before, we had driven back from a big Biology pay party down south, which had spectacularly failed to materialise, and we reflected that we could do better ourselves. Over many drinks in the Golden Fleece pub on Mansfield Road in the following days, we agreed that 'diy' would be our name.

It stuck well, and I can honestly say that, although over the last thirty years we have many regrets as an organisation, the name is not one of them. This book is my attempt to document the story of that organisation and of the simultaneous origins of the free party movement. Writing this with the advantage of thirty years' hindsight, some things have become clearer, others more opaque. At some point, 'diy' became 'DiY'. At another, we had a functioning crew of fourteen DJs, two record labels, recorded an album for Warp, set up a recording studio and became, according to *i-D* magazine in 1997, 'The world's most famous sound system'. We also threw some fairly blinding parties. Inevitably, much detail and clarity has been lost to history; my recall is gratuitously subjective and may provoke howls of protest. For this, I can only apologise in advance, my main excuse being the considerable level of drug consumption involved in these adventures and the three decades that lie between these events and their recording. To misquote the comedian Charlie Fleischer: 'If you can remember the nineties, then you weren't really there.'

It is of little surprise that the three pivotal meetings which would eventually lead to the creation of DiY occurred in the context of a public house, a nightclub and a drug deal. That they all also involved music is perhaps even more predictable. Peter Birch and I both grew up in Bolton, a post-industrial mill town on the northern edge of Manchester, meeting one night in December 1983 in a pub called the Victoria, but known to all as 'Fannies', so named after all the dicks that went there. It did possess one redeeming feature, however, which was that it would serve beer to anyone who looked over fourteen. Our initial conversation was sparked by my wearing an Echo and the Bunnymen badge and their upcoming gig at the Manchester Apollo.

'Oi, mate, you off to see the Bunnymen?'

'Yeah.'

'Any chance of a lift?'

'Dunno, I'll ask my mum.'

Upon such sparkling repartees are lifelong friendships born. With a square jaw, piercing stare and a sharp dress sense, Pete was small in stature but great of heart, and he already had the most encyclopaedic knowledge of music of anyone I had ever met. I was sixteen and he was seventeen, being born eighteen months to the day before me, on the twenty-third of the month. For any William

Burroughs aficionados, Discordians, KLF enthusiasts or ex-members of Spiral Tribe reading this, more about all that twenty-three stuff later.

Cemented by our shared passion for music, William Blake, anarchist politics and heavy drinking, we soon became firm friends. We also shared a love of football, both being Manchester United supporters, which in Bolton is only marginally less disapproved of than being a sex offender. Pete later denied his support for the Red Devils and switched to Bolton Wanderers, although I distinctly remember him possessing a MUFC pillowcase.

Many endless afternoons were idled away listening to music in his bedroom while we got very stoned and surreptitiously necked the cans of Special Brew that his dad hid badly in a cupboard. Pete played me music from genres I didn't even know existed: Fela Kuti, Kraftwerk, Carmen McRae, John Coltrane, Hawkwind and Planet Gong, Crass and Flux, Led Zeppelin, Nina Simone, Pharaoh Sanders, Gil Scott-Heron, On-U Sound. A truly eclectic baptism into the wondrous world of music that was out there, taking us way beyond the confines of a suburban bedroom in Bolton; it was life-affirming, challenging, angry, beautiful, vital, strange.

Where we really met musically was our shared devotion to Factory Records. Devotion is a strong word, but the religious connotation accurately describes the strength of feeling we and many others had for the Manchester-based label that had brought the world Joy Division, New Order, A Certain Ratio, The Durutti Column, and so much more. Beyond the music, everything about Factory – the attitude, the design, the inherently anarchistic approach to business, the contracts signed in blood – became the benchmark for Pete and I on many fronts, and remained so for decades.

At the house parties we frequented, the Human League's 1981 album *Dare* had been the staple musical fare, and many adolescent fumblings had taken place on piles of coats in a spare bedroom as the proto-house electronica of 'Love Action' and 'Open Your Heart' had spun on a single turntable downstairs. In March 1983, however, New Order's 'Blue Monday' was released and nothing was ever the same again. From the haunting, glacial and sombre songs of Joy Division, which still remain some of the greatest music ever made, via the grief-laden electronic experimentation of New Order's first album, *Movement*, the band had arrived at this.

Still the biggest-selling twelve-inch single of all time, and co-produced by New York electro pioneer Arthur Baker, 'Blue Monday' was huge in every way, from the enormous kick drum and the ruthless four-four beat, the production was in your face, the beats and syncopation relentless, the vocals cryptic yet somehow profound. I first heard this monster at the glamorous setting of Bolton's Cinderellas Rockerfellas nightclub. Having over-indulged in a rather dodgy combination of magic mushrooms and tequila slammers at a mate's flat up the road, I had just left the club to vomit over the edge of the fire escape as vivid hallucinations warped the sky into some kind of living Turner landscape. When I staggered back inside, those vast sparse bass kicks were so intense and demanding that I was simply halted in my tracks and stood motionless for the entire seven minutes and twenty-nine seconds. It would have been beyond me to explain precisely why this piece of music created by a band twelve miles down the road sounded so revolutionary. Within five or six years, I would have the innate understanding that this was a very early version of what would become known, via electro and Chicago, Detroit and New York, as house music, and that this music would take over my soul and provide the soundtrack and driving force of my adult life.

Over the next couple of years, and expanding from that initial meeting with Pete, our circle of friends grew. This was my first experience of being in a gang – not a gang in the sense of violence and money, but in a like-minded group where somehow the whole had a separate existence greater than the sum of its individuals. Ours was a mixed crew with both male and female members, attending various local schools including Smithills, Bolton School, Dean High School, Thornleigh, and a crew from Turton school who turned up at my first proper party. My family lived in a modern, red-brick, four-bedroom house off Chorley New Road in Bolton. My mum worked for Salford Social Services and my dad was by that point the chief executive of Greater Manchester Council, later responsible for the renovation of Manchester Central Station into G-Mex and a frequent guest on BBC's Look North and ITV's Granada Reports, where a certain Tony Wilson was the anchor, with whom he had a friendship going back to the seventies.

It was in their house, having somehow persuaded my parents to go out for the night, that I held my seventeenth birthday party. Contrary to the prevailing wisdom of the time, I just invited everyone I knew and told them to bring everyone they knew. Even in that pre-Facebook era, this proved to be a foolish move. Several hundred teenagers turned up, many from the sixth form college I attended but many more from the other schools of the new friends I had made. People rolled in, filled the house, trashed it. Echo and the Bunnymen, The Jam, Teardrop Explodes, Stiff Little Fingers, The Damned and the Human League were played very loud on my dad's stereo, his whisky was drunk, there was much vomiting, and all my mum's confidential paper records from social services were thrown out of the window and sent fluttering down the stairs. All fairly standard teenage fare, but two things made that night noteworthy. Firstly, the fact that I had never felt so satisfied in my life at this wonderful chaos, and the thought that I had organised it. Incredibly, my parents let me do the same thing a year later for my eighteenth birthday, when even more people turned up, including some of the Bolton punks who ripped the front door off its hinges and stole my dad's car.

The second noteworthy event was meeting a remarkable young man called Whitey. At the height of the teen madness, having just asked some random person not to set fire to the curtains, I looked up to see a tall guy in a raincoat, black drainpipe trousers and brothel creepers descending the stairs. With his blond floppy fringe, he was the embodiment of the post-punk alternative look. Although I have never told him this, my immediate thought was that he was Bolton's coolest teenager, cemented in my estimation when I discovered that he had a car. He later divulged (thirty-three years later, Boltonians not being noted for their fulsome use of praise) that he thought I was alright, as he'd just been through the records in my bedroom and found some Killing Joke.

Whitey, Pete and I became firm friends, and this became the nucleus of our gang, certainly the musical nucleus. Just as obsessed by music as Pete, and a highly competent drummer, Whitey would go on to join many bands, including the Electro Hippies. These two individuals were the first people I would meet for whom music was not just a background soundtrack to life but front and centre in terms of importance. To them, music was life. Whitey was a great admirer of Crass, had been to stay on their commune in Epping Forest and was the first person I had met who would have called themselves an anarchist. We were to meet many more. Although greatly influenced by the politics of Crass and Flux of Pink Indians, and the whole anarcho-punk scene, in all honesty I was never a big fan of the music, although their rejectionist politics became increasingly influential. I understood that their almost shouted, relentlessly polemical lyrics and jagged music reflected their inherent anger at the world, which we intuitively shared.

Along with two of Whitey's friends, Dave Hayes and Coupey, and a genuinely committed punk from Edgeworth called Miles who introduced me to the music of the Mob, we began to frequent alternative discos in Bolton, Wigan and Manchester. There we would dance, or more likely sit and drink, to Southern Death Cult, Bauhaus, the Birthday Party, Theatre of Hate, Joy Division, plus, of course, classics by The Clash, The Stranglers and other punk greats. On a Monday night, up to fifteen of us would pile into Dave's decrepit transit van and scream down the A666 to the alternative night at the Ritz in Manchester. Dave was a mechanic and prided himself on his reckless driving abilities, each week timing how fast he could get from the Golden Lion in Bolton to the door of the Ritz in Manchester, a journey of around twelve miles. His record was nine minutes.

If this was a time of musical discovery, then it was equally a time of sexual and chemical discovery. Part of our rapidly expanding gang, Sarah was a pupil at a different school but lived nearby and together we mutually discovered the delights of sex and drugs , initially in the form of cannabis. She and her best friend Sheila became obsessed with David Bowie, particularly the *Hunky Dory* and *Ziggy Stardust* albums. She had very tolerant parents, and often we would gather, my mate Chris from school in attendance too, and get very stoned in her parentless house and listen to Bowie endlessly. Compared to the remorseless and debauched chemical consumption that the nineties would bring, there seems now a touching naivety to our exploits, but at the time it felt pleasingly deviant. As in the Howard Marks biopic *Mr Nice*, the first time I got stoned the world seemed to change colour; no longer was I marooned in a dull, monochrome northern mill town but now possessed the means of instant, dreamy escape.

Looking back with the bonus of hindsight there have been several pivotal nights in my life that have changed everything, shifted the parameters of my thoughts and attitude. One such night occurred at this time, at some point in 1983, at my friend Chris' house in Adlington. While our gang had all been smoking draw, as it was then known in the north-west, for a while none of us had actually done a trip yet. We had begun to hang out with the polydrug-using Bolton punks, who would frequent the moors surrounding Bolton and Rivington in the autumn months to look for magic mushrooms and who could obtain microdots and small blotters of acid.

As a group, we had many stoned discussions around whether we were ready to take a trip, in between giggling and going to the garage for munchies. I wish I had taped those conversations, as they would be comical to listen to now: four or five stoned but earnest seventeen-year-olds worrying about the kid who jumped off the bridge thinking they could fly and the guy who took too much and never came back. So eventually, we thought fuck it, let's do it. Around six or seven of us gathered at Chris' mum's house and, with some trepidation, all stuck a little serrated blotter on our tongues.

There was then the waiting phase, familiar to anyone who's ever done acid or mushrooms, where nothing happens. Someone had heard that it was important to be comfortable and so we sat on the bed, on cushions, on a beanbag. And then, slowly and imperceptibly, that feeling diffused from my stomach, my guts and into my throat, my mouth and my brain. And it grew and removed me to a very different place.

Many years later, in a farmhouse near Exeter and following a particularly spectacular night of indulgence, our friend 'Dangerous' Dave would crystallise this as 'acid is spiritual, ecstasy is emotional and ketamine is just plain surreal'. Perfect summary. As the trip and the night wore on, my mind opened up to places I didn't know existed. Everything seemed fresh and painted in new colours. A drab semi in Lancashire became a palace of earthly delights. We were doing William Blake at school and I somehow knew that his lines about holding 'Infinity in the palm of your hand, and Eternity in an hour' was not just a metaphor but somehow a fundamental truth. I felt linked to these young friends, who incidentally looked equally as overwhelmed as I felt, not just as casual acquaintances but as microcosmic parts of a cosmic whole. We spent some hours bewitched by a poster from The Clash's *Combat Rock* album. There are several hanging baskets in the back of the café where the band members are sitting around drinking. In our collective brain, these baskets turned into beehives, into great dangling swarms of bees. It was not so much that they looked like bees; on LSD, they were bees, alive and real and yet not dangerous or threatening, something to be marvelled at, like a great painting coming alive.

No doubt all this is from the rose-tinted vantage point of decades later. At the time, I probably just wanted to laugh uncontrollably, and yet afterwards I was unquestionably altered. Inevitably, given the ying-yang of all things, the comedown was not too pleasant, my cheeks hurt from laughing and in the harsh light of morning, my hands seemed to have gone a strange greeny-purple colour.

Word spread at school that week that we had taken acid and a couple of my mates gave me sincere warnings that this path would lead to disaster and mental breakdown, but I wasn't listening. I wanted to do this again, and soon, this staying up all night to greet the dawn with my mind on a different plane. For a few hours, it felt as though all the tedium of my sixteen years of existence had briefly fallen away as the doors of perception had opened in just the way the poets and the counterculture legends had said they would. Our small gang of aspiring psychonauts had crossed a line, one which we would and could not step back across and which proved to be the first of many lines we would cross in the years ahead.

# 2

Away from the psychic and sensual awakenings of a group of teenagers in Bolton, this was a time of wider political and cultural extremes and social polarisation. In the UK, Margaret Thatcher had been in power since 1979 and had, in her brutal determination to reduce inflation, destroy union power and introduce free market economics, pushed unemployment to over three million. She had, in the process, and for reasons which our fledgling political brains could not comprehend, won a second election in 1983 with an increased majority.

Her transformation of the Conservative Party to a radical, neo-liberal free market philosophy, rejecting any notion of the collective spirit was further proven, if proof were needed, in the titanic struggle of the Miners' Strike in 1984–5. While operating behind the smokescreen of Ian MacGregor and the National Coal Board and publicly remaining above the fray, behind the scenes Mrs Thatcher employed all the dark arts and might of the British state to bring down the miners and consequently crush union power.

For those of us growing up in such dark times there was another reality which pushed things towards the apocalyptic. We lived in constant fear of the four-minute warning, which would apparently be broadcast, through some unnamed medium, upon the launch and detection of nuclear weapons by the two great superpowers, America and the Soviet Union. Life in the European Theatre (as Europe was then known militarily and which provided the title of a great compilation album) was set against this ever-present threat.

At school, we would discuss what each of us would do when this incredibly short warning of impending doom was given, and sombre government pamphlets were distributed advising that an all-out thermonuclear war could best be survived by placing some doors and cushions against a wall and waiting a week or so before emerging to carry on as before.

It was within this unsettling social and political environment that for many the genuine street anger of punk took hold and mutated into a philosophy of rejection of conventional politics, religion and society. This anarchism was not the comic-book pastiche of Johnny Rotten snarling at a generation to 'get pissed, destroy' but a genuine libertarian wholesale refusal to participate in any societal norms, to reject authority in all its forms.

Spearheading this movement were Crass, who were living in a collective spirit in Epping, from 1978 issuing their black and white singles and albums with provocative titles and 'pay no more than' stickers, which some workers at the pressing plant refused to handle due to the inflammatory and blasphemous nature of the lyrics. Their uncompromising attitude and approach, unifying a militant approach to politics, environmentalism, feminism and animal rights, combined with their adopted uniform of all black, mainly ex-military clothes and stark slogans ('There is no Authority but Yourself'), caught the imagination and fervour of whole swathes of disaffected youth.

This was not the politics of an occasional demo or a meeting, this was immersive and holistic, and certainly for individuals such as Crass, living almost completely outside the system, this was not about voting every five years but about living by example, every minute of every day. This anti-authoritarian rejectionism was not new, of course. Collective, pre-industrial communes and societies could be traced back millennia across the world and certainly in the West to the feudal era, which many thinkers have seen as a golden age predating the innate brutality of capitalism.

Magna Carta itself was a very early example of the commoners laying out their demands to wrest absolute power from the hands of the monarchy, which then was synonymous with the state. England had its own revolution and civil war in the mid-seventeenth century, becoming the first nation to execute its own king and replace it with an early notion of a democratic republic or 'commonwealth'. Leading directly from this came the thoroughly radical demands of groups such as the Diggers and the Levellers in the 1650s, who called for a 'levelling' of wealth and the division of land into small, sustainable communes.

In the eighteenth century, the French Revolution had led to the removal of the monarchy and the execution of virtually the entire aristocracy in the name of 'liberty, equality and fraternity'. Across Europe in the nineteenth century, the great political movements that are still with us fired generation after generation into the radical restructuring or wholesale overthrowing of society. Communism, socialism, anarchism; all huge social movements which in different ways sought the downfall of capitalism. Of these, the influence of Karl Marx and Friedrich Engels through their books such as *The Communist Manifesto* and *Das Kapital* is well documented and widely known, particularly as Marxism went on to become the official doctrine of the new Soviet government in Russia following the 1917 revolution.

Anarchism, however, never really became a mass movement, apart from a few notable exceptions, and has been much misunderstood historically. Etymologically, the word combines the Greek prefix 'an', meaning without, and 'archos', meaning leader. Ideologically codified by nineteenth-century agitators such as Bakunin, Kropotkin and Proudhon, anarchism has many layers of meaning. While its basic definition is clear – a political structure without rulers – on a deeper level, anarchism as a philosophy is opposed to all hierarchical structures and pyramids of power imposed from above. So, while any state run by an elite class in collaboration with the monarchy, church and military is clearly to be opposed by an anarchist, so is any other power structure where all are not equal, be that a school, union or even the family. Although traditionally associated with violence, many strands of anarchism have been pacifist in nature, and those approving of violent means have done so only as a last resort, feeling it necessary to smash the illusion and structure of capitalism's stranglehold on modern society.

Often emerging seemingly from nowhere and then disappearing just as quickly, this rich vein of thought was effectively temporarily buried beneath the avalanche of state communism in the early twentieth century, emerging again in Europe following the First World War. Many artists, exemplified by Marcel Duchamp, horrified by the state-sanctioned slaughter during the war, were highly influenced by anarchism, with movements such as Dadaism, Cubism and Surrealism incorporating its inherently subversive ethos into their breathtakingly radical new art.

Simultaneously, during the great civil unrest in Spain during the 1930s, anarchism found probably its most successful adoption as a practical day-to-day system for running society. Promoted by the huge anarcho-syndicalist union CNT, large sections of the Spanish working class adopted anarchism as their creed and briefly ran their factories and communities along non-hierarchical lines with mass democracy and workers' committees replacing top-down power structures. Such revolutionaries would lead the fight against the emerging fascist forces of General Franco and his Falangist nationalists.

During the 1960s, across Europe and indeed most of Western society, profound battles were fought between a world of opposites, between young and old, between left and right, between the forces of repression and those of freedom. These events culminated in 'Les Evenements' in Paris and the rest of France in May 1968, when it seemed that a grand alliance between the ultra-left student radicals and the massive industrial unions could genuinely topple the regime of De Gaulle and the entire edifice of the state.

Many differing strands were interwoven into the fabric of this rebellious left. One of the crucial ones, overlooked at the time but gaining more weight since capitalism has entered its hyper phase, was Situationism. Although founded in 1957 and emerging from a group calling themselves 'Lettrists', this avant-garde movement really emerged in the sixties, integrating politics, art and performance into 'situations' or applied surrealisms which, its activists hoped, would expose the futility, hypocrisy and decay at the heart of modern society.

Its leading light was Guy Debord, a French theorist who in 1967 published 'The Society of the Spectacle', a book whose central tenet was that civilisation had become passive and non-participant. Society had, he felt, acquiesced into the narrative of late capitalism through constant and endless consumption and through observing reality via the organs of the mass media, all of which now seems remarkably prescient seen from our vantage point fifty years later in the age of the internet. The Situationist's artistic, shocking style would be copied endlessly, most famously in Jamie Reid's artwork for the Sex Pistols and the clothes and attitude of The Clash, and it would find monochrome expression in the slogans and critique of Crass. Not for them the electoral system and the occasional change of captain to steer the ship through minor change. They wanted to throw the captain overboard, sink the whole ship, and build a new one.

And so back to mid-eighties Bolton. Our growing gang, having discovered the delights of sex, drugs and rock 'n' roll, were discovering the political and cultural lineage outlined above. Frequenting the Golden Lion and the Blue Boar pubs in Bolton town centre, we had begun to associate with the punks of Bolton, and they were merrily putting the politics of Crass into action, fired by an uncompromising attitude and dress sense, and fuelled by a diet of snakebite and cheap amphetamines.

During the eighties, I encountered many young people from many different nations calling themselves punks, but I don't think any of them matched the authenticity, post-apocalyptic dress code and chemical intake of the genuine British punk. Although the word 'crusty' had yet to emerge into the extensive slang vocabulary so beloved of British youth, the clothes, music and attitudes of this urban tribe were extreme.

Although all wearing black and grey clothes in many layers so ripped and torn that you could often still see knees and elbows, there were divisions within this subcult, reflecting the schism that happened within the British punk scene in the early 1980s. There were clear differences between those followers of the more cartoon punk ethic of The Exploited, Chaos UK, GBH and the Anti-Nowhere League and those immersed in Crass, Conflict, Poison Girls, Flux and the other political bands.

Fanned by the inflammatory commentary of writers such as Gary Bushell, the initial minor differences between the two groupings became more marked, with the politics of the first group moving to the right and becoming influenced by the Oi! movement and the rise of the skinhead extreme right. On the opposite flank, the punks who were genuinely committed to radical change adopted the militant manifesto of the anarchos, dressing all in black with fewer studs, leather jackets and Mohicans, and more ex-army cast-offs, vegan footwear and dreadlocks.

It was exactly around this time that our crew of relatively fresh-faced school kids, smoking some pot and having done a few trips, encountered the righteous anger of the anarcho-punks and their concomitant ferocious attitudes. Mostly living in the high-rise council flats ringing Bolton town centre, especially the aptly named Skagen Court (skag being global slang for heroin), these refuseniks lived in a world of benefit fraud, polydrug use and loud, spiky music. What set this particular bunch apart was their organisational positivity; collecting for the Miners' Strike fund, organising free gigs, being influenced by Hinduism and Buddhism, veganism and attending free festivals. This last indicator of a crossover or merging between the angry young brigades of the urban anarchists and the traditional traveller movement was to be pivotal in the counterculture of the eighties and nineties, leading to the Peace Convoy, the huge free Stonehenge festivals, Greenham Common, the mass eco-protests of the nineties and, most importantly for this story, the explosion of the free festival/party scene.

Pete, Whitey and I had already been interested in the traditions of anarchism and protest in general when we encountered the activism of the punk crowd. That we shared a fondness for extreme intoxication was a bonus. In fact, these twin and often contradictory impulses, on the one hand searching for enlightened meaning and noble ethical standards and on the other the self-destructive urge to drink and drug to excess, were not seen as paradoxical at the time, either by ourselves or by most of what became known as the ecstasy generation. This was exemplified for me when I attended my first free festival at Pick Up Bank near Darwin, north Lancashire. I'm not sure what year this occurred, I'm guessing 1984, but this was another of those pivotal nights that revolutionised my thinking and my worldview.

Heading up there on a Saturday night, I think Whitey was driving, five or six of us jammed into his car. We were stoned, of course. In those days of limited income, we would chip in together for a sixteenth or an eighth of flat-press or squidgy black, these being long before the days of skunk and hydroponic weed. Upon arriving at the festival, a fairly small affair in the wilds of the north Lancashire moors, we did what we would do at countless festivals over the next decades: form a pack and hunt for drugs. What amazed and delighted us was the sheer conspicuous blatantness of the range of drugs for sale. Outside many of the tents, benders, tipis and trucks were chalkboards where the range of chemical intoxicants for sale inside was proudly displayed. 'Line of coke £5, Line of speed £1, Acid £1, Mushrooms 50p'. This was, if not a chemical supermarket, then certainly a mini-mart, and we shopped enthusiastically.

Fast forward a couple of hours and we were successfully intoxicated. Our limited budget had stretched to some lines of speed and some mushrooms, and with the cans of Skandia lager (39p each) they had definitely done the job. I was genuinely amazed by the friendliness of those assembled. They may have looked scary from the outside but everyone seemed happy to let us on their bus or sit around their fire. This was a revelation, this combination of cheap, easily accessible drugs and music in the great outdoors. The sheer visceral excitement and wonder of sitting, shit-faced, under the great dark canopy of nature with none of the queues, the aggression and barked out last orders of a Bolton town centre pub was revelatory.

I wandered around in a haze, feeling a deep affinity for the elements: the ground beneath my feet, the fires, the wind. At some point, I found myself sitting, or more probably, lying inside a larger tent, where giant rugs, cushions and beanbags had been scattered. As I lay gurgling in my psilocybin reverie, a band was playing somewhere. Free festivals in those days were the musical preserve of bands like Hawkwind, Ozric Tentacles and the amplified music of Planet Gong, with some reggae thrown into the space-rock mix. At some point, and this vivid memory has stayed with me ever since, the singer began, over a wall of electric psychedelic cacophony, to intone the lyrics: 'Oh, I'd rather be a free man in the grave than living as a puppet or a slave.'

And I got it. I really got it. I would find out many years later that these words came from the Jimmy Cliff song 'The Harder They Come' but that didn't matter at that moment. For me, as a seventeen-year-old ingénue lying on the highly patterned carpeted floor of a marquee which felt like it was floating through deep space, it was profound and I wanted, then and now, to be a free man and not a puppet or a slave.

I can't remember how I got home or how I managed to hide my comedown from my mum the next day, but I was, in some small but important way, changed. Simultaneously with the new horizon of free festivals, we attended a growing number of gigs in Manchester. No decent bands ever played in Bolton apart from when Joy Division supported the Buzzcocks at Silverwell Street leisure centre in early 1979, and to my eternal chagrin, my mum wouldn't let me go. She let me attend my first gig later that year when my older brother took me to see The Police at Blackburn King George's Hall in September 1979 at the tender age of twelve, although Sting was a poor substitute for Ian Curtis. However, if the standard of gigs in Bolton was poor, then Manchester more than made up for it. I feel blessed to have grown up in Greater Manchester in the 1980s, as the bands that came from this post-industrial wasteland were unrivalled globally.

In mainstream society, shiny synth-pop dominated the charts, with Culture Club, Wham!, Pet Shop Boys and Depeche Mode being in the ascendancy. Although these bands were obviously not to our tastes, it is curious how popular music becomes throwaway and shallow when society as a whole seems mired in conflict and strife, as though music is used as escapism. In reaction to this glossy, Thatcherite commodification of chart music, the opposing, independent wing thrived, most noticeably with the arrival of The Smiths, another Manchester band whose first single 'Hand in Glove' was released in May 1983. Immediately dividing opinion between those who cherished their poetic, melancholic songs and those who just plain detested them, The Smiths attracted a huge and devoted following, probably the most fanatical since the heyday of The Jam. Pete, finger on the pulse as ever, went to one of the first ever Smiths concerts and attended their legendary gig at a new club that had opened in Manchester known as the Haçienda.

Opened in a former yacht warehouse in Whitworth Street (I never did work out how they got the yachts in and out or who would want to buy a yacht in Manchester city centre), this most infamous of clubs was initially poorly attended, freezing cold and came very close to closing. That would all change in a few years, of course, and little did I know that ten years later, we would be DJing there ourselves, but it did host some great gigs in its early years, including an unknown Madonna.

Pete being Pete, he had one of their first numbered membership cards, and we saw some great bands there: Sonic Youth, a very early Nick Cave and the Bad Seeds, Big Audio Dynamite and, in another momentous experience which altered my course in life, New Order. As they actually owned the club and were from Manchester, this gig was a triumphant homecoming. The band had just become internationally famous following the success of 'Blue Monday' and their masterful album *Power, Corruption and Lies*, released in late 1983. I went alone, although to her eternal credit my mum gave me a lift in her Ford Fiesta and waited around until the end of the gig at around two in the morning. That night the Haçienda was the most packed I had ever seen it, with God knows how many people crammed into every nook and cranny, and a trip to the bar taking a good thirty minutes.

New Order did not take to the stage until nearly midnight, and in the almost football-terrace atmosphere inside, large, grown Mancunian men were being dragged from the crush at the front to prevent them from fainting. By the time the band emerged, the air was electric and wild. Bernard Sumner, unsmiling as ever, walked over to a bank of electronic equipment and pressed a button. The huge, sledgehammer blows of 'Blue Monday' thudded from the sound system and as the other members of the band stood motionless, the crowd erupted. Without a word to the crowd or the hint of a smile, they played for two sweat-sodden, elegiac hours and blew the roof off the place. It was a mesmerising, hypnotic assault on the senses and I have described it since as not just the best gig I ever went to but surely the best gig that ever happened, anywhere, ever.

Transfixed, the thing that really struck me was that the ululating, primal heart of this music was electronic. Yes, they played bass, drums and guitar over the top, but this astonishing live performance was achieved by utilising these mysterious electronic devices of which I had no understanding. This was not disco, or even the basic and frenetic imported electro beats that Pete and I had been listening to; this was orchestral in its scale and demanded that you dance in some way. It was euphoric. And as I sat in my mother's Ford Fiesta heading up the M60 back towards Bolton, wide-eyed and electrified, I wondered idly what would happen if this new electronic medium was cross-pollinated with that lust for freedom and chemical experimentation I had witnessed in a field near Blackburn or allied with the angry political purity of Crass.

# 3

Back in the real world, our disparate gang were dealing with school, signing on, government training schemes and shit jobs. As noted above, we were drawn from many schools across Bolton, and indeed across social classes, and I think this made us slightly different. Within our crew, there were kids in sixth form college and heading towards higher education, those who were signing on and having a laugh with no real plan, and some who were planning to travel.

Some, like Dave, worked. He was a full-time mechanic with a council flat and disposable income. Then there was the phalanx of full-time punks and travellers, and, in a category of his own, a sixteen-year-old punk named Cookie who was attempting, with minimal success, to stay within a Youth Training Scheme making PVC windows. Thrown into this mix were a group of psychobillies, several hairdressers, a crew of hunt saboteurs and some cool Manchester types. Many of us wore the all-black post-punk uniform – many did not. A teacher at my school named us the 'armpit gang', stating that if society was a body, we would be the armpit.

And so these weeks and months of experimentation and discovery, wrought variously with exhilaration, angst and tedium, led inevitably to the disintegration of our first social faction. I decided to study in Nottingham, where I was accepted on a degree course in law and politics with vague thoughts of becoming a human rights lawyer to fight the system at its own game. On such seemingly random decisions do futures hang.

In the meantime, I decided to wait a year to go and, in what seemed like a great idea to me but perhaps not so to my mum and dad, I moved in with Dave above a wool shop on Wigan Road and signed on for a year. This year before my big move was, I have to say, not spent gainfully but in a fairly continuous benefit-funded whirlwind of gigs, clubs, parties and festivals, and a gleefully ramped up diet of hot knives, psychedelics and amphetamines.

The psychedelics came mainly in the form of magic mushrooms, which we often took trips to gather in the wilds of Rivington. Usually, we would fill bags to be dried at home and partaken of at a later date, although often we would simply eat the mushrooms as we picked. While presenting real problems over who was to drive home, this was a good example of our inability to exercise any form of basic impulse control. This characteristic would become definitive in later years and came to an end when, having sat one sunny day in a field near Ramsbottom eating dozens of mushrooms afresh, an old lady came over to ask what we were doing and it turned out to be Kirky's gran. A difficult conversation ensued, and the episode put paid to further al fresco tripping.

Amphetamines were usually scored from the crusty punks, one of the goodies available on their long menu of drugs along with Nembutal, Morphine, Largactil, LSD and a poky opium tincture called J Collis Browne's Mixture. Speed, as so memorably described in the film *Withnail and I* as 'like a dozen transatlantic flights without ever getting off the plane', was available in the form of amphetamine sulphate, having been around forever and popular among most youth cults, including mods, bikers and punks. Once snorted, it produces a feeling of alertness and euphoria, a feeling of wellbeing and an intense desire to talk shit. Sleep can be held at bay for days at a time, and excessive use can produce hallucinations and symptoms which mimic those of psychosis, but in a fun way. Combined with hallucinogens, there is an all-out assault on the senses which can last for the eternity of a very intense night and well into the next day. These would be the drugs of choice for several years until a certain substance named MethyleneDioxyMethAmphetamine arrived and moved the chemical goalposts.

Pete had by this time moved to Liverpool, where I would often head over to drink and drug with him on Lark Lane, often ending up at one of the wild squat parties in the rambling mansions dotted around Sefton Park. This would be another eye-opener that alerted our impressionable minds to the possibilities of just how unhinged parties could be: urban gatherings of hundreds of people, bands in front rooms and gardens, fires, joyous and intoxicated chaos. Another was the somewhat deranged 'Crystal Day' in Liverpool in 1984, organised by Bill Drummond, manager of Echo and the Bunnymen and later of KLF notoriety, involving thousands of Bunnymen fans traipsing around various city centre landmarks and having a banana fight on a Mersey ferry before the legendary gig at St George's Hall.

In Bolton, our gang was now notorious and unwelcome at house parties and most birthday celebrations in general. We would still gatecrash such parties, including an unfortunate evening where we accidentally ran over the birthday girl's dad in someone's mum's car, hospitalising him and getting on the front page of the *Bolton Evening News* ('Crashers Bring Terror to Party'). At the events to which we were allowed admission, rejecting the then-current dancefloor staples of Duran Duran, Madness or bad seventies disco, we would pester the DJs at towny clubs for Southern Death Cult, Sonic Youth or The Birthday Party, only to be met with blank stares so often that we ended up having to take our own records.

Disc jockeys then were strange beasts with uniformly big hair and those flashing rope lights, desperately wanting to get a slot on local radio where they could mimic the mindless shite of their heroes on Radio 1 (with the honourable exception of John Peel, of course). They would end the night, inevitably, with the slow tune when couples would smooch to sickly smooth slowies. One particular venue exemplified this strange dichotomy in which we existed: one week at cutting edge gigs in Manchester, the next at mundane parties in Bolton.

Rivington and Anglezarke form a wild and rugged expanse on the edge of the West Pennine Moors, between Bolton and Chorley. Its centrepiece is Rivington Barn, an ancient hall originally built in distant centuries and rebuilt in the Tudor era. Miles from any neighbours, this graceful and classy building became a very popular venue for disgraceful and unclassy teen parties. We would sit in the corner, drinking heavily and refusing to get involved, whether invited or not. If you're wondering why we went, it was because they would sell beer to anyone, there were lots of drunk people to cop off with and they occasionally played some acceptable Two-Tone records.

It was here that I met a young lady named Barbara, although she promptly told me to 'fuck off'. We would overcome this initial hostility and be together for fourteen years. Barbara was, and still is, a big-hearted and sparky Bolton girl, the daughter of a plumber, with a mane of ginger hair and a love of the theatre which caused my dad to compare her to the flame-haired actress Sarah Bernhardt. She had a broad northern accent, an effervescent approach to life and a dry sense of humour, qualities which would prove to be essential over the years. She would be a frequent overnight guest at our flat during the year leading up to September 1986, still taking her A-Levels, as she was a year younger than me, and causing her parents some disquiet at becoming involved with a bunch of druggie refuseniks. This was further compounded by us dreadlocking her hair while her folks were on holiday, her mother laughingly telling her to wash them out, not quite realising how much soap and backcombing had gone into those locks. They would remain for ten years.

Another visitor at our flat of iniquity was the young punk Cookie. I had first encountered him on Bolton Town Hall steps where the punks and the crusties would hang out during the week, especially Saturday, misbehaving ingloriously in the most prominent point in Bolton town centre, much to the disgust of the upstanding public and the police. Even amid the sartorial carnage of the hardcore punks, Cookie stood out. Firstly, due to his age – despite claiming to be sixteen he looked about twelve – secondly for the unfeasible thinness of his legs, but mostly because he was glue-sniffing in public and had a red 'V' symbol shaved into the side of his head, explained by his obsession with the then-current television programme about alien invaders. Somehow Cookie ended up staying at our place on Wigan Road the first night we met him, and somehow he also stayed for another six months. Having been thrown out of his family home by his step-dad, he soon made the front room his own, sleeping on an old mattress in the corner, a pile of records and a bong his only possessions. He never changed his clothes.

Disaster nearly struck when a team of dodgy Bolton builders were attempting to repair the bowed-out end terrace wall and managed to push the entire top section of the wall inwards at 9am one winter's morning. Rushing through the dust cloud and chaos and bumping into a naked flatmate, I looked up to see two grinning builders silhouetted against the grey sky through the new gap in the wall, who looked down from the scaffolding and said simply, 'Sorry lads'. We then turned to each other, thought of our young squatter in the front room where most of the bricks had fallen and rushed into the lounge, only to see an empty mattress with fifty or so bricks on top of it. Luckily, Cookie had stayed out that one night and had escaped serious injury. There would be times over the next fifteen years when I would wish he had not had such a lucky escape.

And so, with an extensive and fairly deviant posse established, we spent our time in the pursuit of life, liberty and happiness. In June 1985, a small number of us decided to go to Glastonbury Festival. This was a big decision for us. These were not the days of the festival being transmitted live on the BBC or police being allowed onsite. It was much more lawless, with a huge free festival adjoining the official one, including most of the travelling community and their vehicles. There was also, and this seems incredible by today's standards, hardly any fences or security. It never occurred to us to buy a ticket, not at the astronomical price of sixteen pound. Glastonbury Festival, or Pilton as the travellers continued to call it in line with the original name, had first happened in 1970, with a line-up including The Kinks and T Rex and at the cost of a pound, with free milk thrown in. Since those early days of the British festival scene, Glastonbury had mushroomed and around forty thousand tickets were sold in 1985, although the actual attendance was probably at least twice that total.

While the modern festival scene had started initially in California with the Gathering of the Tribes in San Francisco in 1967, it had spread across America to culminate in the epoch-defining Woodstock and the concept of large gatherings where rock music was played and drugs consumed had become popular in the UK. Since the very early days of this movement, with events such as the Isle of Wight Festival, the dynamic had split between those who charged money for such events and those who wished for them to be free, the latter current leading to the huge Stonehenge free festivals of the seventies and eighties. A matter of weeks before we travelled down to Glastonbury in 1985, following an injunction regarding Stonehenge, the free festival had been violently and permanently prevented by the joint actions of English Heritage and the police.

This historical impulse to celebrate important events in the pagan calendar at sacred sites was one that went back millennia, along with the accompanying desire to become intoxicated and submit to the bacchanalian ritual of shamanic celebration. We still do not know, and probably never will, exactly what Stonehenge, Avebury and the other surviving thousand or so stone circles across Great Britain were used for in the druidic era and before, but I would be willing to bet that hallucinogenic mushrooms and some kind of music, especially drums, were involved.

Certainly, those who lived full-time on the road and believed that mass gatherings of the people should be free saw themselves as continuing a tradition going back to the times of the druids and beyond, long before the advent of recorded history. Although this strand of thought would be of pivotal importance to the story of DiY and free parties some years later, back in 1985 our youthful and amateurish attempts to get to our first big festival had ended in disaster when Dave and I were arrested at Bristol train station following the purchase of tickets using a dodgy discount pass.

Despite our protestations we were taken to the transport police cells, where they made us empty our bags and found a flattened joint in what would prove to be a long personal and collective series of conflicts involving the authorities. After a few hours, they released us, although annoyingly I gave my real address and Dave didn't, and so I was prosecuted and later fined for defrauding British Rail. And so we took a packed special bus from Bristol train station to the world's biggest festival and arrived amid a sun-drenched maelstrom of confusion, chaos and wonder. If our collective experiences at the Pick Up Bank festival had been a revelation a year or so earlier, then our three days at Glastonbury were transformative.

We simply walked into the festival site, with the fence as it was then only extending a few hundred yards from the main entrance. Nowadays, there is a massive double fence with concrete footings guarded by security patrols and watchtowers. This reflects the fact that, in the mid-eighties, attending a festival like Glastonbury was very much a minority interest. There was no need for draconian measures to keep people out as relatively few wanted to go. There was very little else on the pay festival circuit back then except for Reading, and the days of hundreds of thousands of tickets being sold in a day and hundreds of festivals happening over the British summer were still far away. This was not yet a leisure option involving yurts, offsite accommodation and VIP areas; it was still raw, anarchic and felt genuinely liberating.

Somehow managing to find our fellow Boltonians who had travelled down by coach without getting arrested, we set up our two tents under a zinging electricity pylon, this being the only space we could find. These were the days before mobile phones, when losing a friend at Glastonbury could result in not seeing them for days, or even until you got home, so establishing a base was critical. We were then free to explore the festival, of which none of our youthful eyes had ever seen the like. It was simply mind-blowing, especially at night when the festival lights stretched as far as the eye could see like some huge medieval town, an all-out assault on the senses, and that was before the purchase and ingestion of any drugs.

Again, in those pre-police days there were chalkboards outside tents offering a smorgasbord of chemicals. However, I noted they were somewhat more expensive than those at Pick Up Bank, a clear indicator of the north–south wealth divide. There were also very shady gangs aggressively touting a range of substances, all seemingly from Liverpool and Manchester. We spent three glorious days on Worthy Farm and, although it rained a lot, we had to listen to Joe Cocker, and we only had one big potato burned in a fire to eat in two days, I knew I would be coming back. I would not miss another Glastonbury Festival for the remainder of the century, some fifteen years away.

And so, on a wet Monday morning we climbed onto a bus back to Bristol, muddy, skint and somewhat less innocent than we had been a few days before, wide-eyed at the realisation that some people lived like this. I can't remember seeing a single proper band that weekend, but I had seen some sights in the free area that had been burned into my retina; trucks called 'Fuckpig', beautiful dreadlocked women in big boots, Mutoid Waste Company's giant welded sculptures from the post-apocalyptic future, wild all-night bars filled with amplified noise, open and unabashed drug-taking, frenzied hedonism.

It was not lost on me that this had all occurred within the safe confines of a pay festival and that the real free festival scene, which had key dates at weekends over the summer, had been brutally repressed only three weeks earlier. In what became known as the Battle of the Beanfield, although it was more of a massacre than a battle, on a sunny morning near Stonehenge on 1 June 1985, around 1,300 police officers had attempted to enforce an injunction on around 600 travellers to prevent the festival from taking place. This had escalated into a full police riot where vehicles were smashed, pregnant women and children were beaten and 537 people were arrested, dogs were seized and put down. This represented clear evidence of the growing militarisation and politicisation of the police, much of it established during the Miners' Strike, and of how the state was willing to use disproportionally draconian means to enforce government policy.

For us, back in the north, where most people had little interest in the travelling community, we cemented our twin interests of politics and partying. Part of the militant manifesto of what was by then known as the alternative movement, certainly the anarcho wing, was a fervent belief in animal rights. Many of our friends had become vegetarian or vegan at this point, and I was to follow when, following a heavy night's tripping, I was faced on Sunday lunchtime with a joint of beef at the family table. Still hallucinating, I looked at this lump of carved meat and I had a decidedly unpleasant vision of what it actually was. As with William Burroughs's concept of the 'Naked Lunch' being the moment when you see exactly what is on the end of your fork, so this pink and brown object radiated pain and suffering. I couldn't eat it and, even when the acid had worn off. I haven't eaten meat since.

Much time was spent hanging out in Bolton pubs at this time, going to the 'alternative' discos, in our hometown and in Manchester. In addition, we travelled over to Wigan Pier frequently on a Wednesday night, an interesting outing until the vegan punks decided drunkenly to trash the burger van, meaning a whole crowd of us had to make a quick exit before the police arrived. We thought we had got away without bother until two police cars pulled over our transit van on the M61 and hilariously demanded that the occupants disembark, only to watch wide-eyed as twenty-six young men and women, all very drunk and crusty, fell out of the van onto the hard shoulder. It was a long walk home.

Many events and situations from the summer of 1986 still evoke vivid memories from that year before leaving the north-west. The highlight of these was the Festival of the Tenth Summer in Manchester, a week-long celebration of the tenth anniversary of the legendary Sex Pistols gig at the Free Trade Hall in July 1976. Various events, including a gig from a then fairly unknown band called Happy Mondays, culminated in a huge 12,500 capacity all-dayer at G-Mex featuring a line-up which seems frankly unbelievable now: The Smiths, A Certain Ratio, OMD, The Fall, Cabaret Voltaire, John Cooper Clarke and a transcendent New Order, featuring Ian McCulloch guesting vocals on 'Ceremony'. This was a confident Manchester, proudly demonstrating a swagger that often threatened to spill out of control. Firmly anarchist that sunny day and attending that seminal concert were a few of our gang, who, not wanting to wait to be served in a busy off-licence round the corner from G-Mex, just simply walked out with bottles of brandy and were chased down the street by the owner's irate sons.

At the other end of the spectrum, that summer also saw our attempt to get to the Stonehenge free festival, setting off to the now injuncted event with Miles and his mate Ean in a brown and yellow Fiat 127, little knowing that we would have to live in it for a week. This was just a year since the trauma of the beanfield and the approaches to Stonehenge were blocked in a way reminiscent of the Miners' Strike, rows of razor wire, riot police and armoured vehicles. While not matching the state-sanctioned police violence of the previous year, the authorities made it only too clear that we would not be allowed anywhere near the stones, and that indeed anyone even resembling a traveller was not welcome in Wiltshire.

Thousands of people in hundreds of vehicles were effectively kettled up on various sites and we ended up spending several days at Hanging Langford, around ten miles from Stonehenge. The three of us had first called in at a house in Warminster, which I suddenly realised was the home of some of the members of Culture Shock, previously the Subhumans, one of the biggest bands on the free festival circuit and certainly the most articulate and funky. Over the next few days, I saw how driven and idealistic the hardcore travellers were. For all the crusty clothes, clapped-out vehicles and crazy hair, there was a genuine drive towards being allowed access to what they considered to be the people's temple of Stonehenge, and they certainly aligned themselves with an ancient tradition of pagan spirituality. They, of course, never stood a chance.

Pitching such a disparate contingent against the full weight of the British state, which had been so effectively militarised during and after the 1981 riots and the epic Miners' Strike, which had only ended a year before, would only ever end one way. I witnessed for the first time the capacity of the police to effectively act as the aggressor in a public order situation and to employ escalating tactics and levels of violence to achieve their aim. We were verbally abused, threatened, chased and harassed as we played a surreal game of cat and mouse through Wiltshire woods and chocolate box villages under a burning sun. Eventually, dispirited by the ferocity of a government that had just labelled travellers as 'medieval brigands' and having tired somewhat of our cramped Fiat home, we decided to get out and head to Glastonbury.

That this level of draconian power and resources had been allocated to uphold a civil injunction (on behalf of English Heritage, let us not forget) was astonishing. I would reflect many times in years to come that such forces had been mobilised not to prevent a revolution or a serious threat to society but to prevent a celebration. Arriving at Glastonbury felt like coming home that year, and after strolling in for free again we quickly hooked up with our other Bolton friends, finding the punky traveller crew in the free field. My other mates camped, with better tents, more food and alcohol and numbering around fifteen but still, sadly, under the same electricity pylon. I have a fantastic photo of twelve or so of our gang, posing in front of our borrowed family tent, smiling and looking young and innocent in the Somerset sun. To the side flies our hastily cobbled-together flag, the black on white letters proudly proclaiming us the 'Couch Potatoes', a then-current moniker for our ever-growing gang.

Again, few bands were witnessed, although I think I watched The Cure, but much time was spent in the adjoining free festival which was, quite simply, more debauched and deviant, light years away from the Babylon of the main commercial area; it was still a riot of trucks, music, stalls and the smell of the earth below. Apart from the overwhelming feeling of freedom following such a frustrating week trying to get to Stonehenge, my most vivid memory is of a marauding gang of Bolton punks, spotting a seventeen-year-old Cookie at dawn around our campfire and dragging him off to that most gruesome of locations, the Glastonbury long-drop toilets. Three of them proceeded to dangle the young man down into the pit, filled with the most unmentionable and hideous waste matter imaginable, chanting "you're going in" and cackling demonically. Cookie screamed and begged, his head inches from a ghastly fate, but despite our encouragements to finish the job, they pulled him back from the brink, leaving him a quivering wreck in the mud before they sloped back to the main festival, much humoured.

Looking back some thirty-odd years later, these are the experiences that recall my last summer living in the north-west of England. We are all products of our environment, and these were the environments that had moulded me. I will always be glad that I was born and raised in Bolton against a backdrop of social and political upheaval, as it genuinely felt that during the eighties, the north-west of England was the centre of the musical universe. My departure was a bittersweet feeling: my sadness at leaving my parents, my girlfriend and my friends contrasted with a yearning to leave Bolton, spread my wings and throw myself into new adventures. So, following some tearful farewells, in September 1986 I set off for a new life in Nottingham, armed with a new duvet, a few hundred records, a yucca plant that would never grow, a big bag of speed and a nice chunk of squidgy black hash.

# 4

My first impressions of both Nottingham and student life were far from auspicious. Although I would grow to love the city hugely over the next few years, at first it seemed to be a very poor substitute for Manchester. Sincere apologies to all my friends who were born and raised in Nottingham, but it felt very parochial and humdrum. This was probably not helped by the fact that I didn't know a single soul. Surely there can be no lonelier feeling than wandering aimlessly around a city centre, lost in existential isolation amid seemingly happy crowds and knowing that you do not have a single friend within a hundred miles. If Nottingham itself felt mundane, then the reality of being a student on the three-hundred-acre university campus felt repellent. What I had envisioned of student life was a non-stop whirl of gigs, drinking, drugs and sex, so that I could pretty much carry on where I'd left off in Bolton. What I witnessed, with mounting horror, was thousands of very clean-cut young people, most of whom seemed to be from the south of England with appallingly middle-aged taste in clothes and with no interest in getting wasted at all.

By week two, I went to see the student welfare team and asked to be transferred somewhere less like the 1950s, but they informed me it wasn't so simple. So, I settled for a move into the city, ignoring the year-long contract. Just before Christmas 1986, I moved into a house on Albert Grove in Lenton, sharing with two other students I had met, Tanya and Aub. Equally horrified by the student bars and parties as I was, we started exploring what nightlife Nottingham had to offer. It was here, sometime around November 1986, that I sat down at a table in the café on the top floor of the Garage, as it still was. Overhearing the conversation of a young man at the next table, it became obvious he had also just arrived at the university and was equally unimpressed. Recognising a kindred soul, I leaned over to his table and introduced myself. His name was Rick and he was from Stockport.

Instantly we struck up an animated conversation about Manchester, marijuana and music, and we've never really stopped. Rick was tall, six foot three or so, eccentrically dressed in large jeans, stripy top and a beret, with a self-evidently voracious appetite for getting stoned, and came across as a larger-than-life cartoon character. Our friendship was to blossom and, unbeknown to us on that otherwise uneventful midweek night in Nottingham, we would become not just firm friends but real comrades in arms for decades: living together, partying and getting arrested together; always joking and laughing, and occasionally crying. Sparking instinctively off each other creatively, we would have many very stoned and speed-induced late-night conversations over the next few months about music, regarding which our influences were very different. Rick seemed to have few possessions. Apart from several huge pairs of trousers, he owned a battered old suitcase filled with disco, soul and funk seven-inch singles and an equally battered blue Triumph Herald.

One of the more idiosyncratic features of the old classic car was the system for braking. As the brake cable had snapped, Rick had instead employed a large sponge in its place, which mimicked the actions of the cable, sort of. The main problem with this, apart from the inherent danger, was that due to a hole in the driver's footwell, the sponge got wet during any period of rain, so that every time the driver pressed the pedal, a cascade of water would squish out of both sides of the sponge. This mechanism seemed to sum up my new friend. It was both ingenious yet sloppy, fascinating to watch, risky but, ultimately, it worked.

What also shouldn't have worked but did was the unification of our fairly polarised musical tastes. As mentioned above, Rick seemed to possess only hundreds of old disco, soul and funk 45s, while my collection of albums and overflowing bag of cassettes was predominantly indie, punk and noise. While I already had a fondness for Curtis Mayfield and Funkadelic and much reggae, I essentially saw such music as dated and no longer relevant, especially in comparison to what felt like the zeitgeist-defining, and fresh, music of New Order, The Smiths, The Jesus and Mary Chain and Sonic Youth, and the angry, political diatribes of activist punk bands such as Fugazi and No Means No. While Rick, in retrospect, already saw music in terms of dancing and mixing in the way a DJ would, I saw music in terms of expressing darker concepts: dislocation, injustice, anger.

Where we really bonded musically in that pre-house era was in a joint love of the emerging genre of hip-hop. Run DMC had popularised this new music across the globe, followed by LL Cool J and other Def Jam artists. The definitive first album by Public Enemy and tracks by EPMD, Stetsasonic and Eric B & Rakim would be released during 1987 and managed to combine the realities of street life or, in Public Enemy's case, coruscating political anger with clinical, driving beats. You could say that, whereas my new friend showed me the funk, I introduced him to the fury. These two historically opposing impulses would be the twin entwined drivers of all that was to happen to us over the next ten years.

During these times, the mainstream cultural backdrop was of Live Aid and MTV, vacuous synth-pop and big haircuts, a growing obsession with material wealth, the seeming triumph of Thatcherite economics and a fascination with yuppie lifestyles. For those resistant to this brash, shiny new world, the options seemed limited. Having been exhausted by the Miners' Strike and the internecine battle over entryism by the hard left, the Labour party seemed incapable of preventing the ongoing, crushing juggernaut of Thatcher's Conservative Party, who would go on to win a third consecutive electoral victory in 1987. For many, the only alternative manifesto to rally to was that bequeathed by Crass and the wider punk movement, that of becoming political refuseniks, living on or outside the margins of society and following a variety of radical single-issue politics.

This rallying cry for a radical new political activism was most powerfully articulated for me in Chumbawamba's seminal album *Pictures of Starving Children Sell Records*. Composed as an angry reaction to the self-congratulatory posturing of Live Aid, the ten tracks on this record dealt with the standard themes of the anarchist left but in a way that was not only empowering and humorous but brilliantly produced, melodic and, dare I say, danceable. While retaining the blistering anger of earlier anarcho bands, this was new and, along with the controlled rage of the Mob's 'Let the Tribe Increase', focused my own disillusionment with society and gave it a powerful voice. Many years later, when we made a joint record on the One Little Indian record label opposing the 1994 Criminal Justice Act, I would mention to Boff, a founder member of Chumbawamba, that their record had changed my life. He simply replied, 'Me too.'

Within the frustration that the system could not be brought down or changed electorally, single-issue politics and escapism dominated. Still utterly unmoved and unconvinced by the navel-gazing of conventional student politics, Rick and I became heavily involved with animal rights and became vegans. We were the main organisers within the university animal welfare society, which we slowly moved from uncontroversial vegetarian lunches to direct action demos and hunt saboteuring. Involving 5am starts and exhausting running over hill and down dale, we became devoted hunt sabs for several years until it began to interfere with our party lifestyles. Then, unfortunately, the Land Rover we were saboteuring on one Saturday morning accidentally ran over the fox and that was that.

It was during these days that we began to establish a working relationship, throwing crazy, impractical ideas at each other and talking them into some kind of realistic shape. Rick was always very creative, and while I would lionise musicians and writers, he idolised conceptual artists such as Nam Jun Paik, Bruce Nauman and, of course, Andy Warhol. He would spend hours messing around with a photocopier, distorting the copying process by physically moving the original image or photo as the green copying light went across. The university had just purchased some of the first Apple Macintosh personal computers, featuring the first diskette storage discs and a strange new device on the end of a wire, apparently known as a 'mouse'. Intended for students to write essays on, Rick used these new gadgets to produce innovative posters for our events, again spending hours messing with images and experimenting with fonts. The way in which we worked, where we would often brainstorm seemingly ludicrous ideas and then mould them into existence, with me supplying the theory and Rick supplying the design, would be repeated ad infinitum over the years to come.

As we moved into 1987, we began to familiarise ourselves with Nottingham and, more specifically, the like-minded individuals we began to meet through attending gigs and our animal rights activities. Benefit gigs were endemic, with monies raised in sweaty rooms above pubs usually going to militant groups such as the Animal Liberation Front. With few exceptions, the music at these events was hardcore punk with its accompanying mosh-pit. For the uninitiated, this involved a seething mass of, usually male, bodies down by the front of the stage, forming into a whirlpool of tribal combat with individuals pushing, punching and grabbing each other into a frenzy. I had personally tired of this testosterone-fuelled ritual and distinctly remember seeing a big punk with 'CRASS: Fight War Not Wars' stencilled onto his leather jacket repeatedly kicking someone in the head with no sense of the deep irony involved. Similarly, at several concerts I had witnessed this supposedly harmless fun spill over into disturbing mass violence, most notably during The Damned's set at the huge 'Save the GLC' concert in Brockwell Park in 1984. Stage diving was also a popular sport at such gigs, and although less macho than the moshing, probably more physically dangerous to the diver. With his tall thin body and reckless regard for his own safety, Rick came to specialise in this pursuit. I will never forget his majestic stage dive at a Fugazi concert, just as singer Ian MacKaye stopped the music and launched into an impassioned diatribe against stage diving, Rick ran from backstage and launched himself in the air for all the world like an enormous, elongated flying squirrel and came crashing to the floor as all those in the crowd moved out of the way.

Music itself was now rapidly morphing into something new, as always. Hip-hop had exploded from a quirky New York borough scene to a global behemoth, driven by the availability of cheap drum machines and now samplers. As so often with the introduction of new technology, the seismic shifts in application can be very unpredictable. While by 1987 the distinctly American music of hip-hop and very early house records were being released, in the UK, our homegrown bedroom producers were also experimenting with cut up and paste techniques. During this year, the early proto-house of outfits such as Coldcut and Tackhead began to emerge but were somewhat overshadowed by the release of the KLF's '1987 (What the Fuck is Going On?). Created by Jimmy Cauty and Bill Drummond (the former an ex-member of Brilliant and the latter the ex-manager of Zoo Records, Echo and the Bunnymen and The Teardrop Explodes), the Kopyright Liberation Front broke all the rules in this, and all subsequent recordings and activities. Sampling ABBA, Led

Zeppelin and Elvis, among others, without permission, all existing copies of the record were ordered to be destroyed by the courts. Although our paths would cross with the KLF many times over subsequent years, at that stage Rick and I just found the whole approach viscerally exciting, uniting as it did our passions for technological innovation, music and provocative art.

Meanwhile, back at my Victorian red-brick terraced house in Lenton, Cookie had turned up with his dog and a bottle of sherry. My old friend Miles had been persuaded to give him a lift, although he looked like he was somewhat regretting it. Cookie begged to stay the night and took his traditional spot on a mattress in the front room where he, unsurprisingly, remained for several months. Pete was also a regular visitor, although, unlike Cookie, he never seemed to wish to move in, not yet at any rate. He had been visiting regularly since I arrived, including one memorable occasion when he and I went to watch Nottingham Forest play Manchester united, and the United fans kept up a near-constant barrage of 'scabs' for the full match in response to the Nottinghamshire collieries policy of working through the strike.

And so, at some point early in 1987, I was able to introduce my old friend Pete to my new friend Rick. We sat in my front room in Lenton, talked, smoked, drank late into the night and played a lot of music. We shared many things in common, our northern attitudes, an almost sacred belief in the transformative power of music and, it has to be said, a real passion for inebriation in all its forms. Between the three of us, there was a genuine meeting of musical minds. With Rick's love of soul, funk and disco, Pete's already encyclopaedic and eclectic knowledge of jazz, electronica and afrobeat, and my passion for punk, reggae and indie music, we had just about all bases covered, barring opera and country and western. Although at these first meetings we could not know what the auguries of the future would bring, that the three of us would end up living, working and partying together for most of the nineties, we certainly intuitively understood and fired off each other's imaginations.

Another Bolton wanderer who gravitated down to Nottingham that summer was Barbara. Having stayed at home to re-take her A-Levels, she and I had remained long-distance partners and were now re-united as she moved into what was becoming a fairly crowded house. My fellow housemate Aub now had to contend with not one but three fairly messy Boltonians, plus the dog. However, we muddled along quite nicely. The place became something of an urban commune with vegan cooking, rampant drug use at weekends, and a series of foster animals provided by Nottingham Animal Accident and Rescue Unit. For a year or so, these totalled about twenty dogs and fifteen cats, including a dog called 'Frisky' who certainly lived up to his name when I took him home for Christmas and he bit my mum. We also temporarily housed a feral cat and a ferret called Freddie, who Cookie would gleefully take for a walk around Lenton in a very small collar and lead.

During the spring of 1987, my mum decided to donate her old car to me, the same Ford Fiesta in which she had waited so patiently outside the Haçienda and other insalubrious nightspots. In this battered vehicle, we spent the summer attending festivals, some free and some officially paying, although we didn't pay for any. As the annual solstice attempts to get to Stonehenge were now effectively policed out of existence, we headed again for Glastonbury. We just got there in time to catch New Order play a sublime set late into the night while torrential rain poured down from the heavens. Not that this concerned us as we tripped ferociously yet merrily, so much so that Cookie repeatedly shouted through the torrential rain that he couldn't see the band, only for us to point out that he was facing the wrong way.

During these times, there was an established summer circuit of free festivals, many of which had been going since the seventies.

Travelling from festival to festival, and then wintering at a small site out of the way somewhere, was how the Peace Convoy and the wider traveller movement had emerged, via semi-permanent peace camps such as Greenham Common and Molesworth. Traditionally arranged around Stonehenge and the June solstice, the season featured events such as the Avon Free Festival at the end of May, always free and considerably more lawless and anarchic than any pay festivals. Ribblehead Free Festival was another such event, and we headed off there in August of that summer. Meeting up with some of the Bolton crew on the windswept moors near Settle, Yorkshire, this was a different experience, more a matter of survival than celebration as we spent days sitting in the Fiesta beneath the silent, bleak beauty of the Ribblehead viaduct.

This was beginning to be the heyday of what became known as the Brew Crew, a vanguard of particularly crusty traveller punks who gained their name from their voracious appetite for Carlsberg Special Brew (9% ABV) and any other mind-altering substance, and whose behaviour was shockingly fucked-up, even for mainstream travellers never mind the general public. This tension between those on the road who saw it as a viable alternative lifestyle, who made things and had children, and those who just cared about getting obliterated, was coming very much to the fore at this time. This dichotomy between the positives and negatives of site life would assume great importance in years to come. One great example of the depths to which some traveller behaviour had sunk was nevertheless very funny, assuming you like dark humour.

There was a fairly forlorn pub near the festival in Ribblehead and it was jam-packed with soggy festival-goers. The elderly and upstanding landlord clearly hated us all but was making so much money he stayed open for days on end and probably made enough to retire on. What did tip him over the edge, though, was when he emerged from his bolthole behind the bar to collect glasses and one of the hardcore Bolton travellers, a lad named Gaz, was merrily pissing in the corner pocket of the pool table, his urine trickling into a puddle below. We had to laugh, although the landlord didn't see the funny side. It was a strange thing: even though we had no tent and had to sit in a small car for three days, the windows opaque with condensation and weed smoke and the Yorkshire rain falling incessantly, we had a great time. I think it was the feeling of freedom that, despite the material inadequacies we were suffering, the spiritual emancipation of being away from the city, within nature, with no fences, tickets or security was liberating.

Around September 1987, Rick did me a huge favour when he and some mates rented a big, rambling house in Church Street, Lenton, and allowed Cookie to move in. This house quickly took the heat off my own and became the session place of choice. A drum kit, guitars and amps were quickly set up in the huge upstairs front room and lazy afternoons were spent jamming. Bands were started one weekend and finished by Tuesday. The most transient was Sledgehammer Massage, featuring me on drums, Cookie hitting a bin with a hammer, two mates on feedback guitar and Rick singing dementedly. Unfortunately, our one and only practice session was cut short when two uniformed police officers walked into the room. The front door had been left unlocked and they had let themselves in after the old lady next door had repeatedly phoned the authorities and they had arrived to find her weeping in dismay at the racket.

Around this time, the first house tracks were beginning to come out of America, but we were still focused on noise and hip-hop. 1987 was a great year for both genres with the release of Butthole Surfers spectacularly weird 'Locust Abortion Technician', Erik B & Rakim's 'Paid in Full' and, above all, Public Enemy's debut album *Yo! Bum Rush the Show*, the latter showing exactly how political anger could be merged with electronic beats into an irresistible force. It was very much in this vein that Rick got his first DJ slot, playing hip-hop at the Garage basement in support of MDC, a Texan hardcore punk band. As mentioned earlier, Graeme Park was beginning to play an eclectic mix of early house and electronica upstairs at the weekend. We would often frequent the 'alternative disco' in the basement on the same night, sometimes checking out the music being played upstairs but not quite getting it. And then, one night in 1988, acid house entered our lives and nothing would ever be the same again.

# 5

It must be remembered that at this time, in mid-1988, the sensation-
alist media frenzy over acid house and its associated drug, ecstasy, was
just beginning to erupt. From the vantage point of the third decade
of the twenty-first century, it is hard to remember or imagine the
sheer, ill-informed hysteria that the tabloid newspapers, in particular,
spewed out regarding acid house parties. However, it certainly acted
as the most effective magnet possible towards those young people
who might be drawn towards this new social phenomenon.

Every ten years or so since the global eruption of rock 'n' roll, a
youth movement had exploded which captured, through new, revolutionary musical forms and usually an accompanying drug, the
primal excitement and possibilities of being young and free. This had
occurred ten years after rock 'n' roll with the cultural rebellion of
the international hippy scene and LSD, and again in 1976 with the
snarling, shattering year zero of punk rock. A decade had now passed
since then and not only did a generation of young people want their
very own insurrection, but they were also about to collide with new
technology and a new drug to ignite it.

For Rick and I, this ignition occurred in the unglamorous location of Nottingham's Rock City. This venerable old venue had
played host to thousands of gigs over the years across the musical
spectrum, and in the mid-eighties occasional soul and funk all-dayers would happen there. The soul-funk scene, much like the early
northern soul scene of the seventies and the warehouse parties in

London in the early eighties, would all eventually feed into the voracious monster that acid house would become; it was the end point of so many musical narratives. At this time, for those of us outside London and Manchester, acid house was pretty much a thing of the media, spoken about in hushed conversations, misinformation and longing. Yes, house music was being played in Nottingham, but the whole 'acid' part had not yet arrived. I doubt that anyone in Nottingham had even taken ecstasy at that point, certainly no more than a handful of people.

So, when a night named 'Acid House Frenzy' was advertised at Rock City in the late summer of 1988, Rick and I simply had to be there. Walking into the city centre, we discussed how we thought the night would go with our friend Andy Wood, a serious devotee of all things thrash and hardcore punk. Rick and I were full of slightly nervous anticipation and had brought along a pocketful of magic mushrooms, unable as we were to obtain this mystical new drug ecstasy but figuring that as the word 'acid' was involved, mushrooms would be the next best thing. While we had been going to clubs for several years, as soon as we got in, this was very different from the start. Coachloads of people had come up from London with the DJs, and they were already clearly dancing to a different drummer. Each person was dancing in an individual space, oblivious to the gyrations of their neighbours, all moving frenetically to the beat and wearing the sort of colourful, bright clothes and big smiles that everyone I had ever known would rather die than be seen wearing. They looked happy, for God's sake, which to us northerners was pretty much the ultimate sin.

Having never experienced records being mixed together before, it was impossible to know where one record ended and another began; all sorts of shrill electronic noises and melodies floated in and out of the pulsating, four on the floor, metronomic beat of the kick drum, familiar vocal samples merged with the crisp fluctuations of the hi-hats, some bhangra wobbled in and out somewhere within the sensory overload. Smoke machines belched out some flavoured fog and strobes illuminated the scene, for all the world like some Dionysian ritual of the ancients. Rick and I just stopped and stared; we had no adequate response. At all the discos and clubs we had experienced, people would get up, usually drunk, and maybe dance or push their mates around to a favoured track or two, before drifting off to sit down again or head to the bar. This crowd were not drunk, they were not sitting down and they certainly weren't heading to the bar. Their collective body rose and fell, rocked and jerked to this music which sounded as though it had been beamed directly from a different planet that was thousands of years more technologically advanced than ours. I turned to Rick and mouthed the word 'mushrooms' and he nodded enthusiastically. We got some water from somewhere and gobbled half the dry liberty caps each and wandered onto the dancefloor. And that was that. Two hours later, drenched in sweat, we had still not left the dancefloor, not even for a piss. I had certainly never danced like this before, or for so long. It felt sensual and safe, liberating and divinely pleasurable.

With the mushrooms further distorting sound and vision and feeling like a spiritual part of a great organic whole, I could have danced all night, and as the music finished at what I suppose must have been two o'clock, the whole crowd just stood and smiled and cheered and hugged each other. My mind suitably blown, I embraced and chatted to my new friends whom I had never met before and would never meet again. I then went to profusely thank the DJs, where I found Rick demanding that they tell him where this music came from and where it could be purchased. As we finally stumbled out into the dark Nottingham night, we found Andy, and the three of us set off walking home towards Lenton. As we reached the brow of the hill, and I will never forget this, Andy turned to us both and said, 'Well, that was shit.' Rick and I could only look at him in pity, lost for words for once and knowing we had just glimpsed the future, our future.

What the future brought very quickly – in fact, the next day – was a visit to Nottingham's premier record shop, Selectadisc. Although Graeme Park no longer worked there, they stocked the most eclectic range of music in the city, and we strolled in and asked for some 'acid bhangra', as you do. Being too cool for school, as is compulsory with all record shop workers, the guy behind the counter waved us over to the end of a rack. We went over to look and inspected their 'House' section. No genres yet to come, no techno, garage or hardcore; no chilled, drum and bass or deep, and definitely no acid bhangra, just a sticker saying 'House'. There were probably ten records in there; I think we bought five of them and left.

If one of the main themes of this book is the convergence of the urban club scene with that of the travelling festival movement, then our trip to Wick Quarry that year clearly illustrates how far that union would have to travel and showed how fragmented things were at that time. As mentioned above, certain dates occurred annually in the travelling summer calendar, and after Stonehenge, the most cel-ebrated of these was the Avon Free Festival, which took place every bank holiday weekend at the end of May. It was the pressure of this ritual festival date in the calendar that in future years would force the taking of a site, and that would lead to the large gathering at Chipping Sodbury in 199,1 and, of course, the epoch-defining Castlemorton a year later. In 1988, however, house music had not yet married into the festival world. Although on the other side of England the Orbital parties were in full swing within the M25 motorway, at the quarry in Wick, the music and the vibe was altogether less fresh. It has to be said that the weather was appalling and, though some may disagree with me, the festival felt like a pretty joyless affair. Again, the nihilist antics of the Brew Crew were in full effect, the location was some sort of old tip and there was clear evidence of widespread heroin use.

Many would argue in the years to come that the influx of acid house and raving would destroy the free festival scene, but I would argue that things were already pretty bleak and near to irrelevance, the belief and cosmic optimism I had witnessed years before at Pick Up Bank seeming to have withered. Admittedly, five of us spent three days in a badly erected and leaking tent, not lending itself to a positive frame of mind, but the general atmosphere was flat, self-destructive and stale. We still had a laugh, of course, sitting in the tent snorting microdots and guzzling cheap cider and amphetamines, but I had a feeling that something new was needed to give this movement fresh impetus and positivity if it was not to become even more irrelevant and moribund.

By this time, in the autumn of 1988, things had changed again domestically. Barbara had by now moved to Liverpool to finally take up her drama degree at the polytechnic, and Rick and I, plus two friends, Jez and Kay, had moved in together, still in Lenton on Johnson Road, another row of terraces adjoining the former Raleigh bicycle factory. This was now the West Indian community hub known as the Marcus Garvey Centre, in honour of the early twentieth century Jamaican leader who had inspired the pan-global African consciousness movement that had led to, among others, the Nation of Islam and Rastafarianism. To us, who effectively shared a back wall with the place, it was mainly a place of quite incredible bass from their reggae all-nighters which rattled the kitchen windows and went on until 6am, holding as it did the only all-night 'dance' licence in the city. It was here, less than two years later and totally unforeseen, where we would promote Nottingham's first rave.

Rick and I were still students at this time, technically. We had long eschewed the social scene on the big campus, which lay just outside Nottingham's city centre, and looked for both our entertainment and our friendships in the real world. However, we decided that the central student's union bar, the Buttery, was the appropriate location for our first foray into promotion. Our night was to be called 'Different Disco' and the poster featured a skeleton playing records on some turntables, with the words 'Grind Yer Mind and Rattle Yer Bones at a … Different Disco'. The plan was to alternate DJ duties, with Rick playing some disco and soul for a while, then I would take over and play some vaguely danceable noise and punk, followed by both of us dropping some hip-hop, then by our five acid house records. When we arrived with about ten of our mates, what greeted us on the night was a pair of substandard decks and a dodgy mixer, a small, tinny PA and one light.

Although we had no intention of beat-mixing any of the records, we still had to quickly familiarise ourselves with the concept of fading one record into another before the expected onslaught of people attracted by our renegade poster campaign. However, our initial crowd of ten or so remained stubbornly static, leading us to get drunker and drunker in a vain attempt to pretend we were having fun. About an hour or so in, there was a sudden influx of thirty or so very drunk medical students. Rick saw his chance to lock in the dance floor, dropping some disco classics. I was by now pretty smashed, and being somewhat disgusted by the type of punter we had attracted and by their wedding-reception style dancing, decided to play Sonic Youth's 'Expressway to Your Skull', which as the title suggests, is a seven-minute-long epic which begins in a fairly upbeat groove, albeit with sinister lyrics, and builds inexorably into a scream of discordant, crashing guitars and feedback, a paean to the activities of Charles Manson and his Family. This had the desired effect of simultaneously raising a cheer from our mates, clearing the dancefloor and pissing Rick off all at the same time, creating our first fallout over musical differences. As Rick retook the decks and attempted to entice the students back onto the dancefloor, I headed for the bar, reflecting on the innate pressures of DJing.

Over the autumn and winter of 1988, further events took place which would prove pivotal to this story. My former housemate Aub, who had arrived from Coventry with a full head of fine dreadlocks and a very sunny disposition, had given up college as a bad idea and had started work at Rita's, a vegan café situated in Hockley in Nottingham's city centre. It was through this bustling hub of collective food production and general animal rights activity that Rick and I began to connect with a new group of friends who were radical, lawless and risk-taking, much more like my old friends in Bolton. Aub had moved into a sprawling Victorian mansion on Magdala Road in the Mapperley Park area of Nottingham, which had been converted into flats, beautiful and elegant with high ceilings and original fireplaces but now in a state of faded disrepair. The flat into which Aub moved had handsome French windows, huge original ornate mirrors and, reflecting the low rent, a five-foot square hole in the wooden bedroom floor and no heating other than two open fireplaces. Fully detached on a wide, private road with overgrown gardens, a big walled yard and tenants who were themselves noisy and laid-back, entering this lovely house felt much like escaping the city and was a natural place for parties.

Living above Aub's new ground-floor flat, Dave and Julie seemed an unlikely couple but were both bohemian, cultured and alive. Dave hailed from near Newton Aycliffe, gobby with a heavy north-eastern accent, and Julie was an elegant, elfin dancer from Basingstoke. Both had worked for the Michael Clark Company, Dave on set design and Julie as an actual dancer, and they were full of wild tales of touring and Michael Clark himself, to whom Dave bore an uncanny resemblance with his shaved head, full lips and challenging attitude. They had also been to Shoom, the seminal London club run by Danny Rampling and generally considered the birthplace of acid house. Among this new circle were other fascinating characters: Jean, a warm and funny lass from near Liverpool, and Damian, a man who it was impossible to pigeonhole as he seemed to be ageless, appearing to have originated from another planet with the powers of a super-hero. He also had a perma-tan, a blond Mohican and a lightning bolt shaved into the side of his head, leading immediately to us nick-naming him 'Flash'. I can't remember the particular meeting which prompted his visit, but what I do remember is that another associate of our new gang turned up at our house late one night looking for Rick and I. Having heard that we had a Butthole Surfers video and keen to potentially sell us some speed, he knocked on the door and I welcomed in this slightly dishevelled figure wearing an old mac and looking like he hadn't slept in days. We sat him down in our front room, where he proceeded to talk for hours before finally telling us his name. It was Simon.

Much would be said and written about Simon in subsequent years, when he would become the Keith Richards of British house music and DJ of the month in *i-D* magazine, *The Face* and *DJ Mag*, among others. I have personally always said that he is the best person in the world at something; I've just never quite worked out what it was. Certainly, on that first night, there was something extraordinary about this man, something attractive and fascinating and yet some-how tragic. Simon was a paradox: a boarding-school boy with the common touch and no interest in wealth or status, shy and yet com-petitive and confident, empathetic and yet completely self-absorbed. We would soon discover that he had a beautiful soul, an almost pre-ternatural passion for music and a pathological ability to fuck up. Although we didn't know it that night, he would be just the man we needed, and I would still contend that he became the greatest DJ I ever heard, although obviously I'd never tell him.

Shortly after this meeting, and in terms of import equally as momentous to this narrative, I consumed ecstasy for the first time. I can still pinpoint the exact day, Wednesday 23 November 1988, my twenty-second birthday. Rita's was the location. We had gathered for a birthday meal after the café had closed, putting the tables together so the fifteen or so of us could sit around the long table. The evening had progressed in a fairly standard manner with a lovely spread consumed, beer and wine on the table and joints being rolled. Sat next to me was my mate Jim Phillips, who had been my cocaine buddy for the last year or so, on account of him being the only person I knew who could get it. We would often meet round his house for poker nights fuelled by cocaine and Jack Daniels, but I had always had a strange, ambivalent relationship with coke. Although I would consume horrible amounts of it in later years, it certainly never did much for anyone's spiritual wellbeing. That night, he leaned over and whispered, 'I got you this from London. Happy birthday.' He held out his open palm and sitting on it, yellow with a split down the middle, was a small, round tablet. Sensing my simultaneous visceral excitement and surprise, he continued, 'Yep, it's ecstasy, a New Yorker. Twenty-five quid'. My immediate reaction was, 'How much?' This was the eighties, and you could buy a weekend's worth of speed and acid for that amount of money and have enough left over for a packet of fags.

My second reaction was to take it out of his hand, place it in my dry mouth and wash it down with some Red Stripe. And then wait. And wait. There I was, at the age of twenty-two, on the vanguard of the biggest chemical explosion in British youth history, primed for a life-changing experience on this, my maiden voyage on a journey of discovery that would become the symbol of a generation. And nothing happened. It was a dud. To say I was gutted would be an understatement, but hey, at least I hadn't paid for it. As 1989 arrived, I involved myself less and less with the small, fleeting bubble of student life, feeling far more comfortable and inspired by my new friends centred around the big house on Magdala Road. This new gang had much more in common with my old Bolton crew. They were vegans, unconventional, drawn from a range of social classes, genders and sexualities; they were bohemian, with a fondness for experimentation in drugs, alcohol and culture in general. In early 1989, I finally moved in, sharing a flat with my old friend Aub, and a short while later, Rick moved in upstairs, sleeping on a raised bed above Dave and Julie's front room. It was in this faded but beautiful house, with its secret yard hidden by high, ivy-clad, red-brick walls, that we communally converted to the new and wild electronic music known as house, not as observers but as fully committed participants. We wanted to live it.

Probably our favourite band in common at that moment was the Pixies, sharing as we did a love of post-punk and noise; they exemplified the controlled but occasionally explosive noise that combined intelligent sentiment with raw aggression. Bands, however, were rapidly becoming irrelevant. Cassettes were being made, twelve-inch singles being bought, beats sought out. There was an irresistible musical current bubbling under everywhere if you allowed yourself to feel it. In the charts, which still mattered in those days, tracks such as D-Mob's 'We Call it Acieed' could be heard in taxis and open windows, and much better tracks such as Mark Moore's 'S'Express' were played on quality radio shows such as the ubiquitous John Peel. And yet, outside London and certain small pockets of knowledge, apart from the huge Orbital pay parties, the acid house revolution was very underground. It feels today that if any comparable musical revolution occurred, then the ravenous twenty-four-hour media cycle, driven by the universal smartphone camera, would locate and expose it instantly; the revolution would be digitised, the magical secrets tarnished and the scene would instantaneously become commercialised and ruined.

And so, in the spring of 1989, following my disappointment with my first experience of ecstasy, the last piece of the jigsaw would, inevitably, fall into place. Where? Well, obviously, in an abandoned tile warehouse in Mapperley, a nondescript suburb of Nottingham up Mansfield Road. Organised by James Baillie, more of whom later, this was undoubtedly an acid house party, of which the key ingredient which sets it apart from mere clubs is the illegality. Throughout the next decade and beyond, it was perhaps the extra frisson of law-breaking that turned a potentially joyous experience into a truly thrilling one. Supplying the music that night was Graeme Park and, I think, his protégé Allister Whitehead. Our gang had begun to associate with some of the ultra-fashionable Nottingham crowd, many of whom worked within the Paul Smith fashion empire, which had originated in Nottingham. This cross-pollination of previously diverse scenes was to become one of the defining features of our adventures, and it was this hip crowd who informed us of this party, and it was them from whom ecstasy tablets could be purchased. Ones that worked. These were the days when parties wouldn't even start until midnight and would go on until dawn or until the police turned up; I'm guessing we arrived around two o'clock, mob-handed as ever, probably around seven or eight of us. As serious drinkers, we headed straight for the bar, only to be told there wasn't one. While this would make complete sense from that night on, we complained loudly to each other until someone, I really can't remember who, came back with a handful of pills. Twenty pounds each, again small and yellow.

Whatever was going on in that space, that temporary autonomous zone, something was working. Nottingham's beautiful people were, as they say, on one. And yet the place was something of a dump, the toilets were fairly vile, but it mattered not. Much like the night at Rock City a few months earlier, the music was all-encompassing, the dancefloor an ecstatic, writhing, unified mass. Simultaneously, we swallowed our tablets, washed down with the last can of Tennant's Super we had brought. I started dancing, probably more like wobbling, half-drunk and still not entirely comfortable on a dancefloor. And slowly, imperceptibly at first, a feeling, a fluid emotion, began to seep through my body, starting from my stomach and then out, slowly, sinuously and sensually, like someone had poured liquid gold into my veins. Then up my throat and into my brain, a feeling of invincible, deep wellbeing took over my senses. Looking round to see my friends, they were clearly in a similar state of rising transcendent joy, smiling from ear to ear. And dancing. And then Mr Park played the opening bars of FPI Project's 'Rich in Paradise' and that was the moment, and I'm getting goosebumps right now, thirty-odd years later, even thinking about it. Within minutes, all my cares in the world had evaporated; I had become the music, electronically spliced into these thudding beats, sinuous, dirty bassline and enormous piano chords.

I had consumed many drugs by this stage of my life, but had never, ever felt like this, like all the good bits of acid with all the good bits of amphetamines, and my mind, to quote Jack Kerouac, began to burn, burn like fabulous yellow roman candles exploding like spiders across the stars. Until the day I die, and it may sound crass so many decades later, but this was one of the most important moments of my life. Millions of other people, a generation even, experienced this moment somewhere, be it in a club, a field, on a beach, an abandoned airfield, a boat or in their own front room; in that ubiquitous and universal moment, it matters not about the morality of drug-taking or about the debate about the synthetic nature of these emotions and all the hugging; it just was, and it was important. This moment would provide a deep, abiding bond between people and cultures separated by geography, class and tribal loyalty. In the UK, it would halt the endemic violence of rival football firms; it would see north and south and all compass points in between integrate and unite; it would cause very hard people from the estates of Manchester and Liverpool, Cardiff and Swansea, Glasgow and Edinburgh to hug each other. This moment would cause hundreds of thousands of city dwellers to head for the fields and mingle with travellers to challenge centuries-old land rights, the evangelists of this experience spreading around the planet as emissaries of this brave new synthesis. It would instigate a global movement based on equality and a genuine outpouring of love, and it would change the face of popular culture forever.

But right there and right then, I realised I needed a piss. I tried to find toilets in the confusion and swirling fog, brushing past people whom I knew or half-knew or had never met – they were all smiling. Finding the toilets at last, it felt like someone else was peeing for me, and then I sood in front of a mirror, staring at my reflection, not finding fault or freaking myself out like on other drugs, but just smiling, grinning, chuckling and full of innocence. Over the years, I came to realise that for all those countless millions who had a similar night of almost religious conversion, whatever music you were listening to would define your experience forever, and that once experienced, you would probably wish to recreate it endlessly. As we walked home, collectively jabbering and laughing, the majestic dawn breaking above Nottingham's skyline looked so exquisite and beautiful that it was like seeing it afresh. As a group, we had been changed forever; we had no idea what the future might bring but we knew that we wished for these moments to happen again. They would happen again, frequently, as we began to organise our own small house parties and enthusiastically embarked on our own homegrown summer of love.

# 6

And so began Year Zero for our clan, based around a large Victorian house in Nottingham, signing on and claiming housing benefit, bewitched by this new electronic music, little knowing but perhaps intuitively guessing that it would take over our lives and the world. With six flats consisting of huge open rooms and no neighbours, 30 Magdala Road could have been specifically designed for our purposes. Our first ever party was gleefully thrown in the downstairs flat at some point in early summer of 1989, long before we had a name or decks or a mixer. A strobe and a smoke machine were hired from a 'disco accessories' shop on Mansfield Road, and Damian, due to his line of work and obsessive nature, owned the best quality speakers, tape deck and amplifier, which we duly employed. Music came from tapes of the few records Simon had bought, un-mixed but recorded in the old way using the pause button. A very do-it-yourself party, which around six people attended. Dave and I constantly filled the flat with noxious smoke to hide the fact that no one was there, and with the strobe going and the large hole in the corner of the floor, most people who did enter took one look and left.

Nursing serious hangovers the next morning, Rick, Simon, Dave, Julie, Damian, Jean, John Ousey and I discussed where we went wrong. Clearly, the alternative community in NG7 had not yet caught the acid house bug. The epicentre for those that had remained was the Garage, or the Kool Kat as it now was. In what became the first of many club pilgrimages over the years, every Saturday night would find our scruffy little clan locked in that black sweatbox while Graeme Park spun the magic, dancing collectively to tracks such as 'Pacific State' and 'Sueno Latino'. After several weeks, our appearances began to change (well, some of us anyway). Simon's look never changed and Damian, with his platinum blond Mohican or multi-coloured plaits, would always resemble someone freshly arrived from another planet. I bought my first pair of trainers since school, t-shirts with fluorescent motifs were sported, someone bought some dayglo goalie gloves. In the dark of the Kool Kat, we were mixing with Nottingham's hippest fashionistas, and although we would dissolve these barriers in time, it was initially an uneasy social mix. Becoming genuine mates with this crowd would be our first example of the ability of house music to build bridges and bring down walls, but initially they looked down their noses at us; we had dreadlocks, spiky hair and baggy clothes, wore few labels and the wrong shoes, but in that club at midnight beneath the synthetic beats and under the influence of the new communion drug, we gave not a shit.

Among these knowing regulars was Matthew Collin, whose partner Steph and friend Jag had started a fanzine named *Duck Call*, named after the hunting accessory which mimicked the call of a duck and was now employed every Saturday night to quack along with the beats. It's fascinating how such behaviour seemed entirely normal practice at the time. Matthew would become a firm friend and go on to become editor of *i-D* magazine and, many years later, author of the seminal acid house book, *Altered State*. Other characters were based around the clothes scene in Nottingham: Scully, Ainsley, Osborne, Jay Mooney, Adam, Craig, Marcus, Timm, Laurie (and several women whose names escape me, sorry), and slowly our mutual suspicion disappeared beneath the twin camaraderies of clubbing and ecstasy, of which the latter we had by now established a regular supply. Our traditional approach to drinking (super-strength lager, constantly), inherited from the punk approach, was fading. Before the summer was out, Rick and I would give up alcohol completely as we handed our souls to this new unknown substance that kept you up all night, forced you to dance and brought barriers crashing down.

If we pause there for a moment and pan back to look at what was occurring elsewhere in the UK in the spring/summer of 1989, then there were clear signs of a profound shift. In March, the Stone Roses released their eponymous debut album; April saw Soul II Soul release *Club Classics Vol One*, containing the near-perfect beats of 'Back to Reality' and 'Keep on Movin'; a few months later Primal Scream's *Loaded* would be released, produced by the already legendary Andrew Weatherall. All these now-classic albums seemed to be converging, heading inexorably to the same end point where indie, pop and dance music would coalesce. Along with the now constant stream of quality house music coming from the US and the output of homegrown British tunes such as Orbital's 'Chime', electronic production was sweeping all before it. The availability of cheap Akai samplers, 808 and 909 drum machines and a range of Roland keyboards was now being exploited by the nimble fingers of producers everywhere. Throw in a cheap Atari computer and some sequencing software such as Cubase and the democratic demystification of studio production had arrived. On *Top of the Pops*, in clubs, booming from cars in the streets, electronic beats were becoming ubiquitous. The much-vaunted 'Summer of Love' in 1988 had occurred the year before, but this had been mostly confined to pay parties in the south-west of England, within the M25, the Orbital motorway which gave them their collective name. Ideas filtered through much more slowly in those pre-mobile and internet days, but by the summer of 1989, there were very different developments in very different parts of the UK.

Located in the post-industrial wastelands of former mill towns dotted around north-west England lies Blackburn. Much like Bolton, this whole region had long suffered economic decline, and this had greatly accelerated under the London–centric and ruthless market economics of Margaret Thatcher. As to why a genuinely working–class explosion of illegal parties exploded here of all places during 1989 has been explained in many ways. Possibly its proximity to Liverpool and Manchester, or the handy availability of empty old mills and warehouses, but equally likely because there happened to be a well–organised crew of promoters there, particularly the Blackburn Self Help Group, a loose organisation involving Tommy Smith, Tony Creft, and Neil Shackleton, stated: 'Obviously it was anti–authoritarian. You could even say we were anarchists. We were sick of the violence, the tension, the animosity and commercialisation of nightclubs.'

These were pay parties but not in the same vein as the hugely expensive Orbital parties where ticket prices ranged around the thirty or forty pound mark and someone hoped to get rich quickly. The Blackburn parties may not have been 'free parties' in the strict sense of the word, but they certainly shared the convoys, the attitude and the sheer illegal bravado of what was to come later. Pete didn't move to Nottingham until May 1990, and so he attended several of the Blackburn events, only a short drive from Bolton, with thousands of others, including the infamous gathering where a police car was overturned and set alight. When we next spoke, we could hardly contain our delight that acid house had turned political.

Also located in the north-west of England, of course, was what was fast becoming the world's most famous nightclub, the Haçienda. As remarked in an earlier chapter, Pete and I had been going to the former yacht showroom turned Factory Records owned club since not long after it opened in 1982. In fact, Pete cherished his membership card (number 23, of course) for the rest of his life. Although it had been mostly half-full, except for a few big gigs, this was changing fast. By 1989 the 'Hot' and 'Nude' nights were becoming the premier house nights in the north, with Mike Pickering and Jon

DaSilva playing the crop of early imports, many of them purchased at Eastern Bloc Records, run by an old acquaintance of ours from Bolton, Martin Price. As I was often visiting Bolton to see my family, Pete and I would attend some of these early Haçienda house nights, witnessing a level of hedonistic indulgence we had not known possible. Around this time, it was rumoured that the management had put poppers (amyl nitrate) in the smoke machine and it certainly felt like it was possible. As recorded so exhaustively elsewhere, the place was deranged. Having been constructed within a warehouse space, the interior and design felt perfect: high ceiling, concrete, a sea of fog and sweat, arms raised aloft as the DJs pulverised the senses from the booth up in the gods.

Although we would in later years visit and indeed DJ in some of the greatest clubs in the world – Amsterdam's Paradiso, the End Up in San Francisco, London's Ministry of Sound, Space and Amnesia in Ibiza, Body and Soul in New York – nothing would ever quite match the sheer visceral abandon and intoxication of that club in a rundown street in central Manchester. Around the summer of 1989, I decided to buy a van to get around in style and found a VW Type 2 van, the one with the rounded front but no split screen; it was eggshell blue with a foldaway cooker under the front seat. Rick, Pete, Barbara and I would drive up to the Haçienda from Nottingham, a short hop up the A6 through the rugged county of Derbyshire. Parking outside the nearby Peveril of the Peak pub, we would join the queue (not yet so long that it snaked down the street, around the corner and over the bridge) and, well, get on one.

Emerging drenched in sweat at 2am, we would simply pop the roof in the camper van, fold the bed out, jabber excitedly about the wild scenes we had witnessed and skin up until we fell asleep, waking up to city centre Manchester and a hearty veggie breakfast at the nearby Eighth Day Café. That was apart from one memorable night when we decided to break into an empty warehouse next to where we parked for a laugh, messing around inside until we heard sirens coming. Just before the police cars arrived at considerable speed, we legged it back into the van and lay motionless as they searched the warehouse and stood outside for what seemed like hours before driving off.

Simultaneous to these events in the north and midlands, in the south-west of England, acid house was also beginning to erupt into and disrupt traditional forms of entertainment and gatherings. This was traveller country, based around the ancient counties of Somerset, Wiltshire and Hampshire, where festivals had, as outlined in previous chapters, been occurring since time immemorial. Stonehenge had been the largest, expanding to a huge size to rival even Glastonbury before being violently halted in 1985. Other dates were of primary importance in the free festival calendar, notably Avon Free, to honour Beltane and the arrival of spring. As previously mentioned, me and a small bunch of Nottingham friends had attended this festival in May 1988 when the Brew Crew were at the height of their powers and there was little joy to be found. By 1989, however, things had changed, or rather, they had changed for a tiny minority of those living in the ancient towns of the old counties.

If you listened carefully, acid house could be heard for the first time among the sleepy spires and half-timbered buildings. At the end of May, Inglestone Common in south Gloucestershire became the location for Avon Free 1989. It seems likely that this marked the first appearance of electronic dance music at a free festival, not just cassettes being played over a hired PA system but with the full kit: record decks, mixer, sound system. The sound system belonged to Sweat from Farnham. It has been rumoured that Tonka from Brighton were also there, but I've never had that confirmed. Tonka, with their bright yellow sound system based on the famous tough toys, will certainly feature in this narrative at a future date, and in the debate about which was the first house sound system, it was probably one of these two. Either way, we were not there to witness it, but that weekend represented the beginning of a generational shift that would change the face of festivals and leftfield culture completely.

Glastonbury 1989 would be the first time I heard house music being played at a festival, three weeks after Inglestone Common. Not a free festival, of course, but there were a couple of stalls in the main site belting out acid house, although they did not appear to have decks or a proper sound system, the music being more of an incentive to buy. I don't recall any house being played in the much more lawless traveller's field either that year, although this would change dramatically by 1990. Our Nottingham crew were too busy taking horrible amounts of acid to care. It was a messy event for us, exemplified by one of our cohorts ruthlessly pushing a Portaloo portable toilet over on its front while Damian was taking a shit. Collectively, we watched horrified as he rocked the plastic box from inside and finally emerged to horrified gasps, covered in the most heinous deposits of excrement and sanitary waste. Damian went berserk and, with superhuman strength, picked up the culprit, ran fifty yards or so and threw him into a large fire, shocking a group of what looked suspiciously like Christians sitting around playing acoustic guitar. Obviously, this was not part of our summer of love.

Nor for that matter was our next road trip down south at the end of July, a festival which became infamous in traveller lore, the Treworgey Tree Fayre. Taking place near Liskeard in Cornwall, I think the byline in the *Western Morning News* the week after caught the mood perfectly, describing it as a 'dustbowl of drugs, dreadlocks and dirt where rumours of death and depravity spread at lightning speed'. This event still echoes down the decades in festival veteran conversations. Everything went horribly wrong. Although supposedly a pay event with tickets, any notion of paid entry or security imploded under the sheer weight of attendees. Around 40,000 turned up by Saturday and the infrastructure collapsed. On an incredibly dusty site, there were only a handful of toilets. The Cornish sun beat down relentlessly and the water supply dried up. On Sunday, a dead sheep was discovered to have blocked the water tank. Dogs died, children were violently ill, extra police piled in and 300 arrests were made. Bad acid and technical disasters finished the job.

If Castlemorton three years later would prove to be the zenith of the sound system festival and its Woodstock, Treworgey was probably the Altamont of the crusty festival, reminiscent of the infamous Californian event in 1969 where Hell's Angels acting as security rioted and murdered a black member of the crowd. Having said that, our Nottingham bunch thoroughly enjoyed ourselves. We always did to be honest, no matter how unpleasant the environment, a quality that would prove invaluable in the years to come. Lying drinking in the sun on a sparse patch of grass, we watched in amusement at the demented antics of the Brew Crew, some of whom were trying to run a café called the Black Hag. As they rolled around in the dust in the crusty uniform of dreadlocks, several layers of encrusted t-shirts, ripped black trousers and big battered boots with no laces, throwing full cans of Special Brew at each other and popping inside occasionally for a bosh of gear, I remember mentioning to Rick that this was probably the lowest form of behaviour in Western society since the Black Death. Joking aside, this was no potential alternative for living, nobly rejecting consumerist society to live free on the open road; this was just nihilism and mindless idiocy. There was some evidence of the new paradigm that was to come amid the chaos, a drop-sided van turning up and playing acid house on the Saturday night, but apart from our gang who wobbled around under the lone ultraviolet light, few people seemed interested, although we did clock a group of travellers, dreadlocked for sure, but clearly attuned to the beats, well dressed in Kickers and trainers. Our paths would cross again.

Back in Nottingham, we plunged headlong into the world, which represented a polar opposite to the psychedelic mess of these festivals. The Kool Kat was now too packed and finished at 2am. Soon Graeme Park would leave to move to a residency at the Haçienda. Although replaced by the perfectly competent Allister Whitehead, many punters considered this treachery. Allister was even unfairly booed at his first couple of Saturday night slots, and we decided we needed more. More volume, more hours, more freedom, more everything. From the late summer of 1989, we began to find our groove. Various house parties were arranged in houses dotted around the large urban park in Nottingham's NG7 postcode known as the Forest. This park, or 'recreation ground', was certainly not an actual forest, but it was a very handy green space of roughly forty acres just outside the city centre. Over the years, it would provide a focus for many of our escapades, essentially providing a big playground for those who lived in the endless terraced housing of Forest Fields, Hyson Green and Radford.

Having blown Damian's speakers several times by this stage, we began to rent small PAs. Attending several blues parties, we could only wonder at the mind-numbing bass and shrieking treble of the sound systems, and indeed, how the fuck they had fitted through the door of a council house. Hyson Green was the 'front line' in Nottingham, almost an autonomous zone where the police would mostly not interfere. While nothing like as large or as lawless as Toxteth in Liverpool, Manchester's Moss Side or Bristol's St Paul's, we certainly raised a few eyebrows by walking into some of these all-night reggae and dancehall parties and some gigs at the nearby Marcus Garvey Centre. Although almost exclusively black when we clearly weren't, we never got any attitude; I think shoulders were just shrugged and our ballsy attitude accepted. This was not the music for us, but boy did we clock their systems. Much has been written about the evolution of the reggae sound system, originating in Jamaica and travelling to England as an idea from the West Indies in the sixties and seventies. Within the much-deprived areas of the inner cities, a sound system could provide not just noise but an income, a focal point and a source of pride for the community.

Later, as the house parties grew in regularity and size, it became apparent that we needed more equipment; we couldn't afford a sound system but we could just about scrape together enough for some decks. These, of course, would have to be Technics 1200s, first made in 1972 and the DJ's turntable of choice to this day due to the direct drive action and the pitch control, which allowed, with a mixer, for records to be beat-mixed seamlessly. Technics were not cheap: with a mixer thrown in, you probably would have got little change from eight hundred quid. Simon was the driving force behind the obtaining of decks and with some quick transactions of a not entirely legal nature, he had his first gleaming turntables. There will be several occasions in this narrative where large sums of cash just seem to appear and, as none of us had jobs at the time, I will leave it up to the reader's discretion to ascertain exactly where they came from. Before our purchase of appropriate turntables, another chance meeting would greatly embellish our nascent little band. Hearing there was a house party happening on Mapperley Top, a stone's throw away from where we lived, we naturally had to pile up there and check it out. From down the road, the house beats were audible, thumping away in the dark night. This was so rare that we were intrigued. Having entered the house, we pushed past the mass of bodies to check out who was DJing. It turned out to be a young man sporting proper dreadlocks swept back from his head, some decent clothes and playing good music on what turned out to be his own Technics. His name was Jack and we would get along well.

Jack was on our wavelength from the start and would become, with Simon, our main DJ for some time to come. Naturally cool but with a piercing, dry wit, Jack had grown up in Oxford. He had spent his teenage years in Kendal and then Bristol, before arriving in Nottingham in 1987 to study creative media at Trent Polytechnic. Much like some of the others in our group, the degree had been more about moving to a new city and messing around for three years than any attempt at a career. It has been said many times that the system of free higher education, which existed until the late eighties, was responsible for nurturing a generation of creative talent. Jack had his own flat on Gregory Boulevard, which we began to frequent, often having all-night sessions there or even morning sessions after a party.

Rick and I needed somewhere to go as our stay at Magdala Road was becoming chaotic and probably overlong. Although we had experienced some truly magical times and blissed-out dawns there, it was time for Dave and Julie to have their flat back. Of those wondrous mornings, they represented the honeymoon period which we all had with ecstasy. It must be remembered that we had no idea what this wonder drug was. We knew its initials were MDMA and that was about it. Google lay a decade into the future and we simply had no means of finding out what this was other than word of mouth. It seems so quaint now that this new synthetic drug which would sweep all before it, chemically speaking, replacing all other drugs and even alcohol as the choice of a generation, was considered such a secret and almost sacred communion. In those days, we would only take one tablet, twenty pounds each and not to be contaminated with any other substances, except perhaps for a few spliffs. However, it was not long before we would start necking another half a tablet around 6am, justifying it to each other as a 'tactical half'. Those were the days, it has to be said, as fast forward about two years and the idea of a single tablet would be seen as pathetic and we were into double figures over a big weekend.

And so, needing to find somewhere new to live, the idea of a squat was considered after a three-storey house on nearby Vickers Street was found to be empty. I can't remember who found it exactly or who cracked it, but Rick moved in alongside Miles, my old punky mate from the Bolton days, and a highly eccentric musician called

Stream Angel, although I'm assuming that wasn't his birth name. Probably Victorian or Edwardian in era, it was a neglected but beautiful building, with all its original features, high ceilings and many rooms spread over its rambling three floors. In this building, at some point in the early autumn of 1989, we broke on through to the other side. To optimise the three floors, we decided to have three different sound systems: acid house on top, noise and industrial on the middle, and Stream Angel doing his thing on the ground floor. Silhouetted against a series of mind-bending projections, Stream would link six Roland TR 303s (the machines on which the 'acid' part of acid house was first synthesised) to trigger randomly off each other and then wail in what sounded like Gaelic, all while rolling around on the floor. Quite a remarkable performance for which there are no adequate adjectives.

For the first time, we had a real crowd that kept on growing, finally packing out all three floors. Finally, we had a real acid house party on our hands, and over the Saturday night it escalated, evolved and erupted out of control, which was exactly what we had been waiting for. Here we had combined dance music with sufficient lawlessness for the police to turn up. Pete brought records with him down from Bolton and we spent days making tapes. Somewhere in the house, Rick was playing his beloved hip-hop. And for the first time we saw in the Sunday dawn with a heaving dancefloor, a sea of smiling euphoric faces lit by the shafts of late autumn sunlight piercing the room. We were off. There was some collateral damage; someone had scrawled dayglo figures on the walls and Pete and I joined Dave Hayes, who had driven the two of them from Bolton, in throwing a heavy wooden door out of a top-floor window, only to narrowly miss his own car.

One thing that was definitely not euphoric was our attempt to get to a proper Orbital rave two weeks later. This is the first time I have used the word 'rave' in this book; it didn't come into use until around this time in late 1989. Dropping into a fashionable clothes shop in Nottingham city centre one Saturday around then, I still recall the pride I felt when one of the Kool Kat crew asked me if I was a 'raver'. And so, on 21 October 1989, six or so of us with a small bag of pills set off for Hampshire to a Biology party, having paid (to us) the astronomical sum of twenty-five pounds per ticket. Crammed into my VW van, we were hugely excited. Driving down the M1 from Nottingham, as we would come to do so many countless times ahead, we followed the directions to the M3. We then stopped at a service station to ring the number on the tickets.

With mobile phones a decade away, this was the only way to find a party. Promoters of such early raves used industrial-use answer machines such as those used by the NHS to handle thousands of calls simultaneously. In the phone booth, a grating cockney voice told us to head for Guildford, pull off at a certain exit and drive five miles on a random 'A' road. Exhilarated, we drove as fast as the old bus would go up the M3 to the junction, someone holding the map, all of us shouting and throwing shapes to the mix tape. And then we ran into thirty-thousand other people in probably ten thousand vehicles, all trying to get to the same junction. The traffic ground to a halt, the slip road and two motorway lanes jammed for miles. We sat there for about five hours as our rave dreams died and frantic police vehicles tried to move everyone along and clear the motorway.

Personally, I've never had much time for the classic myth of the origins of acid house. As a northerner, it all seemed very London-centric that Oakenfold, Rampling and Weatherall visited Ibiza in 1987 and, having had their brains suitably blown at clubs like Amnesia, brought the vibe back to London and started the whole scene. However, having gotten to know all these legendary individuals since, at least they clearly had a vision and they wanted everyone to have a good time rather than just make big bucks. Obviously, there was a preponderance of acid house clubs and parties in London. It is, after all, the biggest city in Europe and had a tradition of warehouse parties stretching back to the early eighties. And indeed, perhaps the big pay parties which began to emerge in 1989 were initially done in the spirit of unity and hedonism, but at this point in late 1989, pseudo-yuppie promoters such as Energy's Tony Colston-Hayter and the man we were cursing that night, Jarvis Sandy, had taken over. These guys were brash, London-based venture capitalists who were only interested in making money. The initial police clampdown on these huge pay parties during 1989/90 was highly successful as the organisers had no interest in throwing a free party that could be hidden from the police or from five hundred people. No profits there. Indeed, when the Freedom to Party organisation held a rally in Trafalgar Square in 1990 to oppose the Parliamentary Bill introduced by Conservative MP Graham Bright, it was a cabal of the Orbital Mr Bigs who funded it, not because they believed in the freedom to party but because their profit margins had been decimated.

Driving back up the M1 on the Sunday morning, despondent and a hundred and fifty quid lighter, we discussed the situation. Between us, we had now attended all the manifestations of this radical new youth cult, be it Blackburn, the Haçienda, the Garage and now a big pay party. Dave and Julie had been at Shoom and spoke of its idealism and its genuine barrier-free bonhomie. That was what we wanted, but more. What we had experienced was great individually but there had to be a better, more idealistic whole. If the rave scene had lost its way and its idealistic origins, then someone needed to put them back. A few weeks later, the Berlin Wall would come down. Margaret Thatcher was introducing the Poll Tax. Could we possibly organise parties using these twin drivers of house music and ecstasy but mould them into something new? Perhaps this new joyous paradigm could be utilised for political and social ends? Perhaps, as it was my birthday on the twenty-third of November in a few weeks, we could book a venue and try to do it ourselves.

# 7

Or maybe we just wanted to take drugs, dance all night and have a laugh. This dichotomy between social anger, a wish to change society and downright hedonistic indulgence would remain our driving forces, sometimes gloriously unified and sometimes in direct conflict. It had been that way for the hippies and the punks, too, and would be for many of our generation. Either way, we now had about a month to prepare for our first event in a licensed venue – and we had a name. Researching this book, Simon tells me that we kind of hijacked someone else's club night. A friend of his, John Stripey, had booked the Garage for some celebration with the owners, Ian and Tricia, the latter being from Bolton and coincidentally a friend of Pete's. Stripey had invited Simon to DJ and, not for the last time, we took this as a cue to take over. The 23rd of November would become DiY's official birthday. We had no inkling of the cosmic importance of the number 23, being the twenty-third day of the month and my twenty-third birthday, which makes the synchronicity of that night, whichever way you look at it, seem genuinely written in the stars. Or perhaps it's all bollocks, who really knows, but the number which has maintained spiritual significance from the ancient Kabbalah, via the Discordians and William Burroughs, through to the discovery of twenty-three helixes in DNA and the KLF, Spiral Tribe and beyond seems to have had some mystical importance over our long journey.

Whatever the esoteric significance of the chronology, our first event as DiY went well and we were hungry for more. Just over a month later, the turbulent era of the 1980s would end. Amid another house party on New Year's Eve in Nottingham, the nineties slipped out of existence without fuss or fanfare; in fact, we hadn't even started the party at such an early hour as midnight. The 1990s began for us in typically chaotic fashion as the PA hire place had closed early and we had to revert to using Damian's even posher new hi-fi speakers. One of the needles on Simon's decks was malfunctioning and the smoke machine wouldn't work, but the party rocked anyway. Looking back, these were all quite appropriate auguries for the decade ahead.

No one could know what the nineties were to bring, or that it would prove to be the most hedonistic, debauched and downright liberating decade in recent British cultural and musical history, with the possible exception of the sixties, of course. It always struck me that the sixties had been over-hyped and that, although much progressive legislation had occurred, such as the abolition of the death penalty and the legalisation of homosexuality and abortion, there were little practical effects on the lives of most young people, mostly those living outside London in places such as Bolton, Bath or Bulwell. As eighties Britain recedes further into the history books, the more discordant and polarised it appears. Framed by the eleven-year reign of Margaret Thatcher from 1979 to 1990, the stark effects of mass unemployment and neo-liberal economics split the UK into those who benefitted and those who fell by the wayside. In the early eighties, the Falklands War and the Miners' Strike seemed to perfectly encapsulate the bitterness of the fleeing decade, and now bridging the gap into the next was Mrs Thatcher's new crusade, the Poll Tax. Announced optimistically as the 'Community Charge' during 1989 and introduced to Scotland that year and England during 1990, to many this tax demonstrated unequivocally that Maggie had finally lost her marbles. As the saying goes, power corrupts and absolute power corrupts absolutely. As if to demonstrate this, Thatcher had decided to abolish the system of local authority rates that had been in place for centuries and which had a sliding scale of payment based upon income and wealth. This tried and tested system would be replaced with, to quote Wikipedia, 'a tax levied as a fixed sum on every liable individual (typically every adult), without reference to income or resources'. In effect, everyone would pay the same, be they a duke or a doctor, a nurse or a single mother. Flying in the face of a hundred years of progressive taxation, Thatcher also ignored the lessons of history, as when a similar tax was introduced in 1377 (from which the name 'Poll Tax' was derived) it led directly to the Peasants Revolt of 1381, when large parts of England rioted and a peasant mob took over London and burned it to the ground. And this is pretty much what would reoccur in March 1990.

Although now throwing most of our energies into parties, our growing collective was still mostly composed of outsiders, political nonconformists and anarchists. When a date was announced for a huge demonstration in London against the Poll Tax, we began organising coaches. The date would be 31 March and it would prove to be a watershed in British political history. Eventually, twelve coaches would go down from Nottingham, of which we organised and funded several. As we alighted near Kennington Park, south London, the sheer scale of what was about to happen became clear. I was a veteran of demonstrations, attending and organising them since the early eighties. Whether they had been in favour of animal rights, opposing the Conservative government's anti-gay Clause 28 legislation or any other cause, I had never witnessed anything like this. It was clearly going to be huge. Later estimates were around 250,000 people. And, apart from the birth of my children many years later, it would prove to be the best day of my life. More and more coaches arrived, spilling their passengers onto the common. It was not just the sheer volume of demonstrators that overwhelmed, it was the variety. Never before had I seen such normal people attending a demo. This was no 'rent-a mob' and included families from the Midlands, pensioners from Yorkshire, queer activists from Bristol, students from Exeter, trade unionists from Scotland. It was white, black and brown; a large group of Sikh families rolled in. A genuine grassroots reaction to the shameless and ill-conceived change to the taxation laws that would punish all but the wealthy across the land. By the time the leading cohort of this vast assembly had left the park and set off for Trafalgar Square, the multitude was still assembling at the rear. Indeed, the word on the street would be that by the time the vanguard had actually reached Trafalgar Square, miles away, many were still waiting to leave the park.

The atmosphere was carnival-like, anger being dissipated in the glorious spring sunshine. However, as the crowd pushed into Trafalgar Square and filled it to capacity, large splinter groups began to protest loudly in Whitehall and outside Downing Street. Sending in mounted police, the authorities completely misjudged their tactics. In short, by 2.30pm the more militant sections had begun to fight back. By late afternoon, one of the most serious riots in London's history, and the most violent for a century, had exploded across the capital. What followed was a spasm of political violence in which all the repressed anger of the eighties erupted. A few of us, trapped by police tactics and the sheer volume of the crowd, climbed up onto scaffolding next to the South African embassy and watched with a mixture of disbelief and jubilation at the scenes playing out below us. Waves of protestors were fighting back against the police, hundreds of anarchists using scaffolding bars, bins, dismantled bus stops and anything else available to hand to force them back out of the square. And then, below me and fifty feet to my right, someone broke into South Africa House and set it on fire. This was, of course, during the days of apartheid. Nelson Mandela had been released from prison only a month before; it would be another four years before multi-racial elections. A huge cheer went up from the crowd. After years of largely ineffectual marches and boycotts, the despised South African government's embassy seemed a legitimate target.

In effect, we took over central London for several hours, the rioting lasting long into the night. Trafalgar Square and its environs were a melee of smoke, the sounds of breaking glass, shouting from all sides, the clattering of hooves. At one breathtaking point, I watched about ten lads drop a ten-foot-long concrete block from four storeys up directly onto the roof of a riot van and watched them cheer as the riot police within spilt from the crumpled vehicle only to be engulfed by the crowd. Heading back to Nottingham, we learned on the radio that 339 people had been arrested, including some of our party. One of our gang, Pete Kenny, a lawless anarcho-punk living well beyond the fringes of society but who had also now gravitated towards acid house, had been detained and it would take him four days to get home following release. Charged with assaulting a police officer, he would return to London, only for the charges to be dropped.

Much has been written and debated about the relative merits of violence and non-violence for political means. Personally, I think that in certain situations, especially where the state is employing extreme violence, as in apartheid-era South Africa, it is legitimate to fight back by all means necessary. If you shoot our children, as happened at Sharpeville, South Africa, in 1960, then some of us will shoot back. All governments and states are, after all, founded and maintained through the use or the threat of violence. This is always manifestly obvious in the case of dictatorships or failed states, but the ruling class seized the land and wealth so many centuries ago in England that state violence no longer needs to be overt. Whether this particular situation required such a destructive response is open to debate, but it made the Conservative Party fully realise the sheer folly of the Poll Tax as a policy and led directly to the ousting of Margaret Thatcher as prime minister within a few months. Perhaps this is not the book for such a long description of such an event, but it perfectly encapsulates the political focus that ran parallel to our burgeoning party activities. The yawning gap in consciousness between the quite awesome display of righteous anger we had just witnessed and the apolitical Freedom to Party rallies held in the same place only two months earlier could not have been more acute.

Another clear example of where the original Orbital rave scene had exhausted any radical status it may once have had would come a few weeks later when Rick and I travelled down to a licensed Energy event at London's Docklands Arena on 14 April 1990. Since our aborted mission to get to the Biology party a few months earlier, we had been to another big pay party, Raindance. Although that one actually happened, it was still very underwhelming. These were the days when events started to boast competitively about 50K rigs, bouncy castles and three coloured lasers. At the Raindance party, they had dodgems. Again, it just appeared that the whole underground, illicit excitement of acid house had been commercialised and rebranded into a soulless and anodyne imitation. However, the Energy event was a new low. To be blunt, it was fucking awful. Having forked out forty quid each, we hooked up with our old friend, the wonderful Eleanor Bailey, queuing up for admittance to the vast and charmless arena. Even the area itself, the London Docklands, reeked of the ruthless venture capitalism so beloved by the Thatcherite right. Although the line-up featured some individually excellent acts such as 808 State and Orbital, collectively it just didn't work. Finishing at the laughable hour of eleven, there was just no atmosphere, just groups of bewildered teenagers wandering around looking lost in their smiley face t-shirts and baggy trousers. The final straw was Snap playing an obviously mimed version of 'The Power' with those awful formation dancers so beloved by massive commercial artists ever since Michael Jackson's heyday. It was like being trapped in the *Top of the Pops* studio on bad drugs for hours, and they weren't even selling alcohol.

Travelling back to Nottingham, Rick and I decided that we had seen enough of what remained of the big-name pay parties based in London and the Home Counties. We began to plot our next club night and turned our attention to planning a big party in Nottingham, still awaiting its first rave. Having finally found somewhere to live, we would now be hugely assisted in that task when, on 23 May, on his twenty-fifth birthday, Pete moved down from Bolton as we took joint tenancy of a three-bedroom terraced house on Alma Street at the top end of Forest Fields. Having been working on a building site in Bolton for the last year or so, Pete was clearly able to see that things were starting to happen in Nottingham, things that met all the requirements of his various loves. From this point, the three of us would live together, in various houses and with various partners, for the next seven years. Even though we would live and work together constantly for those years and despite all the ensuing chaos, euphoria, arrests, lack of sleep, drugs, endless days on the road and trips abroad, I don't think there was a single argument between us. What we did suddenly have was all our records in the same place, and collectively we had quite a collection. Between us, we bought one, then another Technics deck and a mixer. Although within a musical Venn diagram we were all enthralled by the shiny new sounds of house music, we all had different musical lineages. Rick knew his way back through disco and funk but his first love was hip-hop. I was an indie kid at heart, always prone to slipping on the Happy Mondays, the Stone Roses or New Order. Pete had quite simply the most varied and mind-blowing record collection of anyone I knew. Tunes as varied as Roy Ayers, Funkadelic, EPMD, Fela Kuti, Joy Division, 808 State, Chic, Orbital or Lee Scratch Perry would all be played long into the night, every night as we rotated on the decks.

Simon and Jack, meanwhile, had become house obsessives. For the next five years, I don't think Simon bought anything other than house twelve-inch records, including food. He was born to spend his life under the artificial light of record shop counters, and by 1992 he would have the most unrivalled house collection of any DJ on our scene. Apart from Selectadisc, his main source of vinyl would be Arcade Records in Nottingham, staffed by the legendary music obsessive Jonathon. He and Simon looked like brothers separated at birth, both clearly creatures of the night, tall and gaunt and smoking all day heavily in the Arcade shop basement. Jonathon was a real expert in all genres of music, be it death metal, electro or hip-hop, and used to play records at the legendary Rock City dance all-dayers, which predated the arrival of house music. I recall Jonathon telling me that he would go months without seeing daylight except on a Sunday as it was dark in the winter when he opened up the basement and dark when he locked up. When the house scene became increasingly dominated by US imports, focused on labels such as Bottom Line, NuGroove, Trax and, above all, Strictly Rhythm, Simon always seemed to have access, and Jonathon should take much credit for this alongside Simon's incredible determination to have the best house records and his total devotion to the cause.

Simon was at this point living on the other side of Forest Fields and the three of us were constant visitors at his house. Following our ongoing house parties, the after-party would continue at his for days. Back at Alma Street, the heavy rotation in that spring of 1990 was what became known as the 'bleep' sound, emanating in vivid purple sleeves from Warp Records, twenty-seven miles up the road in Sheffield. Having formed at almost exactly the same time as us in 1989, this nascent record label and shop run by Steve Beckett, Rob Mitchell and Rob Gordon had made a real impact in UK dance music circles. Commencing with Forgemasters' 'Track With No Name' in 1989, they pioneered a minimal, vocal-free electro-house sound, replete with robotic bleeps and tones, which became instantly identifiable. Through tracks such as Sweet Exorcist's 'Testone' and

Nightmares on Wax's 'Dextrous', Warp demonstrated that a new independent label in south Yorkshire, so close to us in Nottingham, could produce records to take on the world.

We had an idea. We had a lot of ideas in those days, possibly due to the copious amounts of hash that we were smoking at the time. As we were all claiming benefits (we were far too busy for jobs) and could ill-afford the cost of getting stoned every night, we inevitably began to sell it. More of that later. Anyway, our idea was to find a licensed all-night venue in Nottingham and put on a big party featuring Warp artists, figuring that this would generate the large crowd we needed. Remember, we had not even done our first club night with a flyer yet. None of us had been paid to DJ; we were unknown outside Notting-ham. Knowing all the clubs and venues as we did by now, it was com-mon knowledge that the only place in Nottingham with an all-night licence was the Marcus Garvey Centre. For years, this community centre had been the main reggae and dancehall venue in Nottingham. Rick and I had been to see Burning Spear and Misty in Roots there, although noting with some trepidation that we were the only white kids in a crowd of several hundred. Some crew from London had actually organised, in the loosest sense of the word, an all-nighter there in November the previous year. Rick and I, plus Damian and his mate Josh, had gone to check it out, only to find that the promised coach-loads from London had failed to materialise and the crowd ended up being about thirty-strong. Again, we knew both that we could do bet-ter and that this was the only all-night licence in Nottingham.

Either way, a few weeks before there had been a pitched bat-tle involving machetes in the car park outside the Garvey between the Nottingham crew and their Birmingham equivalent. It was that kind of place. Simon knew everyone in NG7 by this point. A walk across Forest Fields or Hyson Green could take hours as every sin-gle person under the age of fifty, black, white or brown, would stop him and chat. This pattern would always remain. Simon was and remains probably the most loved person I've ever known, but boy can he be infuriating. Anyway, he knew a couple of the engineers at the community studio attached to the Garvey, as everyone knew it, and got us an intro to see Les, the main man. God knows what he thought when two cheeky young white boys (I was twenty-three, Rick twenty-two) stumbled into his office one day. Les was in his fifties, tough as old boots and brutal with the insults. As we explained our intentions, he slowly shook his head in disbelief. Not for the last time, I think our sheer bravado carried us through and he agreed to give us a date, Friday 6 July, licensed until 6am Saturday morning. It would cost us a grand. As we shuffled out of his office, he stated, 'You seem like a pair of cunts but I kind of like you and your money is as good as anyone's.' Taking this as a compliment, we set to work on our first big party. Warp agreed to supply Forgemasters live, Winston and Parrot as DJs, and in what was to be their first-ever live performance, the outfit behind a huge track that had just been released and had swept all before it, LFO.

Simultaneously, we decided to book another club night, and after some negotiation with Ian and Tricia, we were offered a Thursday night on 28 June back at the Kool Kat. Rick, who would handle the graphic design for DiY from then onwards, quickly threw together a photocopied flyer. We called it Rhythm Religion and it was the first flyer ever to have the name DiY on it. It simply states 'house – hip-hop – visual FX by Sirius'. No DJ names yet – such simple times. Sirius was the stage name of another new Nottingham contact, Rob, known by all then and now as Rob Lights. Beloved of what could vaguely be called the 'Zippie' ideas epitomised by Fraser Clark and his *Encyclopedia Psychedelica*, Rob was a gangly and well-read enthusiast of the sixties counterculture, keen to meld it into a nineties technological lifestyle. Very knowledgeable about Terence McKenna, Timothy Leary and Robert Anton Wilson, Rob became our projections and lighting guy.

Clearly, the flyer for the Garvey would need to be done properly; it needed to be printed and look good. DJ wise, we booked Allister Whitehead to attract the Kool Kat crew and local hero DJ SY, who was then the most prominent of what would become known as rave DJs. Not still entirely sure who would be playing among our own DJs, we just plumped for 'DiY DJs'. All we needed now was a name for the event. Of all the protracted and absurd negotiations and discussions we had about names over the years, I think this one went on the longest – not just days but weeks. Our growing collective now numbered about ten, and although such non-hierarchical structures are wonderful on paper and will no doubt one day bring capitalism to its knees, they are truly shit at making decisions. I remember us all drawing up lists of potential names and spending hours failing to agree, not wanting it to sound too ravey but not too punky or anarcho. It had to sound similar to other event names but different. Finally, I offered a name taken from an album by the British punky-dub band Ruts DC: 'Rhythm Collision'. There was silence and some nodding of heads and that was enough. Last-minute as ever, the flyer details needed to be with the printers by the end of the day, and now we had a name.

With several large boxes of flyers to distribute, it was during these weekends that we began to drive long distances, racking up endless inter-city miles. One of our main destinations was Liverpool. Barbara, my long-time partner from the Bolton days, had moved there to do a drama degree and had established a new set of friends based loosely around the Polytechnic and independent theatre scene. Much as in Nottingham, this ever-growing group lived in a series of dodgy houses, squats and, later, several of them shared a rather lovely townhouse at Bold Place next to the Bombed-Out Church, a shell of a building destroyed by the Luftwaffe during the war and never rebuilt. By this time, the Haçienda, thirty-five miles down the road, was well past its prime. Britain's first ecstasy death had occurred there in July 1989, the gangs had moved in and the queue was now composed largely of tourists and students. However, in a rough Merseyside suburb, stepping into the vacuum most admirably and in perfect continuity of the intense and decades-long Liverpool-Manchester rivalry was the new north-western rave Mecca of Quadrant Park. Not long after it became a dance music club in early 1990, Pete and I had visited 'the Quad' together and couldn't quite believe what we were witnessing. Although large, the Haçienda had been broken up by pillars and staircases, different floors and bars. You could see across the dancefloor but had your own space as a group, as outlined so memorably by Shaun Ryder in his autobiography.

Quadrant Park was a huge space, reminiscent of football terraces, packed to its 2,500 capacity and, without wanting to sound cheesy, a veritable cathedral of ecstasy. Originally formed by the trio of local DJs John Kelly, Andy Carroll and Mike Knowler, the Quad set new standards in many ways. Although the car park and the toilets could be very dodgy, and the all-nighter which opened in October round the corner was the dodgiest place I have ever been, it was a truly magical sight to see five thousand hands raised to the heavens in ecstatic worship as a huge classic record was dropped. Very working-class, very Scouse, very exhilarating, Quadrant Park would probably never be topped as a temple of excess and high tunes. The era of such piano-driven classics as N-Joi's 'Anthem', Asha's 'JJ Tribute' and Double Dee's 'Found Love' would reach its zenith at this rundown warehouse in Bootle. In particular, the brutal opening stabs of 808 State's 'Cubik' would send the place into complete meltdown. In the meantime, despite our endless trips up and across the country to promote Rhythm Collision, with long, cold hours spent flyering outside Occasions and the Leadmill in Sheffield, the Warehouse in Leeds, the Kool Kat and the freshly opened Venus in Nottingham, we needed to get ready for our next adventure. Happening in a few weeks and offering potential delights in total contrast to those big northern clubs was the small matter of Glastonbury.

# 8

During the intervening thirty-odd years, so much has been written, discussed and debated about what exactly happened at Glastonbury 1990 and who was there that it really deserves its own book. I personally don't recall Avon Free Festival taking place that year and can find no record of it, nor has anyone that I interviewed as part of my research. As outlined in earlier chapters, in 1988 it had taken place at Wick Quarry, and in 1989 on Inglestone Common. So, in its absence on the bank holiday weekend ending May and with the ongoing prohibition of all Stonehenge gatherings, especially around the Solstice on 21 June, Glastonbury was the first big festival of the year. We were no ingenues and this would be my sixth Glastonbury and umpteenth festival, but over the winter and spring things had changed. In a perfect summary of the convergence of indie and dance music, Happy Mondays were playing on the main stage. However, no explicitly dance acts were appearing, and the days when the festival included a massive dance tent were still years away.

Michael Eavis, the farmer who had run the festival on his farm since 1970, was still allowing travellers to set up an independently huge free field next to the main festival. Security was still relatively relaxed; there was no police presence on site. Drug gangs still blatantly lurked at the edges of the main drag but now they had added ecstasy tablets to their menus. Of all the fifteen Glastonbury's I would attend that century, this would be the sunniest; the infamous muddy quagmires would not make an appearance. And above all, people were heading there in buses, cars and hire vans who had little intention of participating in the 'Performing Arts Festival'. They wanted house music, they wanted to dance and they wanted to party all night, all weekend.

Our merry band set off early on Friday 22nd, having watched the England football team beat Egypt in the World Cup qualifying rounds the day before. Italia 90 would add another magical ingredient to the weekend as hundreds watched the later matches in the sun in the wonderful and highly ramshackle 'World Cup Café'. I think Simon may have driven, or perhaps our friend Doug may have hired the white Luton van we travelled down in. He was another long-term resident of 30 Magdala Road, a chipper and handsome fellow living in a lovely old flat with a couple of lurchers. I always thought of him as the Last English Gentleman. Smart but very laid-back, he kept a fleet of somewhat shabby diesel vehicles just about in service and would later become our consultant mechanic. In addition to myself, the passengers in the van, as far as I can recall, were Simon, Rick, Pete, Jean and her new boyfriend Ged, an implausibly well-dressed young fellow who was part of the Nottingham fashionista crowd — we all connected via house music. Damian drove down separately as ever, possibly with Dave and Julie. If you are wondering how we got so many people into a two-seater van, then the answer is simple: in the large box on the back, sitting amid the record decks, mixer, several crates of records and many crates of beer. Throughout our adventures, it has to be said that we paid scant attention to the rules of road safety, one of the many features of the era that you just couldn't get away with now.

Arriving at Glastonbury on a glorious Friday afternoon on the first day of summer, we now had to work out how to get all these people and our kit inside the festival. Glastonbury was much less popular back then and still considered way outside the mainstream. The thought of paying the outrageous ticket price of thirty-eight pound again never occurred to us. Having attended free festivals for years, I would in fact never pay to go to Glastonbury, or any other festival for that matter, until well into the second decade of the twenty-first century. Sorry, Mr Eavis, we owe you. And so, into combat – we had done this many times before. This year it proved quite simple; we just drove around the back and finally ended up somewhere on the edge of the free fields. Grabbing a crate of beer, we set off into the melee. Friday afternoons at the world's biggest music festival are beyond chaotic, especially so back then. What we needed now was a venue, a tent or a marquee with a sound system so we could go back and get the decks. In one of the great moments of synchronicity that seemed to occasionally step in and guide our fate, as Simon, Rick, Pete and I strolled along into the heart of the beast, a familiar figure came striding towards us. It was Jack, all big grin and dreadlocks. We hugged, we sat down, we cracked a beer. Jack excitedly informed us that some travellers he knew had set up a marquee at the bottom of the main drag in the free zone. They had a sound system, he had records, he continued, but did we know anyone with decks and a mixer? Well, funnily enough, we did.

Hurrying back to the van, we got the equipment and headed the long way round into the unfenced unofficial field. Walking down the drag, this was a very different environment to the main site, or 'Babylon' as it was universally known in these quarters. Big boots and dreads were still de rigeur, reggae and space-rock belted out from the post-apocalyptic vehicles and ramshackle vegan cafés. I spotted my favourite old truck again, sprayed black with huge wheels and 'Fuckpig' painted on the front. Not having yet obtained flight cases, we attracted a few funny looks carrying a mixer and records decks, still in their plastic lids, with Simon and Rick jointly carrying a big red crate of records behind. And then we walked into a marquee with white sides and green, red and yellow patterned squares, the pyramid roof supported by scaffolding, and our world would never be the same again.

Inside the marquee, speaker cabinets were being lifted into position, a lighting platform was being constructed, and cables were being gaffer-taped into position. Waving to a guy in dungarees who seemed to be vaguely in charge, Jack introduced us to Chilly Phil. Living on the road since 1987, Phil was one of those rare people who naturally exudes quiet authority and wisdom. Straight away, we warmed to him and felt at ease within the calmness that he projected. Phil seemed markedly different to many of the travelling clan; no big boots, less attitude and a genuine thirst for house music. A long-time veteran of Stonehenge, the pyramid marquee was his, although he was always at pains to make it clear he was just minding it, the tent being on long-term loan from Hawkwind's Nick Turner. In the years to come, Phil would prove to be probably the single most influential and pivotal individual of the entire free party scene, and that weekend he would be a star. I would describe him a prince among men, but he would hate that.

Later I would discover that Phil had travelled up to Glastonbury the week before with Jack and a small group of his traveller friends. Jack had headed down from Nottingham with his friend Irene to meet up with her buddy Jamie and his site companions, including a couple named Boysie and Emma, before they travelled up to Glastonbury together. Along with Phil, this couple instantly stood out from the crowd and this trio would provide the central focus of our alliance with the progressive travelling fraternity. Although together at the time, Emma and Boysie had moved onto the road separately, Boysie in 1985 and Emma in 1988. Hailing from Hampshire and West London respectively, they had both grown up with musical tastes very different to the standard site variety: Emma had a deep love of beats and breaks, and Boysie had a life-long affinity for reggae and dub from the records his mum brought home from her job as a secretary at the BBC. Our paths must have crossed many times without us knowing before that pivotal summer of 1990, most noticeably at Treworgey, where we must have been wobbling around in the dark by the drop-sided van playing acid house, probably having consumed the same tablets. Emma was at that point in a relationship with a chap named Roger, who would also play a pivotal role in this tale. Either way, they had sampled the delights of the early rave scene, inviting opprobrium when slipping back onto site in fashionable clothes and trainers after a weekend dancing in London.

Back in the action, from Friday until Sunday night, we would fight a kind of running battle with various other factions for access to the marquee and sound system, which belonged to a guy named Lynn, his blue double decker-bus being parked behind the pyramid. In the mix was a variety of bands, including a travelling hardcore punk collective called 2000 DS, who wanted to play live and most definitely did not want our music played in what they considered the sacrilegious environment of a free festival. For the first of untold times, we were told that we couldn't play 'that disco shit'. Phil was caught in the middle of the debate but, as Friday wore on, we were able to set the decks and mixer up, and Simon and Jack began to DJ. They played pretty much all night and it was wild. Rammed from the off, it soon became clear how many people had come to dance. And dance. For us, this outdoor setting was an entirely new space in which to party.

From the start, it was obvious on an instinctive level that this freedom from walls, licensing hours and security combined with loud house music was meant to be; the synergy of crusties and travellers and townies and students and just plain weirdos felt electrifying and full of possibility. These guys had generators, marquees and a sound system; we had the decks, mixer and the records, and we both had the drugs and a relaxed attitude to breaking the law. In his book *Temporary Autonomous Zone*, radical sixties philosopher Hakim Bey had proposed that, with the futility of taking on the entire establishment, we could at least create transitory spaces for a night or a weekend where the standard rules of society would be suspended and replaced by a new radical set of rules based on equality or hedonism. This was such a space. However, come Saturday afternoon the traditional bands were not in the mood for any more disco shit. So we reluctantly withdrew as the drum kit, guitars and microphones were set up.

Still buzzing from the night before, we heard that there was another sound system playing house music up the track. Heading there en masse, around a hundred metres up the drag, the same scenes as last night were being played out in another, bigger marquee, which was red and blue and contained a distinctive yellow sound system with a logo that read 'Tonka'. The marquee itself belonged to Circus Warp and would create a legend all of its own. The dizzying light show inside was the work of a certain lanky fellow, who seemed to be known to all as Dangerous Dave. From this point in June 1990, certainly for the next two years, so much would happen at such a dizzying and accelerating pace, so many names and myriad groupings and events would wax and wane into a chaotic dynamic, that although I have tried to be objective and as inclusive as possible, it will always be impossible to fully unravel all the separate threads thirty years later.

Let's start with Tonka, almost certainly the first house sound system in the UK, if not the world. Originating in Cambridge at the tail end of the sixties, this multi-generational party crew had by the late eighties morphed into an acid house collective and painted their sound system in the bright yellow colour of the famous tough toys. Relocating to Brighton, their monthly after-parties on nearby Black Rock beach were all-night, free affairs played out of the back of a bus, and again they would be a genuine contender for the first proper free parties anywhere. There is a great photo of a young DJ Harvey and some of the other Tonka DJs behind the decks in that marquee, looking so young, as we all were, and completely unaware that this seminal Glastonbury moment would later achieve mythical status.

Several of their personnel would later move to San Francisco and establish the Wicked collective, who a couple of years later would become almost a transatlantic sister organisation to DiY. Adding extra sound that weekend were Sweat, whose additional bass bins built by their main guys Justin and Bob arrived at some point over the Friday or Saturday, giving the tent a whole extra sonic punch. Sweat were also among the first sound systems to play dance music, another being Brighton's Sugarlump.

Dave and Circus Warp are another thread in this rich tapestry. Along with another, older collective of festival veterans, the Mutoid Waste Company, Circus Warp had been around for years. Part circus, part Situationists, part party promoters, they were never sound systems but specialists in outrageous environments. Originating from the London squat scene in the mid-eighties, the Mutoids were an art and sculpture collective who gravitated to the festival circuit, becoming famous for their metallic installations and demented vehicles welded into surreal shapes such as locusts or sharks. Most notable of these was 'Carhenge', originally constructed at Glastonbury in 1984 and consisting of a concentric circle of cars placed on end with another across the top, mimicking the upright stones and lintels of Stonehenge.

Circus Warp were from the West Country, geographically where the travelling lifestyle had always been based. Influenced by the fabled antics of the Tibetan Ukranian Mountain Troupe in the early eighties and spending years onsite, main mover 'Dangerous' Dave had been involved in the Stop the City anarchist actions in London in 1983, which coalesced into an outfit known as 'The Warped Ones', from which he emerged around 1987 as custodian of their huge blue and red circus marquee from its previous life as a beer tent around the south-west. Dave and the other Circus Warp crew, such as Jess, Pod and others, had created this environment, including lighting, scaffolding gantries and a few sofas. On Saturday, it was heaving from the afternoon through Saturday night and beyond. Later in an *i-D* magazine interview, Rick explained how we had danced for the whole night until 7am Sunday morning, stuck to the same spot for so long in the dry weather that we had created little bowls in the dust.

Happy Mondays had played on the main stage the night before. We had been so lost in our pyramid dream that we hadn't even been over to watch them, but now it seemed they had come to us. Bez appeared on the dancefloor, wearing what looked like nothing but a bright yellow sowester and a pair of wellies. His eyes were popping so far out of his head that I thought we might have to catch them. The sides came off the tent, the sunshine broke in, turning dust into golden pillars. And finally, early in the morning, in a near-perfect piece of symbolism, a traveller appeared on the dancefloor riding a horse. An urban sound system, a figurehead of the new dance-influenced bands and a horse all in one glorious convergence. As Bez and the horse stared telepathically into each other's eyes, a new paradigm was being born into existence.

So many of the individuals who would make rave history over the next few years were there, and I still meet people who recount tales of that pivotal weekend. On Sunday, we again took over the pyramid marquee, Simon and Jack working the assembled mass into an all-night frenzy. At some point, a guy wearing a huge furry hunting hat with side flaps came towards the decks for a chat, clutching a cassette tape. Shouting over the beats, he said he was from the KLF and asked whether would we play the track on the tape. We did so. He turned out to be Jimmy Cauty, and 'What Time is Love?' received its first-ever public performance, later propelling, via various remixes, Jimmy and Bill Drummond into the most successful singles band in the world. I would discuss this moment with Jimmy many years later, unaware that himself, Dave Balfe and their friends Sue and Cressida had driven down very late from London, located the only system still playing before handing over the tape. They had set off with a clutch of white labels but had by then given them all away. It only really occurred to me later, when pointed out by filmmaker Aaron Trinder, that DiY had in effect been blessed by the KLF in a pyramid at Glastonbury at our first outdoor party – that's some serious magic.

Glastonbury 90 had provided the first real moment of synthesis between the travelling community and the urban sound systems and DJs. However, no doubt propelled in part by the appearance of all-night parties in the traveller's field, the fallout from Glastonbury would paradoxically prove to be an end as much as a beginning. In the days following the festival, when the punters would go home and leave their mountains of rubbish and detritus, the travellers would often remain, perhaps working or recharging their batteries before moving on. This year, however, tensions between the hardcore travellers and the equally hardcore security firm flared into outright hostility and violence, resulting in a pitched battle involving weapons, some serious injuries and wildfire rumours that someone had been beheaded with a spade.

Whatever the reality, Michael Eavis would cancel the festival in 1991. When it returned in 1992, the travelling community would be banned, a much bigger security fence with watchtowers and patrolling security would be installed and the police would be allowed onsite. As the eternal barometer of festival life, Glastonbury would never be the same again. But for us, dishevelled and exhausted in the back of a Luton van, we had seen the promised land and wanted to visit again soon. A few weeks later, we would receive a phone call inviting us to play at another event, which would prove critical in this embryonic cultural cross-pollination. But more immediately, we had our first proper club night on Thursday.

# 9

As I recall those hectic early days of DiY, I'm genuinely staggered by our levels of energy and motivation. Yes, we were young and had a certain amount of chemical assistance, but I think most young people might baulk at throwing a first club night three days after such a gruelling weekend. As I remember, the Kool Kat were slightly wary of giving us another night. There had been some sub-standard behaviour back in November, but it was also because we didn't fit into any established pigeonhole within the club scene. We could not give a guarantee of numbers, and so Ian and Tricia no doubt imagined an empty club with themselves having to pay door and bar staff. In the event, it was worse than they could have imagined.

Neglecting the Kool Kat because we had Rhythm Collision the next Friday, I don't think we actually gave out any flyers. In addition, it was on a Thursday and the name, Rhythm Religion, was so similar to the upcoming all-nighter that any potential punters were undoubtedly confused. They certainly didn't vote with their feet. In the end, despite there being eight or ten of our personnel, having put up our newly purchased arctic tank-nettings, a great set from Simon and a rousing light show from Sirius, two people swung by and they were both on the guest list. Gaynor and Trev, I salute you, the first and second and only attendees at the first DiY paying club night, for which you did not actually pay.

After a long and somewhat awkward few hours, we packed up and headed home. In years to come, people would often comment that it was easy for us; our events were always full. Well, they weren't at the Kool Kat that night. It would take a lot of hard work before the multitudes began to appear, and that weekend we drove furiously around the south Yorkshire and East Midlands late-night club circuit, determined that next Friday's event would be a success. In reality, we were shitting ourselves. By midweek, the ticket outlets such as Selectadisc, Warp, Eastern Bloc and BPM in Derby reported healthy sales. As Friday finally arrived, we were in a state of nervous exhaustion familiar to anyone who has ever organised a party and is convinced no one is coming. No matter how full our events were to become in future years, that gut feeling never really went away.

One thing we all agreed on was that the Marcus Garvey Centre, although cavernous and holding the all-important 6am licence, was a dump and needed some cosmetic surgery. We would also need a very loud sound system and a mixing desk, as we had three live acts playing. For décor, we used our new tank nets and bought a few more from a military surplus outlet on Trent Bridge. For the sound, serendipitously, we had at this point just encountered a guy named Julian Hicks, who would put us in touch with the most technically advanced PA hire company in the East Midlands, Entertainment Sound Specialists (ESS). Jules was a techie to the core, easy-going and only truly happy when sticking a screwdriver into a power amplifier or fiddling with a graphic equaliser at 4.15am. He lived in Hyson Green on Gregory Boulevard in a flat packed to the gills with bits of keyboards, desk-top computers, amplifiers, circuit boards and other random technology. Among other things, Jules would gravitate to become our sound technician and remain so for many years, and along with Chilly Phil, would prove to be probably the most unsung hero of the entire DiY story.

Arriving at the Garvey on the fateful day, the ESS boys started to lug their immaculate PA up the steps and into the venue, then returning to their truck to fetch more and more bass bins. Eventually, the entire front of the stage was dominated by two huge stacks of ominous-looking black speakers. We were smitten. Although we had been to blues parties in Nottingham and Manchester and had seen reggae sound systems at outdoor social events, that was not a scene to which we were naturally welcome. The ESS crew, however, especially their loquacious engineer Rowland, were only too happy to talk about W bins, mid-tops and crossovers. Simon, in particular, would pick their audiophile brains all day, mainly while we did the hard work getting the venue ready, a pattern that would be followed for years to come. As Rowland ran through the soundcheck, the bass coming from the speaker stacks was plain monstrous.

Giving that rumble of sonic sympathy deep in the gut, the bass crucially remained clean and true, not distorted, even at such volume. That is quality. Similarly, there was no distortion in the treble, the higher end frequencies that can ruin any music if overdriven. Even a couple of Rastas hanging out in the hall looked impressed. We would work with ESS at three all-nighters that year and, as they were so committed to the principles of acoustic excellence, we would soon ask them to design and construct a sound system all of our own.

And so to the long night of Nottingham's first rave. By the time the doors opened at 10pm, with the netting and Rob's projections plus some hired lights, the Garvey had never looked so good. There had been feedback from the decks on the wooden stage and so concrete paving slabs had been utilised to prevent this, but otherwise, all was running smoothly. At around 6pm, some ladies had arrived to set up a West Indian food stall inside the venue, merrily starting to cook meat in a small mobile kitchen. As militant vegans, after much debate, we ended up offering them a hundred pound to close down and go home, to which they quickly agreed.

Our old buddy John Stripey also showed up with his drum circle of about ten friends, whom I can only politely describe as arhythmic. Five minutes into their accompaniment to a particularly choice cut of Detroit house, I had heard enough and also offered them a hundred pound to desist. They also saw financial sense, hid their drums and took the cash. The cloakroom where the entry money was taken was in a small cubicle at the bottom of the stairs. As always, I would be in there with various other DiY crew. Arriving from Sheffield, the Warp contingent looked around approvingly. And, in sharp contrast to the week before, several hundred people showed up and the party properly rocked until past dawn.

In all, roughly seven hundred people actually attended, mostly paying, and it was packed. This would be the first time we ever made any money, and I'm tempted to say probably the last. Everyone had a great night, everyone got paid, the Sheffield artists were brilliant, especially LFO, who put the sound system through its ultimate test with their eponymous bass behemoth of a track. Dave had made some dance platforms with our new logo on the top and they were working a treat, although sadly they were so heavy we never used them again. Looking back musically, the striking thing about the various DJs on the night, Simon, Allister Whitehead and DJ SY, was that their tunes were not that different. House music was still very much marginalised and there was only a limited number of records available. All that was to change within the next twelve months, though, to the point where it would have been inconceivable for these DJs to play on the same line-up. As so often during these years, the security provided the only real negative of the night, albeit in a darkly comic manner. Around midnight, someone stuck their head through the door of the chaotic cloakroom window and informed me that security were letting people in around the back for half-price. I hurried through the full-on rave in progress and down the back stairs, only to see one of the in-house security nonchalantly taking money off a queue of people to enter through the open fire doors. As it was only a tenner on the door, I was doubly upset.

'Oi, mate, I'm from DiY. Can you please stop letting people in?' I shouted above the din from upstairs.

The guy looked me up and down. He was probably one of the machete crew from the car park the other week, and he certainly looked extremely hard and not overly enthusiastic to take orders from a twenty-three-year-old white raver.

'No,' he replied curtly.

'Come on, mate, it's our night. You can't do that.'

'I can.'

'I'll go and have a word with Les.'

He just snorted in derision. I went up the back stairs and knocked on the office door. Les shouted for me to come in.

'Whaddya want Harry, you cunt?'

'Can you tell your guy on the back door to stop charging our punters to get in?'

'No. Fuck off.'

'Thanks.'

There wasn't a great deal I could do. Heading back through the party and back down to the cloakroom, I figured we'd done pretty well, cash-wise. Dawn came and the crowd dispersed, everyone was paid, even Les managed a thank you when I gave him his cut, and for the first and certainly not the last time after one of our parties, we all went back to someone's house and got very, very messy. Rick, Pete and I had by now settled into our house in Alma Street. We had started buying bits of studio equipment, with the next logical step for lovers of house music being to make your own. Purchasing a cheap Atari computer, plus a Roland SH 101 synthesiser and borrowing someone's Roland 909 drum machine, we soon learned how to make rudimentary tracks, although recording them was a nightmare until we could afford a digital tape machine.

Fresh from the success of Rhythm Collision, we began to befriend an ever-growing band of people from across the social spectrum, although this may have also been to do with our decision to start selling cannabis. One such individual lived in the house behind ours, one of those tightly packed rows of terraced houses sharing a back wall with their opposite neighbour. Our wall had collapsed somewhat, so he could pass freely into our backyard. Hailing from Driffield, Yorkshire, his name was Big Lee. Not particularly tall (or big), it turned out the moniker was only given in relation to another diminutive Driffield immigrant known as Little Lee. I was later informed that there was also a Middle Lee, but I'd kind of lost interest by then.

Big Lee was often in our house, popping by to put records on, be fed and hide suspiciously large bags of white powder in strange places. In theory, he was supposed to be studying art at Trent Poly, but what he really excelled at was talking to people. Being a one-man social dynamo, he gradually introduced us to the entire creative troupe at the Poly, such as Alvaro, Gemma, Alex, Beccy Seagere, Geordie Jason, Becki Pate, and many more. They began coming to our events, forging friendships which have remained intact thirty years later. Little Lee would create an instant affinity with my old mate Cookie and, hooking up with Pete Kenny and other mates such as Angus, Brett and Simon Mee, they became an early DiY splinter group: all unemployable, triple shady with zero self-control over their ingestion of substances but loving a tune and a good party. A testament to the ability of house music and ecstasy to simply eviscerate social barriers, our tribe was growing exponentially and in all directions.

There is, as they say, no rest for the wicked. On the next weekend of July, we headed up to Liverpool as rumours circulated about a free festival at a lighthouse on the Wirral Peninsula. Several of us spent Friday night with our friends in Liverpool city centre at a house on Bold Place. Barbara was living here with a group of friends who, along with many others in the city, would over time become our most bonded comrades outside Nottingham. They were a mixed bunch, for sure. Most noticeable among them was the hard-to-miss

Steve Leech, already DJing as 'Vertigo' due to his height of six feet seven. Originally from Manchester, he had made the thirty-five mile move to study at Liverpool Polytechnic, as it was then. It was around their arts and drama degrees that this bunch met, including the fabulous Andrea, who had moved from Bury and was in a relationship with Steve by the time we met them. Also in the house was Mad Mandy from Preston, a BMX champion for whom the nickname will suffice, and Jonny Pritchard, aka Jonny Dangerous, both non-students. Also residing in this party house were Westy and Chris and, at weekends, a frenetic mix of local Scousers (Emma, Fred and Dave) and out-of-town visitors, including Charlie Bucket.

On Saturday night, we all headed under the Mersey through the famous tunnel and arrived at Moreton Lighthouse. It was a fairly small affair, unlike the huge, chaotic event that would occur there in 1991, but it was a free festival nonetheless. Phil and other travellers were there. Simon and Jack would roll in late. The veteran travelling stage Wango Riley's was present and decks were set up on that veritable drop-sided stage wagon which had been providing staging to festivals since 1981. Located on a large area of land by the Mersey estuary, the lighthouse dates back to 1763, and the land around it was historically claimed by the locals as common land. That year the festival passed off peacefully with little interest from the police, with a couple of hundred people dancing through the night, boosted around 4am when the local star DJ John Kelly turned up, dressed all in white, with a posse of ravers in tow. New bonds were formed: Phil, Simon and John shared tunes and information that would have profound effects along the line.

History often hangs on the slightest of threads; events whose consequences reverberate down the years could so easily never have happened. Just such a moment occurred when, a few weeks later, in undoubtedly the most momentous phone call in the entire DiY story, Chilly Phil rang Damian from a phone box near a site in Salisbury. Having got his number at Glastonbury and cemented friendships at Moreton Lighthouse, he was ringing to see if Simon or Jack would be interested in coming to play at a party at a local National Trust landmark near Salisbury known as Pepperbox Hill. Much like Chipping Sodbury a year later, or Castlemorton in 1992, these quaint English place names would move instantly from obscurity into legend.

There has been endless debate ever since the summer of 1990 about which event constituted the first 'free party'. Much of the problem, of course, lies with the etymology of those words, which are open to as great a variety of interpretations as words like 'democracy' or 'techno'. Clearly, parties that happened to be free had been happening for millennia. I have no doubt that most of the megalithic monuments so prevalent across Britain must have seen some level of intoxication and revelry during sacred festivals five thousand years ago. The basic human desire, perhaps even need, to celebrate collectively with like-minded souls has been with us throughout history. Since the 1960s, with the availability of amplified music and the mass production of psychoactive drugs, many events have become synonymous with chemical indulgence in an outdoor setting. Following the explosion of acid house, there had certainly been parties that were without charge, and since then, various small groups had been organising parties in barns, beaches and anywhere else where they could get away with it. What the parties at Pepperbox Hill represent, though, was probably the first time that differing and previously exclusive social factions had united to throw a joint acid house party. That urban ravers, itinerant scallies and the travellers came together for a series of hit-and-run parties in deep countryside with turntables, house music and no idea of an end time represented not only a revolutionary moment but a genuine cultural milestone.

As with the retroactive documentation of all formative events, establishing the chronology and detail of these parties has not been easy. Similarly to the origins of acid house itself, it depends on who you ask. Through numerous interviews and much research, in addition to my own memories, I have tried to remain inclusive and objective, so here goes. Pepperbox Hill is an octagonal seventeenth-century folly, which, according to the National Trust website, 'commands the high point on the chalk ridge south-east of Salisbury'. During the summer of 1990, a series of unlicensed all-night parties took place at the picturesque monument. So far, so good. When exactly they occurred is a different matter. The general agreement is that there were four parties before the police intervened and stopped them. The first, it seems, took place the same weekend as a festival called Torpedo Town in Hampshire, making it 4 August. There would then be another on either 11 or 18 August. We did not attend either of these parties, being both unaware of their existence and also present at the Torpedo Town event itself, which from recollection was a fairly forgettable weekend.

And so the fateful phone call must have come around the middle of August, Phil inviting our DJs down for the next party on the bank holiday weekend around Saturday 25 August. I have a copy of the flyer, 'Total Recall', offering an 'all-night celebration of light, sound and dance'. Rick, Pete and I didn't go but the party certainly lived up to its claims, Simon heading down with Jack and Damian, then returning to Nottingham to rant for days about this incredible outdoor party that went on all morning and where he and Jack had played for hours and met loads of amazing people. A party with no entry fee, no security, no fences, not even a tent or marquee covering the decks. By this stage, we were veterans of house parties and raves, veterans of free festivals too, but it had not really occurred to us to combine these two concepts into what would become known simply as 'free parties'. Like all great ideas, it would seem obvious with hindsight.

Drawn by Simon's tales, we all headed down in separate cars to the next Pepperbox party, named Earth Magyck, the following weekend, Saturday 1 September 1990. Rick, Pete, Barbara and I went via another big Raindance event, the last big pay party we would attend as punters. It had proved enjoyable but would be nothing compared to the free event, which we drove fast through the night to reach. With the car parked, we walked up to the party site, necking the tablets we had brought with us. In the darkness, we could hear the muffled bass kick, which will be instantly familiar to anyone who has ever searched for a free party in the dark night.

As we entered the circle of several hundred dancers loosely gathered around the decks, it became apparent just what a diverse group this was. In the shadows, some travellers' vehicles were parked up, people climbing in and out of these crazily painted and eccentric machines. There was one strip of lights behind the DJ table, splashing vivid blocks of colour across the trees and occasionally highlighting the old monument itself. Jack was playing, locking the dancers further into the groove as Simon, backed by his guardian Damian, was going through his records; obviously, he would be playing some time soon. And as the ecstasy kicked in, the whole scene reminded me of something imagined from the sixties, a communal ritual under the stars, a congregation free to dance, to talk, to wander off. Freedom made reality. All the wild freedom so promised by early acid house and now so absent from events like the one we had just driven from.

I wondered who had organised such a breathtakingly magical yet brazenly illicit event. In the dawn, as Simon took to his own decks (previously they had been using standard belt-drive turntables) for what would turn into a marathon set in the Wiltshire sunshine, we would find out. Chilly Phil was there, plus several of his travelling companions we had met at Glastonbury: Boysie, Emma, Roger, Gav. Other travellers we didn't know had come over from the nearby site, plus some from Stroud, including a chirpy young chap whose name seemed to be Moffball. A contingent from Bournemouth were dancing together, including Justin and Nige, who DJed together as

North and South (one being from Manchester, the other local), Mark Darby, who would later set up Mighty Force Records in Exeter, Hammy, and some other townies.

Then there was a group of Scousers, identifiable by their track-suits, a group of whom had moved to the south coast of Hampshire to 'graft'. Clearly, the leader of this contingent was a square-jawed bloke resplendent in a gold jumpsuit and headband who would be introduced to us as Rory. Completing the eclectic gathering were the local Salisbury crowd, particularly their main organisers, two seemingly inseparable young men named Oli and Eric. Together they had arranged these parties, and although they were communal affairs where you brought what you could contribute, these two had sorted out the business end: decks, mixer, lights and, most impor-tantly, the sound system. The generator had probably come from the travellers, as they needed them for their way of life. Ingeniously, Oli and Eric had started a club event in the back of a Salisbury pub called the Barron of Beef, ostensibly hiring a PA for this licensed venue but then taking it up to Pepperbox at the end and returning it to the pub before the owners came to pick it up.

As the sun climbed slowly into the sky, Simon would continue to play for hours. He had a different set of records to the other local DJs, as we had musically come of age immersed in the northern club scene. Additionally, he was being supplied with quality Ameri-can imports, which probably didn't make it down to the south-west. Either way, from the start, he acquired a legendary status that would never leave him. As the party continued past 9am, visitors arrived at the popular beauty spot and, inevitably, the police were not far behind. Initially fairly friendly, their attitude hardened as we all col-lectively ignored their requests.

Witnessing this ongoing game of cat-and-mouse negotiation, as support for our comrade we stood behind Simon on the decks. Demanding to know who the organisers were, a question with which we would become wearily familiar, they understandably honed in on Simon, the only person actively doing anything. Excuses were mumbled, ignorance claimed. Simon eventually gave them his real name, which raised a few eyebrows and was to have drastic consequences further down the line. There came that moment when it was time for the party to end, when the realisation strikes that the police really have had enough and arrests will soon follow. Speakers were loaded into vehicles, decks placed in the boots of cars, people tidied up.

As I recall, most people had left as we drove out on the A36, leaving only the travellers' vehicles bringing up the rear, and as Phil's bus pulled out into the road, two police vehicles blocked his way. This would be the first of many, many encounters with the forces of authority around a free party, and as the police entered Phil's vehicle, the feeling of helpless agitation was overwhelming. After an agonisingly long wait, they emerged and drove off, leaving a relieved looking man to drive his bus back to site. Despite the police actions and the realisation that the location was no longer a viable party site, we set off back to Nottingham, elated and reverential over what we had experienced. During the emotional intensity of that party, alliances had been formed and friendships made that would have enormous repercussions for all of us present. Inspired, we wanted to do this again, and soon. We wouldn't have to wait very long.

# 10

Some events encapsulate a moment in time so perfectly that they instantly achieve almost sacred status. Often such events are liminal; they represent a bridge or a transition between two worlds. In the theories of the German philosopher Hegel, the thesis is challenged by the antithesis and this clash of opposing ideas creates a new synthesis. This series of small outdoor parties near Salisbury seemed like such a moment, becoming legendary within weeks to the extent that the PFP was formed: 'People From Pepperbox'. Thirty-odd years later, I would buy a set of badges with that moniker and an image of the folly itself from an ex-traveller for whom the decades had obviously not dimmed its mythical status. There were possibly other people playing house music on site parties around this time and the Sweat and Tonka sound systems were active, but this alliance between DJs, local townies and the travelling fraternity was probably unique. These months were captured brilliantly by Matthew Collin in *Altered State*: 'Together they began to throw free parties in the wide open spaces of Wiltshire and Somerset, where travellers and ravers danced a honeymoon rite together in King Arthur's country.'

There were many roads that led to Castlemorton and this was the start of one of them. Coming only a few weeks after the last Pepperbox party, the next late-night trip down south would be to another bucolic-sounding spot named Barton Stacey, Hampshire, or more accurately, a disused Second World War airfield nearby. This would prove to be a classic early free party: minimal gear and a small system, one strip of lights, a wonky table on the airfield with no cover in the event of rain; a very basic and very mobile acid house party which could be packed and spirited away in minutes if the authorities showed up. Fortunately, they didn't and the party went on well into the gloriously sunny Sunday morning, the sun being so hot that Simon's records began to melt.

My abiding memory of that party was at dawn when a traveller named Critter suddenly pulled onto the airfield in his massive old fire engine, driving towards the party with klaxons going and speakers on his roof belting out house music, for all the world like a rural English incarnation of a scene from *Apocalypse Now*. Totally lawless, inspirational and very funny, all the ingredients of those halcyon days encapsulated together.

Fairly rapidly, we came to exist in two separate worlds. Throughout the week, we were living in inner-city Nottingham, signing on and claiming housing benefit, although working hard to promote our activities. At weekends we were driving fast through the night to parties down south or clubs in the north or both. Such a peripatetic lifestyle would become standard for a whole generation of clubbers and ravers, but then it felt incredibly new and exciting.

Fortunately for us, Nottingham is one of the most central cities in England and lies on a motorway, making it less than a two-hour drive to pretty much anywhere in England. One club that we started to attend regularly was Shelley's in Stoke, a classic seventies giant cave of a nightclub with sticky floors that someone had realised would make a great rave venue. Such clubs were springing up all over the Midlands and the north, in Sheffield, Leeds, Birmingham, Manchester and Liverpool. This second wave of young clubbers, who were probably the first to identify themselves as 'ravers', exploded in number and wanted somewhere to dance.

The illegal warehouse events such as Revenge in Warrington just couldn't keep up and, unlike in the south-west, there were no free festivals or traveller's sites on which to end up. Although there were now several of these really big clubs appearing, Shelley's had a secret weapon, DJ Sasha. Rick had first encountered this Mancunian-based young man at some rave where he played alongside the KLF. We had also bumped into him at the counter of Eastern Bloc Records in Manchester and decided to book him for our next big licensed party, Rhythm Collision II. Sasha would rapidly become the first star DJ of the new rave generation and not without some validity: the boy could mix.

Having been fleeced by security at the Marcus Garvey Centre, we began searching for a new venue in Nottingham for Rhythm Collision II. Such a venue would need to be big, and it would need an all-night licence, the main problem being that no such venue existed apart from the Garvey. Due to our numerous house parties around Hyson Green and Forest Fields, the success of Rhythm Collision and our late-night retail business, we had made numerous connections in the local community. One day a well-dressed young black lad named Kenneth Costello knocked on our door with a business proposal. He was a regular at the Hyson Green Boys' Club, a sports and community centre set right in the heart of Hyson Green, just off Gregory Boulevard. Kenneth was confident that he could persuade the management to let us throw a joint all-nighter in exchange for a cut of the profits. Excitedly, we went to view the place and were ushered through some medium-sized rooms before emerging out into a full-sized, covered five-a-side pitch. Rick, Pete and I glanced at each other and raised our eyebrows. This was a perfect building for a party and, although we must have walked past it hundreds of times, we had no previous knowledge of its existence.

Meeting up with the management, who turned out to be far more polite and agreeable than our old friend Les down the road, we agreed on a date, Saturday 29 September. We could only ever get the Garvey on a Friday night due to 'dances' happening every Saturday, so this was a big advantage. After a few sums on a beer mat, we reckoned we could get around a thousand people into the football pitch (Arena 1 on the flyer), plus a couple of hundred in the backrooms (Arenas 2 and 3). Eight pounds for a ticket, tenner on the door, split the profits after expenses, we shook hands. It was at this point that they informed us they had no licence. Of any kind.

Clearly, advertising and selling tickets for up to a thousand people to rave all night in an unlicensed venue right on the front line could present certain issues with the forces of law and order. Having considered it for all of five minutes, and not for the last time, we decided to just go for it and fuck the licensing laws. After all, what could possibly go wrong? We had smashed our way into a warehouse using sledgehammers only the week before on an industrial estate in the centre of Nottingham and held a party until dawn with no interference from the police. This would just be a bigger version of that. Much bigger.

So now we needed a line-up. Sasha agreed to play; it would be his first-ever appearance in Nottingham at the princely sum of two hundred quid. Within a year, you could probably stick a zero on the end of that. Already a legend in house music circles, Carl Cox agreed to play, and again we asked DJ SY and Allister Whitehead, along with Paul Wain, to help pull in the Nottingham rave and club crews. The Rhythm Collision II flyer is the first to feature various DiY DJs, although with unrecognisable names, apart from Jack. Comically appearing in Arena 1 is the unknown 'DJ Decay'. As his real surname is Smith, Simon had been faced with the agony of having to decide about his DJ moniker and didn't want to be confused with Derby's Simon 'Bassline' Smith. And so we entered the netherworld of Simon's indecision. I fondly remember spending hours, if not days, suggesting DJ names, only for him to reject them. Eventually, I flippantly suggested 'Decay' due to Simon's slightly older age and his scruffy post-punk appearance. 'I like that,' he replied, and although

I strenuously insisted it had been a joke, he chose it and it appeared on the flyer. In time, it would be shortened to DK, and eventually Simon DK would become probably the most renowned free party DJ in the country, and, it has to be said, a legend.

Arena 2 was intended to be a hip-hop room, and so appearing alongside various beats DJs such as Trade, One Step Ahead and Hardcore Trio was another new name, 'DJ Shaggy'. This, of course, was Rick utilising his remarkable likeness to Scooby Doo's sidekick in the famous cartoon. Alongside Jack, Arena 3 boasted 'DJ Wooshmelon', this being another newly adopted handle, this time for Pete, and later be shortened to Woosh. Sound would again be supplied by ESS, an even bigger rig this time, coordinated by Jules.

It was around this time that we started to discuss building our own sound system with ESS. Apart from anything else, each PA booking was costing us several hundred quid and we would clearly save money in the long run if we had our own. Heroically delivered by Barbara to all the flats in the two very close high-rise blocks, we printed flyers apologising in advance for the noise, saying the event would run very late. While this was laudably community-conscious, it turned out to be somewhat short-sighted as a member of the now pre-warned community informed the police. They showed up at some point in the afternoon but were reassured by the management that it was only a small event for local people.

Another factor which would add up to this being a pivotal moment in the DiY story was the arrival of a cohort of our travelling friends from the south-west, following advice from local veteran travelling activist and photographer Tash, parked up next to a cemetery in Wilford Hill, a few miles south of Nottingham. Tired of the constant police harassment and looking for somewhere new to party, they would remain on this site for several months before leaving Nottingham, eventually heading to the much more congenial droves and quarries of Derbyshire.

Looking back at Rhythm Collision II, we must have been deranged to have gone through with the event. Having popped home to sort some tickets and some party supplies, when we arrived back in my old VW bus around six o'clock there was already a crowd forming. These were not Nottingham folk, we didn't recognise any of them, but a quick chat revealed they had travelled from Derby, Sheffield, even Manchester. A quick ring round of the ticket outlets showed clearly that this was going to be big. How big exactly we had no idea, but the absence of a licence was now causing me increasing anxiety. Inside the covered football pitch, the venue looked great, we had obtained a laser from somewhere and ESS had done us proud. One problem with the laser and the size of the PA was that we needed a three-phase power supply. The Boys' Club didn't have one, so we had hired a massive, shiny new 40kW generator. It may have been shiny and new, but it came with one fundamental drawback: no one knew how to start it. As a vague queue began to form in the car park, no one could test their equipment or play a record until, in one of those glorious moments of synchronicity which would randomly pepper our story, a random bloke stepped up, declared he was a generator engineer and got it started. God bless you, whoever you were.

By 10pm, the venue was filling up. As the only non-DJ on the team and probably the gobbiest of mouth, I was in the ticket booth with Kenneth and a couple of young women he had sorted out to take money. This would be the only event we would ever do where the rave promoter caricature would become a reality. We would literally be stuffing ten pound notes into bin-liners; it may have been a pay party but it certainly felt both incredibly dodgy and exhilarating at the same time. I nipped outside. There was now a massive queue snaking around the car park and a couple of police cars. I hurried back inside. Sasha and Carl Cox and the rest of the DJs turned up and, by midnight, the party was going properly mental. We ended up with at least 1,500 people in there; it was chaos. The only way into the football pitch was via a narrow concrete tunnel, but once in there it looked for all the world like a big Orbital rave from 1988. Less than impressed, however, were the Nottinghamshire Constabulary. They were now inside the venue and Kenneth grabbed Rick and me and ushered us into an empty office for discussions. This was no plod; it turned out this guy looked like a high-ranking officer, a chief inspector, and carried a cane. Calmly, he explained that he now had a major public order situation in his hands, in a very sensitive area. What time did we intend to stop the music, considering we had no licence? We went for 6am, he shook his head and said 3. We met at 4.30. It would run until well past 5am before the police's tolerance would finally run out.

'Could you also tell me what sort of music this is?' he asked us.

'Hard funk,' replied Rick, deadpan and also clearly off his face.

'Not acid house, then?'

'No, no, definitely hard funk,' I added.

And so the chief inspector went for a wander, followed by his supporting officers, a growing crew of wide-eyed ravers and ourselves, fervently wishing the place wasn't so packed and infringing every fire regulation in the book. Finally, he wished us good night and left. Just like that. When we finally turned off the music and turned up the lights, I could not believe what we had just done. Our core crew gathered in a circle and just hugged: sweaty, disbelieving and elated. We had also made a lot of money. Kenneth and I had been ferrying thousands of pounds out of the venue to avoid having to split it with the management. I had been driving back and forth to Alma Street to secrete large bags of cash inside the couch until the side door had fallen off the van and I'd had to ditch it somewhere in a side street. Quite a night, really.

Soon after this remarkably benign brush with the law, events in our parallel lives down south would prove to be far less fortuitous. As our closest associates on the traveller scene had now moved to

Nottingham, they would be the point of contact for the free party heartlands. God knows how they, or we, or anyone for that matter, ever found the isolated rural locations where parties were beginning to spring up, but somehow we got there in the end. Although veterans of police violence on the streets and demonstrations of the past, our first realisation that the authorities were prepared to use tactics employed against the miners and the travellers at the Battle of the Beanfield to stop a party came in that autumn of 1990.

DiY were starting to make inroads into the southern club scene at this point; within a year, Simon and Jack would become massively in demand. Following a club night somewhere in the southwest, we headed in yet another 3am convoy to a party near a place called Bloxworth in Dorset. I can't recall who organised the party, DJs North and South strikes a chord, but it was a well-organised affair, certainly in comparison to those earlier parties at Pepperbox and Barton Stacey. A proper sound system, no apparent neighbours, all inside a marquee, hundreds of people partying in a really euphoric atmosphere at four o'clock in the morning. Some kind of heaven.

Then, unbelievably, dozens of kitted-up riot police arrived from nowhere. We watched in mounting horror as they formed a line behind the decks at one end of the tent, turned the music off and walked slowly forward, hitting their shields, pushing and striking partygoers randomly. In seeming slow-motion, they shoved riot sticks through speaker cones, battered the DJ, yanked out cables and threw the decks onto the floor. Hundreds of panicking ravers spilt out of the other end of the marquee, walking and then running away, many onto the nearby road. Having emptied the tent and trashed the equipment, the police then emerged and, in a running battle, began hitting people indiscriminately. A gang of four or five young girls had climbed onto the roof of a car, and I will never forget the sight of fully grown men in riot uniform repeatedly hitting them with full force on their legs as they screamed.

And all of this was to stop a party. Not a riot or a violent demonstration or a terrorist threat but a party that was nowhere near any houses and represented zero risk in terms of fire and safety. There is probably no building or nightclub on the planet which is as safe as an outdoor party, but the police were clearly not there to enforce safety legislation; they were there to teach the ravers a lesson. Well, guess what, boys, it didn't work. That night I think we realised that the authorities were prepared to use as much violence to prevent parties as they had to other perceived threats to the establishment. The travellers already knew this; veterans of the road had dealt with police hostility and brutality as a way of life for many years. For this younger generation, however, as with the mass arrest of over eight hundred ravers many miles north, near Leeds, in July 1990, the police only succeeded in both politicising them and encouraging their cravings for more parties. Just how little their tactics suppressed this nascent movement would become apparent in summers ahead.

Deeper into the winter, we again encountered the hostility and heavy-handed approach of the representatives of the state in the decidedly unglamorous setting of an abandoned air force base near Sopley, Hampshire. There always appeared to be some cosmic rule of karma that applied to our parties. When the vibe was good (it was, of course, usually much easier to start a party than escape from one), we seemed to have luck firmly on our side. The very few which went weird were usually the disastrous ones involving bad drugs and arrests. This was to be one of the latter. Again, we arrived in two cars late on Saturday night; myself, Rick, Pete and DM (he wishes to remain anonymous and who can blame him) in one and Jack, Simon and Simon's new partner Nikki in the other. In the back of Rick's estate car were the decks, mixer and two crates of Simon's records, and on our persons we had, and there's no way around this, quite a lot of acid. Sopley RAF base was a pretty miserable affair with lots of war-era Nissan huts, abandoned in the seventies. The site had recently witnessed the nasty eviction of some travellers who had attempted to park up there; they had snipped the padlock and arranged the party as revenge, although no one had informed us of this. Any criminal damage taking a site could be used by the police as just cause to bust it. As we walked into one of the cold, abandoned huts selected for the party, there already seemed to be a strange atmosphere.

As Simon launched into a fairly dark acid set, we broke out some of the acid blotters we had brought and began consuming, which on reflection may not have been entirely wise. The party never really got going, perhaps because there was an inherent strangeness about raving in an old military base or because it just lacked the critical mass of numbers. We persevered through the night until, around five in the morning, during Simon's masterful dropping of a remix of Phuture's 'Acid Trax', several police officers strode into the building, looking distinctly unimpressed. Stopping the music, standard questions were asked: Who organised the party? Where are you from? What are your names? I think we just stared at the wall. Valiantly, Simon tried to negotiate with them but the game was up. I walked outside into the cold dawn air and saw that there were at least eight or ten police vehicles parked outside the gate, the only exit. Loitering for some time, we kept popping outside to see if the police had gone, which they had not. Finally, we began to drive off, with about five vehicles in convoy, ours being the last. As we neared the gate, the police allowed the other vehicles to leave and then moved in to block our car, probably because we were at the back and had two crates of records and two turntables. Clearly, the ranking officer, a policeman, made the signal to wind the window down and spoke to Rick:

'Did you organise this party?'

'Erm, no…'

'Did you play records at this party?'

'Erm, no. Not really…'

The copper stepped back for effect, glancing into the back of the uncovered boot:

'So why have you got two crates of records and some turntables in the back of your car?'

'Errrm, well...'

'Whose are they?'

'Dunno...'

'Right, I'm going to walk away and come back in one minute. If you are not prepared to tell me who organised this event, you four will be arrested for organising an illegal party and for criminal damage when breaking into a military base.'

Still tripping, we spent the minute battling internal panic and hysterical laughter simultaneously. I was most concerned about the acid blotters I had in my pocket, so I used my minute to lean into the back of the car and hide them inside a sleeve of one of the two hundred or so twelve-inch singles in two red crates. The officer returned:

'Right, are you now prepared to tell me who organised this party?'

'Errrm.'

Five minutes later, we were driving down a beautiful country lane and the sun had emerged, dappling the trees in autumnal beauty. In the front, the two policemen are chatting, passing the time. Occasionally the police radio bursts into life. The big problem is that nestled in the warm leather seats in the back of a police Volvo, we were now really, really tripping. Hard. At the police station, we were formally cautioned and allocated separate cells, again with Rick and Pete in one, DM and I in the other. As we giggled uncontrollably, the police seemed distinctly unimpressed and informed us that we could be looking at four years inside. They then took us out individually for questioning, and as I was led to the interview room, I saw the bright red record boxes sitting on the custody counter. Taping the interview, the officer asked me to make a statement. I refused. Truth be told, I was barely able to speak. Back in the cells, it felt very surreal as the sunlight poured in through the glass window.

DM became quite agitated, but I could hear the other two laughing in the cell opposite, which the police did not appreciate. As immortalised in *Altered State*, they told us we were 'too scruffy to be acid house promoters' after discovering our entire possessions amounted to around three pounds and a half-empty pack of Benson & Hedges cigarettes. After a few hours, they finally released us and we retrieved our vehicle from the car park, driven by the police from the party. To his eternal credit, Simon had waited for us. He now attempted to get his records back but the police declined, holding them as evidence. We shakily drove to the nearest petrol station, where we bumped into Paul Oakenfold (of all people), who recognised Simon and was highly sympathetic. Waiting nervously for weeks, we never had any charges pressed against us, but Simon was finally summoned to the small, rural police station in Hampshire where they gave him his records back, complete with the acid still hidden inside.

There would be some much happier moments through the rest of the year, though, with many small parties in forgotten woods and droves dotted around the south-west. Having now become very friendly with this small progressive group of travellers, we got into a groove of driving south and partying together. I will inevitably accidentally miss some names from this story but alongside Phil, Boysie and Emma were Tamsin and her toddler Jelly, Roger, Laura, Critter, Jamie, Nettie, Martin, Gav, Chris and others. Our beatific existence was further blessed when, following some heart-warming treachery from the Conservative Party, Margaret Thatcher resigned, mourned not by us but offering the possibility of a newer, less reactionary government.

Back in Nottingham, having been given assurance by Les that we wouldn't get robbed again, we booked the Marcus Garvey Centre for another all-night party named Datura on 28 December. Not wanting to go for the name 'Rhythm Collision III', we bickered as usual and failed to agree on a name until Nikki showed Simon a rather beautiful image of the plant *Datura meteloides*. Causing possible death or delirium if ingested, Datura is known as one of the 'witches' weeds'. Although not convinced by the suitability, we loved the image and went with it. Coming three days after Christmas, which we didn't really celebrate, it was as near to New Year's Eve as we could get. Sasha was to play again, with SY and Allister plus Jonathon from Arcade Records. For the first time, Simon was on the flyer as DJ DK.

It was a roaring success numbers-wise, although there was still some dodgy door-work from the security and a worrying moment when local rapper Natz demanded to be allowed to MC using a microphone he produced from one pocket, showing us the gun he had in the other. Our hearts were by now firmly in the fields of the south and this would turn out to be the last ever licensed DiY rave. The last straw came after we had cleared all our kit from the Garvey at 6am, finally got home to carry on the party and then received a phone call from an irate Les around 10am. He informed us that we had taken down all their Christmas decorations for our 'dance' and that we needed to come back straight away to put them back up, which we duly did amid some serious grumbling.

This was probably the last time we would have DJs such as SY at one of our events, as the scene was beginning to split into two. A music known as hardcore was emerging, the beats per minute were rising and harsh metallic or demonic noises were becoming widespread. Driven by such statements of intent, such as Joey Beltram's 'Mentasm' and his remix of 'Dominator', this scene would explode during 1991 and would see young producers worldwide, seemingly unaware of the origins of house music, push sonic boundaries to breaking point. Record speeds would be pushed ever higher from the original house beat of 120 bpm until a Dutch form of hardcore named gabber emerged, clocking in at over 200 bpm. Needless to say, what we saw as this new bastard offspring of real house music horrified us, and we would fight a running battle with it for years as it further fragmented into subgenres such as happy hardcore, trance and what we referred to as 'nosebleed techno'.

Finally, in the closing moments of 1990, we decided to head up to Quadrant Park, now open until 6am, to see our also ever-growing group of friends up Liverpool way. Having now given up alcohol due to our almost religious belief in MDMA, we hired a minibus, driven by myself and with, among others, Chilly Phil on board. As he was by now a lover of what became known as 'high tunes', anthemic garage tracks often with deep vocals and piano high in the mix, it seemed like the cross-pollination between the northern rave scene and the free party domain of the south-west of England was, if not complete, then certainly established. It had been a year of firsts for DiY: first club night, first time DJing at a festival, first licensed rave, first free party. As we threw our hands aloft at midnight in a shady warehouse in a suburb of Merseyside, little did we know that the coming years would see all these firsts explode and become the chosen weekend lifestyle of a generation.

# 11

And so we rolled into 1991, brimming with optimism and a deep determination that we could export our particular brand of collective celebration from Nottingham to the world. It seemed glaringly obvious to us that this was the torch that acid house had lit and then dropped, and which the increasingly morally bankrupt licensed raves could not legitimately carry. In our almost messianic zeal, we wanted to make that torch our own. As this was the winter and the free party and festival season lay a few months ahead, our first immediate concerns were to somehow get our own sound system, to publicise our cause via the national press and to start a regular club night. Although not in that order, all three priorities came rushing headlong towards us in the first months of the new year.

As a chaotic and anarchic organisation who mostly ignored licensing laws and now numbered dozens of fairly unruly members who would dance all weekend given half a chance, where else to start a regular night other than the UK's most fashionable new club? Venus was a sumptuous venue on Stanford Street in the centre of Nottingham, the brainchild of a charismatic Scottish ex-miner named James Baillie. Transforming the club from its previous townie existence as 'The Club', James had ploughed his redundancy money into turning the two floors into Britain's first real Balearic temple. For the uninitiated, further fragmentation had emerged during 1990 between the more upmarket club-orientated fashion crowd, many of whom holidayed in Ibiza (one of the Balearic Islands, hence the tag)

Only surviving photo of first DiY event: Kool Kat, Nottingham, 23 November 1989

Pyramid marquee, Glastonbury, June 1990

Free Party People: Gav's bus, 1991

Simon, Damien, Jack: acid house party, 1991

Early DiY publicity photo, 1991

Still smiling: after the acid party, 1991

Oli and Eric raving hard: Chipping Sodbury free festival, 1991 (Pic: Alan Lodge)

We just want to party, officer (Pic: Sharon Storer)

Basic raving, Derbyshire, 1991

Scoraig party boat, Solstice, 1993

DK in the Dolly

Full rig Plumpton, 1992

Castlemorton at dawn, May 1992 (Pic: Alan Lodge)

Full crew: End-Up Club, San Francisco, 1993

Hothead EP: DiY's first release on Warp Records, 1993

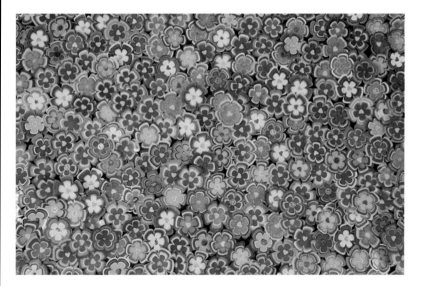

A patch of Love Cabbages

DiY flyers and record covers

Simon DK: New Year's Eve, somewhere near Bath, 1992

DJ Jack with Martin: classic Free Party (Pic: Sharon Storer)

DJ Digs: Reclaim the Streets (Pic: David Bowen)

DJ Woosh (Pic: Alan Lodge)

DJ Emma: the Bomb (Pic: David Bowen)

Harry and some riot police: CJB demo, Trafalgar Square, 1994 (Pic: Alan Lodge)

DiY incognito in the park (Pic: Alan Lodge)

CJB demo Sound System, Park Lane, London, 1994 (Pic: Matt Smith)

CJB demo: Trafalgar Square, London, 1994 (Pic: Matt Smith)

Press photo: Squarecentre Studios (Pic: Alan Lodge)

DiY – the catalogue years: Rick, Harry, Pete, Simon, Wales 2013 (Pic: Dilys Jones)

and the mass of new ravers, whom they had been dismissing as 'acid teds' since the latter days of the legendary Boys' Own parties two years before and whom they considered sweaty, shabby and somewhat inferior.

James was something of a paradox: small in stature but with great charm, tough as old boots but distinctly camp, he was relentlessly driven by the high glamour and excess of this crowd, of whom Nottingham had many. Having already secured the involvement of London's Flying organisation and, more particularly, Charlie Chester, man of the moment and uncrowned king of the Balearic scene, James would succeed in attracting the cream of the trendy international DJ world. And DiY. Although initially mutually suspicious of each other, and with James understandably reluctant to give a night to what he probably perceived as a bunch of crusties, we would evolve a sense of mutual respect, going on to work together for many years.

Starting with a bang, our first night at Venus was in February 1991 and we persuaded Sasha to play alongside Simon and Jack downstairs. Initially outfoxed, James would soon offer this rising star of UK clubland a monthly night called Zoo, eventually becoming his manager, steering him away from the ever more tacky commercial rave scene and into the annals of club and remix legend. In the upstairs bar, Rick and Pete would be playing one of their early Serve Chilled sets under their new name of 'Digs and Woosh', the latter being an abbreviation of 'Wooshmelon' and the former similarly an abbreviation; some sharp observer had clocked that Rick bore an uncanny resemblance to Nottingham's legendary blind solicitor and defender of bad boys, Digby Johnson, and so 'Digs' he became.

In the meantime, we had to fill this club, replete as it was with marble bars, glamorous staff and an ever-growing reputation for opulence and indulgence. Friday 8 February 1991 would prove to be a night of high drama, significant repercussions and some downright farce, but first we needed a name. Again, we spent agonising days throwing names around before we settled on Bounce. Not the most scintillating name ever, but certainly descriptive of the night. Bounce would run for exactly five years and travel all over the UK and beyond, rarely dropping out of the Top Ten club listings in the dance music magazines. That first Friday, however, did not start auspiciously. On a freezing cold night and with large parts of the country blanketed in snow, we wondered if anyone would manage to get there, never mind Sasha.

As always, we had gone totally overboard on sound and put a medium-sized ESS rig in to boost the club's in-house system. James initially thought we were mad but again would end up copying us later down the line. Bodies began to drift in and a healthy queue started to form before the Venus office took a phone call from Manchester asking them to let us know that Sasha was stuck in snow and would not be able to make it. Much of our crowd would by now come to any event we did, irrespective of whether it was a club, a warehouse, a field or a festival, but this was Venus and a certain percentage of this assembly were distinctly more fashionable than our regular punters, no doubt lured by Sasha's advertised attendance. Assuming we would just have to announce the disappointing news, we wondered if they would believe that we had ever genuinely booked him. This was, remember, during the ascendancy of raves offering the world and with no intention of delivering, when a Sasha or a Carl Cox might be alleged to be playing at five different parties simultaneously. We wrestled with this problem for a while until I had an idea. Cometh the hour, cometh the Pezz.

During our visits to Shelley's in Stoke to check out Sasha, also in attendance was a young man who had just started a degree at Trent Poly but to whom Stoke was home. Friends with the rave duo Altern 8 and the about to explode Bizarre Inc, for Pezz the trip to Shelley's wasn't just a night out, it was a pilgrimage. Attending weekly with his old friends Rachel and Claire, Pezz became obsessed with some of Sasha's tapes where obscure and seemingly unmatchable tracks were mixed together with a finesse that defied logic and established his reputation. After meeting Rick in Arcade Records and bonding with us over our shared enthusiasm for house music, Pezz was a great example of how DiY managed to attract such a startling mix of people to our cause. Almost a cultural polar opposite to the travellers and the anarcho-punks we had drawn into our orbit, here was a working-class lad from Stoke who had grown up with electro and break-dancing and was, for want of a better word, normal. A bedroom mixer for years, he had obsessively tracked down all the records that Sasha had played on his last tape and perfectly copied the mixes in private. All that was about to change. Noting that Pezz had an almost identical ponytail to Sasha, although he was several inches smaller, I asked him if he was willing to drive home, get his records and impersonate the missing DJ. Initially and understandably reluctant, Pezz stepped into the breach, drove off into the snowy night in his Mini and returned to a packed club bouncing off the walls, got on the decks and played the most pitch-perfect imitation Sasha set of all time. There were a few knowing glances over the DJ booth but I think we got away with it and Pezz became our saviour and latest DJ, going on to represent DiY for many years.

If that represented the drama, then the farce arrived shortly after when James came running up to me and announced in his broad Scottish accent that there was a dog in the club. Without informing us, a dozen or so travellers had arrived en masse from the now-growing local site and had taken over the foyer, giving the fashionista on the door a heart attack and us another headache. And yes, they had a four-legged friend with them (although it could have been three), about which I refrained from asking James if it was on the guest list, also noticing that Roger, the most visibly wasted and piratical of the posse, was wearing no shoes. To this day, I consider one of DiY's truly great achievements was to get an actual dog into Britain's first uber-cool superclub. Having extracted the dog and found Roger some shoes, the night continued. In true Balearic style, people danced on the marble bar as Digs and Woosh let rip with some eclectic classics, and downstairs hundreds danced to the driving house of Simon DK, Jack and a slightly diminutive Sasha. Despite the sartorial conflict, Bounce remained and blossomed at Venus, our monthly Friday night becoming increasingly popular until we were reluctantly turning people away. Partly thanks to James' relentless publicity skills and our own growing reputation, we were now attracting another element of the night-time cultural spectrum, the fashion crowd. As with free parties yet to come, this remarkable and growing eclectic mix of dreadlock punks, students, dodgy estate ravers, travellers and fashionistas just seemed to gel naturally.

Beneath the coagulating force of underground house music, boundaries really were disintegrating, friendships that would previously have been impossible were being forged and it was wondrous to behold. DiY did not exist in a vacuum, of course. Across the country, this nascent pleasure combination of dance music and ecstasy was quite simply eradicating any opposition and becoming the only game in town. With Simon, Jack and Pezz now forming the core of our house DJs, and with Digs and Woosh perfecting their art of eclectic beats and backroom chill-out, we were now a tight unit with only one thing missing.

Still having to hire a PA for our club night and increasingly spending Saturday night until Monday morning somewhere onsite in the deep south-west of England, we turned our attention to getting hold of our own sound system. Looking back, what now seems like a seminal and radical decision just seemed to us a logical next step. Although we were probably one of the first three house sound systems in the UK and possibly the world, almost certainly the first north of Watford, it didn't feel ground-breaking, only pragmatic. As outlined above, we had grown up going to blues parties and seeing black sound systems playing at various events. We had danced in the dust to Tonka at Glastonbury the summer before and danced in front of shadily hired PAs across the south-west. Being us, we were far too impatient to start building a system slowly, buying a power amp or two with a couple of bass bins and adding to it when we had some money. Having asked ESS to design us a bespoke 4kW system, their price came out at around twelve grand. Unlike when we could purchase our studio in cash thanks to a mystery benefactor a couple of years later, we simply did not have access to this kind of money.

Step forward Simon's dad, who, being worth a few quid, agreed to guarantee a Lloyd's bank loan if we could persuade him that this would be a legitimate business. I'm still chuckling now. Yeah, sure. No problem. I threw together the first of what would prove to be a fairly long list of deeply flawed and totally fictitious business plans based on a certain number of hires per month, and, to our incredulity, he went for it. Having retained a couple of grand from Rhythm Collision II, I went to open a business bank account. Firstly, however, we needed a name for the account. Not wanting to use DiY (for fairly obvious reasons), we had another discussion around names before it was suggested we call our system Black Box. The name stuck, having the double meaning of not only actually being a collection of black boxes but also in honour of the Italian piano-house act who were massive at the time. So, now in possession of a bank account and cheque book in the name 'Black Box PA', the money was duly transferred and we went to inspect our shiny new sound system at the ESS workshop in Mansfield. The repayment arrangement was that we would pay £243.12 per month into the account to pay off the loan and, to our credit, we made those payments every month for many years. Thank you, Mr Smith senior. I don't think you ever quite realised what you did.

Our criteria for the new rig was fairly simple; it had to sound great and had to be compact. The main problem, of course, is that those two principles work in direct conflict with each other. Pulling up at the workshop, we could already hear some deep, quality bass coming from inside and Simon grinned from ear to ear. However, walking in, there was a feeling of instant disappointment. The system that was playing was massive, with eight huge bass bins and four chunky mid-tops. This obviously couldn't be Black Box. We had distinctly requested that it be small enough to chuck into a van on a wet Sunday night, to fit down the steps of a cellar or through the door of a dodgy warehouse. ESS, however, techies to a man, had definitely paid more attention to the sound than the size. And God bless them. It was a beautiful thing and the sound that Black Box produced became legendary. So many systems who came along claimed to have 8/10/15K rigs but many of them just sounded shite, driven too hard and blighted by distortion. For those that care, ours consisted of four 1kW Rauch power amps, eight fuck-off W bins, four mid-tops carrying the mid-range and treble, a crossover and a serious graphic equaliser. And lots and lots of Neutrik cables; never forget the fucking cables.

A slight problem emerged fairly rapidly, however, in that we had no van or truck to transport it in. For the first year of being a sound system on the road, we either had to hire a Luton van or beg someone to let us use theirs. As it was undoubtedly the bulkiest 4K sound system ever made, an ordinary van just wasn't big enough and it only just fitted into a long wheel-base. About two weeks after we took possession of the incredibly clean and shiny Black Box (it would never be that clean again), we used it for the first time at a house party on Mount Hooton Road in Nottingham, where our size-related fears were entirely justified. The first bass bin got jammed carrying it down into the cellar and took about thirty minutes to dislodge. But hey, we were now irrefutably the DiY Soundsystem and were fanatically prepared to make some serious noise. It was at this party that I first attempted to DJ, choosing the name of DJ Decimator. I played out precisely three times over the next eight years before giving up, as each one ended in disaster. At the house party above, the amps blew, at the second a young lady named Mad Debbie threw one of the decks on the floor and smashed it, and at the third I tried to use CDs and they all glitched. Clearly, it was not meant to be.

Obtaining a sound system at that precise point would prove most fortuitous. With what seemed to be becoming a trademark mix of serendipity and synchronicity, in February 1991 our friend from the Kool Kat days, Matthew Collin, wrote the first article about us in the national press, also featuring a history of Tonka going back to the late sixties, most of which we were unaware of, further underscoring future alliances. As editor of *i-D* magazine, he clearly had the editorial muscle to write about leftfield subjects outside their regular fare, and so penned 'Sound Systems: House Music Anarchists', a deftly written four-page article about house sound systems. It would have been somewhat embarrassing if the issue had come out before we actually owned our own system, but as ever, we just about scraped it. Although we would go on to have dozens of interviews and features in national and international magazines in the years ahead, as with your first record, there was something special about seeing yourself interviewed and photographed for the first time, especially in a magazine as fashionable as *i-D* then was. There is also a negative reaction: it feels somewhat icky, and the press would frequently prove to be a double-edged sword in the years ahead.

There would be many articles to come that would prove embarrassing and inaccurate, but this was not one of them. To be labelled anarchists in public was the icing on the cake. However, when shown the article, my mum did not seem to share my enthusiasm, merely responding with an 'Oh dear!' As ever with his writing, Matthew caught the essence of DiY with deep understanding and neat prose.

He got us. With the cultural awareness that landed him the editor's job at an internationally renowned magazine, he also mentions other fledgling party outfits such as Liverpool's Bass Evangelists, and Bournemouth's Unity and Circus Warp. There is also a mention of Oli, noted above as a major player in those halcyon Pepperbox Parties, who is rather wonderfully quoted as saying: 'It's strange, the travellers are starting to wear brightly coloured clothes, rave gear and trainers. They're all changing and mutating again. It's good.'

As if hearing these words and answering Oli's clarion call, two or three weeks after *i-D* was published lay Chilly Phil's birthday; and in what would be the first outdoor free party for our new system and our first in Nottingham, the word went out to the progressive sections of the traveller scene that there was to be a gathering of the tribes at the equinox. Held over the weekend of 23 March on the Nottingham Wilford Hill site previously mentioned, this party was to be another pivotal milestone in the story of free parties. The site had grown since the arrival of Phil, Emma and Boysie in the autumn of 1990. Now, more travellers, equally adventurous and searching for the beats, had made the journey to the East Midlands. A flyer was thrown together, hand-drawn by a young party-head named Scooter, featuring a cartoon Phil on the front, resplendent in dungarees, flying hat and shades. Beneath a banner avidly invoking the invitee to attend the 'Equinoxal Roxoff', he is joyously leaping into a vortex of what look like five-sided flowers but are, in fact, what had become known as 'Love Cabbages'. Over that summer, this innocent-looking creation would become the emblem of the free party movement.

Over the previous autumn and winter, another green shoot in this story had emerged, now centred on a site in Dudbridge, near Stroud. Dangerous Dave, our acquaintance from Glastonbury 90 (over the years, all roads would always seem to lead back there), and his Circus Warp crew had parked on what would become one of those fairly rare long-running and semi-permanent travellers' sites. Although not owning their own sound system, this group of musically and chemically enlightened merrymakers had everything else needed for a party: a marquee, lights, generators, sites, belief, balls. Over the winter of 1990, they had also been partying, in many ways parallel to the travellers with whom we had become symbiotically entwined. They had a new name, Free Party People, and they had an emblem. The Love Cabbage symbol was to become so ubiquitous and universally coveted that years later, decades even, Dave would write a short history of its origins, of which I shall quote at length:

## 'A Short History of the Love Cabbage and the Free Party People' by Dave Langford

This happy little sticker originates from 1990. Shortly after getting kicked out of Circus Warp for being 'too fluffy', Pod and I moved to a traveller's site at Dudbridge in Stroud. We had heard about a group of fun lovin' heads living there. Good move!

One great party later and the Free Party People were born (FPP).

Tet, Roger, Slob, Moffball, Sarah, Jeanie, Laura, Beki, Tamsin and all the others put their heart and soul into some of the best parties ever, bar none.

DiY, the legendary Nottingham sound system, quickly became the FPP's sound system of choice, teaming up for parties and festivals throughout the early nineties.

Pod had been drawing these little five petalled flowers on the flyers, the FPP logo, a sort of soft-edged pentagram with a dot in the middle. Among the art materials we were collecting for the Bristol Children's Scrapstore were coloured rolls of what Blue Peter used to call 'sticky backed plastic'. Back then we didn't have the internet or a hundred other blessings of modern life, but we did have . . . scissors!'

As we later worked out that the average donation into the free party bucket was around twenty pence, the idea was to give away a cabbage with every donation, the donator then sticking it upon their person and avoiding being harassed again. I would just like to make two comments on Dave's evocative story. Firstly, I'm glad that he listed the characters involved. I will need to try to name an impossible galaxy of people involved with the story and will inevitably miss some people out. You can now blame Dave. Secondly, I was reluctant to quote his assertion that DiY were 'legendary', but I just couldn't resist.

And so the party happened over the night of 23 March, next to a cemetery, over the equinoxal night, a time halfway between the solstices when traditionally light and dark are in perfect balance. It was suitably wild and set the tone for much of what was to come. Many of the southern-based vanguard of raving travellers (ravellers?) drove up from the south-west to join those who had already moved full-time. This was unquestionably the first free party anywhere near Nottingham, in fact in the Midlands, and so representatives of many of the young tribes of the city came out to play. Friendships and contacts made over that long night would endure and blossom for many years. Again, the sheer cultural mix represented was unparalleled. Amid the union of local travellers and the cohort of Free Party People were an almost unbelievable smattering of crusties, students and fashion victims, plus a new group, the local football boys, in particular a couple of mates called Adey and Marcus and their associates.

Local working-class lads (and lasses) from the Nottingham suburbs, such as nearby West Bridgford, this group were noticeably dressed in complete inversion to the hardcore hedonists of the road. In contrast to the bright colours and baggy clothes of the travellers, they wore expensive clothes and immaculate trainers, but, as ever, they met in the world of music and drugs and not a shit was given either way as we all danced into Sunday with Jack, Pezz and Simon playing through the night. Black Box performed beautifully at its first party and got its first splattering of mud, of which there would be many more. Jules ran it (him? her?) heroically over a long night and morning and the sun rose over what would become the prototype for a DiY party. Also, we seemed to have a new lighting guy, a dreamy but hard-working young hippy named Moffball, who had been at Pepperbox the summer before.

For me, the night was only topped off with a moment so cross-culturally profound yet comic that it has stayed with me ever since. Around five in the morning, I persuaded Pezz to get onto a bus with me. Now this event alone would never have happened without the cultural melting pot that was house music. Coming from social polar opposites, Pezz nevertheless sat next to me, totally ill-prepared for this scene, surrounded by a smattering of travellers very clearly absolutely off their tits, to use one of the many phrases which sprung up in that era.

Now, when travellers smoke pot, they really smoke it. Like they do in India or Kashmir, where they utilise a long clay pipe called a chillum. With a rag draped over the end, it allows huge amounts of smoke to be inhaled. A three-skinner it is not. Anyway, this chillum was orange in colour, and as a wasted guy with dreads down to his arse passed it to Pezz, he looked at me in some panic, leaned over and said, 'Why's he passing me that carrot?' And I just burst out laughing. I couldn't stop. This was marvellous, just fucking marvellous, and, sitting on a crusty old coach in the mud next to a cemetery somewhere near Nottingham with a puzzled young raver and various intoxicated hippies, it just seemed like the funniest thing ever and I'm laughing again now.

# 12

A pattern would emerge over these years. At the end of the summer, the big outdoor parties and festivals would fizzle out and the action would move back to clubs, warehouses or small sites. This followed the pattern of the free festival circuit established in the hippy hey-day of the late sixties and early seventies, itself following the ancient cycles of the solstice and the summer. No doubt, even five thousand years ago, it was preferable to dance or worship the rising sun than the driving rain. Conversely, as the seasons moved into spring and the countryside once more erupted into life beneath huge blue skies, it was always fascinating to see how much bigger the free party scene had become during the hibernation. In that spring of 1991, clearly, the house music bug had bitten new swathes of the traveller move-ment and the attendant youth of the south-west of England. Avon Free Festival, that annual bellwether of festival size, lay at the end of May over the bank holiday. No one knew where it would be, of course. It was unlicensed and beyond the control of the authorities. Whether it or any free festivals were illegal depended on who you asked. An infringement of local authority licensing laws, certainly, but an actual crime?

Either way, this seems another good place to take stock of just where DiY were at this point in time. We were still glowing from our first free party with our own sound system and preparing for a summer that we sensed would be lively. On a professional level, we had now been organising parties for two years and had pretty much everything in place to start throwing events wherever and whenever we wanted. In addition to our shiny new rig, we had a generator, two sets of decks, various mixers, two lighting guys, access to various marquees and a growing network of travelling friends who could source appropriate sites. Our monthly Friday Bounce night at Venus continued to be packed and wild. We stuck with underground guests, which over the next few months included our old comrade DJ Vertigo representing the Liverpool posse ('Britain's Tallest DJ' the flyer proclaimed, accurately but somewhat irrelevantly). Laurent Garnier played, originally a Parisien and now an honorary Mancunian with a hilarious bilingual answer-machine message, plus Choci from the Tonka collective.

Bounce was now beginning to take off nationally, and throughout 1991 we would cement friendships and club nights across the land. Liverpool, Manchester, Hull, Sheffield, Bath, Bristol, Exeter would all become affiliated with our cause. Simon and Jack, in particular, would become massively in demand, especially in the free party territory of the south-west. Other crew members began to buy records and play wherever they could get a slot.

Saturdays were reserved for free parties and we quickly became adept at setting up and breaking down our mobile party structure, often in some haste. In a very DiY way, just as events accelerated heading into the spring of 1991, we decided that what we really needed, in addition to our already punishing schedule, was a weekly Tuesday club night. This would be somewhere that we could kick back midweek and play some of the other music that we loved away from the tyranny of house, and yes, admittedly continue the party until Wednesday morning before starting again on Thursday night. Dizzy was chosen as a name (a cunning play on the letters DiY). The venue was a fairly run-down club on Nottingham's Alfreton Road named the Stork Club, later the Skyy Club, run by a savvy businessman named Dennis. Dizzy would run for the best part of that year before finding its natural home at a two-storey night-box in the city centre called the Cookie Club and changing its name to 'Serve Chilled'. Memories abound of the Skyy Club, but two would leave a lasting impression. At some point at one of those fairly mental Tuesday nights, long before anyone had a job, we invented a new DJ concept called 'One Tune'.

The concept was simple, elegant and quite brilliant. We cut two eye holes into a plain cardboard record mailer and placed it over the head of whoever wanted to be One Tune for the night. They would then choose a favourite track and hide in waiting at the side of the DJ booth until the actual DJ would stop the music dead, this being the signal for One Tune to leap behind the decks and play, well, their one tune, before slipping away into the night. Surprisingly, this idiocy really caught on, and within a couple of weeks, massed clubbers would be chanting 'One Tune, One Tune' and demanding the mystery figure appear. Clearly, the business ramifications could be enormous. Suppose One Tune could break out and become as in demand as our main DJs. In that case, anyone could stand in and they would only need one record. Imagine getting paid three or four hundred quid to play one record with a bag on your head. Genius. Sadly, One Tune never made it big, and we left him quietly in the back corridors of the Stork Club when we moved on.

The second memory which stays with me involved a strange introduction. One night amid the haze and fog that always characterised the end of a good club night, a figure emerged. Well dressed but eccentric-looking, this prematurely balding figure strode up to me and said, 'Hello. My name's Dick and I thought the music was amazing.' I thanked him and took him over to Rick and Pete, who were putting away their records. 'This is Dick,' I announced, 'and he thinks you're amazing.' They looked up, nonplussed, as this strange new fellow replied, 'Actually, my name's Richard Burton and I don't really want to be known as Dick.' But it was too late and that's probably about as good a portrait of him as you could get. He would join the team and strangely represent DiY as a DJ named Dick for many years.

As we now had a large PA and several thousands of pounds worth of equipment, we needed somewhere to keep it all. Our old friend Doug would step in to suggest a garage behind the old house on Magdala Road. We approached the somewhat dubious Russian landlord and he agreed to rent us one of a row of garages for the princely sum of five pounds a week. Over many years, that garage would witness us exhaustedly shifting those boxes in and out many hundreds of times. Before we could utilise this new space, however, we were forced to think of some very suspect places to keep our beloved system. Undoubtedly the most farcical of these was when Pete Kenny assured us it would be fine to store the PA in the kitchen of his sister Gaynor's council house for a few days. Assuming that he'd actually asked her, myself, Pete and our mate Angus pulled up outside her kitchen at about three in the morning in a hired Luton van.

While reversing into position, Angus crashed the van into a lamp post, bending it to about thirty degrees off-kilter and causing it to start sparking – not an auspicious start. Pete unlocked the back door and we set about our task of completely filling Gaynor's small kitchen with massive black boxes. Relatively quickly, I saw an issue in that she wouldn't be able to reach the fridge, the cooker or the sink, and so we left narrow gaps between the towers of boxes. It was also at this point that Pete remembered that Gaynor had a baby and that he hadn't actually asked her if we could store the system there. This last point was instantly corroborated by the appearance of the lady in question, as a bleary-eyed and furious sister stormed into her own kitchen to be met by a wall of black speakers with thin access canyons. Eventually, she took it well, I blamed Pete entirely, and, to her credit, she let us keep it there for over a week until we could move it into the new lock-up.

Obviously, the business end of any sound system is the amplifiers. They are compact and sit in flight cases and would be much more tempting to steal than our outsize speaker cabinets. In the first of what would become probably six or seven equipment thefts we suffered over the years, Simon's Technics and mixer were stolen during those months from a house he shared with Nicki in Forest Fields. As with most of these burglaries, we would immediately make enquiries through our contacts in the community and someone would inform us that they knew the culprit, obviously without naming them, but that we'd have to buy the equipment back. Initially, this was incredibly galling, but we got used to it. What choice did we have? Better to buy back a grand's worth of decks for two hundred quid than never see them again. A few years later, all our amps were stolen from Squaredance Studios, the recording complex where we would later set up an office after an all-night party. I don't even want to say how much they cost us to get back.

Clearly, we couldn't keep the amps in a fairly damp garage with no security beyond a padlock, and so we would go on to keep them in our houses, often at Jules' place or in our new flat on Vickers Street, the same road that the wild squat party had happened eighteen months or so before. Rick, Pete and I had needed to move out of our Alma Street house, and fairly quickly, due to the increasing levels of police interest provoked by two memorable incidents.

These were the days long before the UK driving licence carried a photo of the driver. The only proof of eligibility to drive was a green and pink folded piece of paper issued by the Driving and Vehicle Licensing Agency. As the UK is also one of the few places in the world that does not have an ID card, you could easily drive a vehicle while pretending to be someone else. It was fairly common to give another driver's name if stopped for speeding, thereby generously donating them the penalty points and fine. Anyhow, Pete decided to hire a car in someone else's name but cunningly used his own signature at the counter of the hire company. Upon discovery, he made a sharp exit, with the problem being that the car hire company had his real address. Rick and I were fiddling around with a drum machine when the police knocked loudly on the door and then entered to search the premises. Not good. Without Pete even being there, they began to turn the place over. Inside the couch, they found some 'decorative brass scales' (written on the top) and crumbs of resin from our ongoing business venture. Some officers went to search the bedrooms. All the while, I was sat in a chair, failing not to stare at a large poster on our living room wall. When we had moved into the property, we thought it would be really funny to put all the utility bills – phone, electricity, gas and so on – in the name of 'I. Raves'. Rick, ever the king of the photocopier, had blown up our entry in the Nottingham telephone directory to A1 size, printed it out and proudly stuck it on our wall, gleefully proclaiming **I. Raves, 2 Alma St, Forest Fields, Nottingham, NG7 7LY**.

As one of the sharper police officers began to look curiously at the poster, it suddenly didn't seem such a clever idea. He asked for an explanation, so I free-formed: 'Well, there used to be a guy who lived with us called Ian Ravez. He put all the bills in his name but they spelt it wrong in the phone book.' Distinctly unimpressed, the copper replied, sharply, 'Just let me stop you there. Before you tell me any more bullshit, it's not actually a criminal offence to put util- ity bills in a false name.' In what must have been one of a thousand occasions over the decades, Rick, Pete and I looked at each for a split-second before Rick declared, 'Really? Didn't know that. OK, it's a false name then.'

Having cleared that legal hurdle, there just remained the matter of intention to sell cannabis, which the police seemed fairly unarsed by. They confiscated the 'decorative brass scales' and that was the end of that, including two mystery pills they had discovered by my bed. I think Pete, who had been arrested, was cautioned and released.

Although that incident turned out relatively well, the second incident involving a brush with the law occurred only a few weeks later. It prompted our moving property and the cessation of our business sideline. James Baillie, the Venus promoter, had opened a new bar in Nottingham city centre called 'Papa Binns' in honour of his grandfather. Much like Venus, it was a stylish and chic establishment, frequented mostly by the city's fashion crowd. One night Simon, Rick and I ended up drinking there and, highly inebriated, set off walking towards the Market Square to get a taxi home. We took a detour through the Broadmarsh, an unprepossessing seventies shopping centre. We emerged on the other side amid a row of typical city centre shops, including a Hallmark Cards outlet. Its large glass window was covered on the inside with Garfield toys, and I remarked on this to Rick.

Little did I know that he harboured a deep hatred of this cartoon cat and all its manifestations, so we were somewhat surprised when he took a feet-first running jump at the huge window, for all the world like a giant flying squirrel. Great shards of glass and a multitude of Garfields, big and small, rained down upon the now prone body of my friend and his ridiculously large fur coat. Things immediately turned even more surreal as four passers-by suddenly piled in and grabbed hold of Rick, who had several lacerations from the window shards and was bleeding profusely. As Simon and I shouted at them to back off, one of them produced a warrant card and shouted, 'Police!'. Oh, them again, off-duty this time but still clearly intent on stopping crime. They proceeded to drag Rick across to some benches and held him down, having radioed for a squad car. Simon shouted at them to take him to hospital, but they weren't interested. A lone Garfield clung to Rick's fur coat, but he threw it aside in disgust. As they drove off with our friend in the police car, we demanded to know where they were taking him, and they responded, 'Central'.

Simon and I set off for Nottingham's Central Police Station

before I suddenly remembered the incriminating materials back at Alma Street, that being our brand-new digital scales, a large amount of cannabis and quite a chunk of cash. We quickly jumped in a taxi and headed back to our house, where Simon and I ran around like headless chickens with the aforementioned items, unsure of where to hide them before I took them outside and hid them inside the wheely bin. Catching another taxi back in the city, we marched into the large central station and demanded that our friend be taken to hospital. Having been completely ignored by the custody sergeant, I then unleashed a torrent of abuse regarding his weight and his job, and we were duly both frog-marched through the revolving doors by two burly officers and thrown out into the night. In the end, the police never did search our house. Rick ended up having to pay £534 to Hallmark Ltd for damage to the window and several Garfields, thus avoiding prosecution. However, this was a turning point for the three of us living at Alma Street. We could no longer take the stress or the risk of being both party organisers and purveyors of cannabis, so the latter had to go. Our old friend Damian and some associates were just moving out of a rather lovely four-bedroom flat at the top of a big Victorian building on Vickers Street and we rapidly moved in, with some relief. Joining the three of us was Rachel, Pete's new girlfriend. She was a native of Stoke, a childhood friend of Pezz and a regular at Shelley's.

Rachel was smart, vivacious and lovely, a vivid redhead – the same as Barbara, who had now returned from living in Liverpool – and so the five of us moved into the flat where we would live for a couple of years, and from where we would plan and plot most of the tumultuous DiY escapades to come. Sitting atop the massive old house on a leafy residential street, the flat was level with the treetops and felt for all the world like a nest, fifty feet above the street below, and much safer than our old terrace. The spare bedroom in the back became our new studio. I had purchased a spanking new Roland keyboard and a small mixing desk to add to the Atari computer and the drum machine. Rick's dad donated his ancient old PC and it became the first DiY office computer, on which we began to enter the names and addresses of our new members, this being so long ago that the printer paper was the green eighties type with holes on both sides and turned by cogs.

Simon and Nikki were still in Forest Fields, Jack was living in a flat on Gregory Boulevard, near Jules, and Pezz was in a shared house in Basford. Those who came to dance at our events were scattered across inner-city Nottingham and the cities beyond. Our traveller comrades had by now moved on from Wilford Hill, via Stathern, where we had another joint party, and on to Derbyshire, a move which would have a huge influence over the years to come. Our sound system was primed and ready. All was in place for the imminent arrival of the festival season, which duly landed over the bank holiday in early May with an event on Hungerford Common, which ran from Friday 3rd to Monday 6th May. This was the first time Black Box had been to a festival and it became clear from the off that things had changed over the winter and spring. Hungerford was probably the first festival where the sound systems and the ravers had really taken over from bands and the traditional festival-goers. There was some tension behind the scenes, but this was minimal compared to the sheer visceral excitement in the air. For the first time, our movement felt like it was beginning to come of age, that it had great import and that it was growing. The feeling was irresistible and exhilarating, and it would reach a whole new level just three weeks later.

# 13

If those who came of age attending festivals since the start of the twenty-first century could travel back in time to the free festivals of the eighties and nineties, they would probably be somewhat bewildered and shocked. The concept of a festival as an expensive weekend leisure option is relatively new. Events such as the Avon Free Festival originated in the early seventies, much like Glastonbury (although Glastonbury itself was never free, of course). With the state elimination of Stonehenge from 1985 onwards, free festivals had come close to petering out in the late eighties but were now about to explode, not only into life but into the national consciousness. But there was to be no expensive tickets, security and high fences, VIP areas, artisan food and drink experiences, the luxury yurt, the BBC onsite broadcasts, the scented toilets, or indeed any toilets at all. And, most crucially, no police. These festivals offered complete freedom, a primal, almost pagan experience where a range of drugs were openly on sale, and where anyone could set up a stage, a marquee or a sound system. An environment within which pretty much anything went, and which carried on for days with no one in charge to pull the plug. Getting out without being pulled by the police was a different matter, but for those two, three or even five days, within a genuine temporary autonomous zone, wild and unfettered hedonism, coupled with an atavistic reconnection with the earth, the sky and fire was possible, even unavoidable.

And so the bank holiday weekend at the end of May 1991 duly arrived, and with it the first big free festival of the year. Unlike Castlemorton exactly a year later, we really didn't know how big it was going to be, and, more importantly for us, whether house sound systems like ours and hordes of ravers who knew little of festival etiquette would be welcome. How these big festivals materialised and how a site was chosen probably warrants some explanation. As the free festivals grew exponentially over those years, the process would come under much press and legal scrutiny. For the Avon Free Festival, there was obviously no pre-agreed venue, no licence from the local authority, no adverts or flyers other than a few photocopies which didn't and couldn't mention a site, mainly because there never was one in advance. At this time the traveller lifestyle, that is the 'New Age' or hippy section as opposed to the Gypsy or Roma travellers (between whom there was little love lost), was much more widespread than it is now. Although effectively harassed out of existence by the authorities by the end of the nineties, in the spring of 1991 there was a large contingent of people living in buses, wagons, caravans, benders and even taxis on sites big and small, on droves and in warehouses, with the majority centred around the ancient stomping grounds of Somerset, Wiltshire, Devon, Hampshire and Gloucestershire. In terms of numbers, it's impossible to know but I'm guessing that seventy-five to one hundred thousand people were living nomadically, outside the traditional boundaries of society.

Amid the chaos there was a certain level of organisation: a magazine, *Festival Eye*, plus traveller welfare services and a school bus. As with any social grouping, hierarchies had formed, and it was the older, more experienced travellers, who had perhaps been on the road since the seventies, who would make the call. It would be among these older heads, many of whom had families on the road, that festival sites would be decided. Often it depended on current levels of hostility from county-based police forces, but sometimes it was simply the discovery of a great potential site, or one of those kept in reserve. Organisation was conducted by word of mouth, a place was chosen, and multiple groups would drive from their own site and congregate simultaneously, usually on a Thursday or Friday, so the festival could be set up for the weekend. A large common, or similar location, was ideal as it was big enough to accommodate all the vehicles, there would usually be multiple entrances and exits, and there might be disputed land rights which would slow down an eviction. In theory, a site could be taken and a small town set up before the police even realised and responded by creating roadblocks.

Even with roadblocks, especially as the new rave-dominated festivals exploded over that year, festival-goers would just abandon their cars and walk to the event, often for miles. It's very tricky to keep thousands of young, excited and determined people away from a large site, as the police discovered. There being no mobile phones, we received a call on the landline sometime on the Thursday. A site had been taken, Sodbury Common near the village of Chipping Sodbury, then still in Avon, later Gloucestershire. Again, with no GPS we had to consult the obligatory UK road map to find the place, and then we loaded our system into a mate's long wheel-base van and set off, having informed all our production crew and associates. Simple as that: no planning, no hesitation, no fear.

Having gained access to the common, it was clear that this would be big. In the end, as the ravers swelled the ranks on the Friday and Saturday night, this would turn out to be the biggest free festival I had ever been to; it was nowhere near the size of the Stonehenge festivals I had just missed years before, or Glastonbury, but much bigger than Avon Free in 1988. Press reports put the numbers at around four thousand, but it seemed much bigger to me, and I reckon there were a good ten thousand attendees on the Saturday night. We set up Black Box in front of our friend Roger's double-decker bus, put the generators around the other side, plugged in the decks and turned up the bass.

It was Chipping Sodbury, the name by which this festival entered folklore, that would prove the turning point in the traveller/raver/free festival alliance. As far as I know, Sweat and Circus Warp were also playing, but we were so locked into our own DiY patch that I don't think I left for two days. Hundreds gathered in front of our speakers, Jack and Simon played marathon sets beneath a clear sky and starry nights. It felt like a real gathering of the tribes. The Free Party People were there. Many had driven from Nottingham, Liverpool, Bath, Exeter, London; the atmosphere was wild, jubilant, ecstatic. People danced on our speakers, danced on buses, the sun shone the whole weekend, and, for the first time, it felt like dance music had not just been accepted at a free festival but had taken over. I sat on a traveller's bus and stared wide-eyed as someone who will definitely remain nameless opened a bag to display five thousand ecstasy tablets and, again for the first time, it felt as though this synthetic new chemical had now become the drug of choice at festivals. And it showed.

On Sunday morning, Digs and Woosh took over the decks for hours, playing a truly eclectic and seductive set, moving from the house music of the night through funk, soul, hip-hop and jazz. In one of those moments where you realise things have truly changed, I watched with delight as hundreds of crusties, travellers, ravers and whatevers danced or sat down and bobbed along together to Lonnie Liston Smith, Roy Ayers and A Tribe Called Quest right through Sunday afternoon. Here was the true spiritual heir to the Summer of Love and the early acid house scene.

Chipping Sodbury was the first free festival so explicit in the presence of dance music. It was from here that most of the traveller's initial hostility to house music began to fade. From here, trainers began replacing boots, ecstasy replacing acid or speed, and the unstoppable juggernaut of electronic beats replacing live bands and space-rock. Not universally, of course, as some travellers never lost their instinctive dislike of house music, and there can be no doubt that trying to put kids to bed with the massively amplified metronomic beat of a large sound system pounding away for days would be a nightmare. But we had tasted the real freedom and joyous abandon that festivals now represented, and we had no intention of stopping.

Crucially, Chipping Sodbury had been a truly collective endeavour. Aside from the decks, DJs and sound system, where Jules was assisted by a growing team of proto-techies, a whole infrastructure of support was emerging. In addition to Rob's projections, Moffball was establishing his own unique and magical lighting show, backdrops and decor. Different people would refill the all-important generators, without which we would have had only silence. Teams of the extended family would comb the crowd asking for donations in buckets, giving away love cabbages in return. Just as importantly, unlike a licensed rave where everyone was ordered to go home at 6am, these festivals went on for days. A truly eclectic mix of people from across the cultural spectrum were able to sit in the sun and talk. Hugs were often exchanged, and friendships were made for life. Mostly we were young, and although some of us were veterans of the festival scene and DiY had already been organising parties for two years, at Chipping Sodbury I was twenty-four years old. Over this summer, our bonds with the travellers grew, and a core group would coalesce around this new, exciting scene. In addition to Phil, Emma and Boysie, others were forming the nucleus of this new rave-friendly gang, including Max and Kizzy, Martin, Sharon and Soma, Roger, Helen, Laura, Sarah, several Petes including Glug, One Dread and Dread, Tamsin, Jay, Austin, Mote and Jeannie, Stig, Dave Blah, Grub, Kate, Demo, Lee Jones, Alix, and many others.

If there is a cycle with all movements, especially musical movements, or indeed with life itself, then the summer of 1991 was a classic example. This alliance between sound systems, DJs and travellers had gestated over the summer of 1990, had been born and was now not only blossoming into life but about to explode. As always, the question is asked: why then? Even with the advantage of three decades of hindsight, it's a difficult question, and one with many answers. Perhaps it should be asked why acid house itself erupted in 1987/88, as the free party was a manifestation of the innate thirst for freedom central to acid house but relocated to a culture which held freedom as its central creed. Acid house itself may have been a reaction to the stark cultural and economic conditions in Thatcher's Britain. Certainly, the crazy, colourful clothes and fevered dancing seemed designed to banish such a drab and colourless decade. As outlined in the early chapters of this book, it strikes me that every generation thirsts for something new, something revolutionary and wild that will not only upset their parents but their big brothers and sisters too. For me, having missed the early days of punk when it was so pregnant with possibility, I became jaded listening to the cultural commentators of the *NME* endlessly recycling the myths of punk rock into the eighties. When you are nineteen years old and something so viscerally exhilarating as acid house comes along, surely anyone with rebellion in their soul would jump on board with both feet?

And yet, there was more to acid house than pent-up teenage boredom. Never has a new musical form and a new drug appeared simultaneously and merged so perfectly, for all the world like some benevolent, genius scientist had sent them back from the twenty-fifth century. House music and MDMA seemed to appear through a tear in the space-time continuum, and yet they were just harbingers of a new digital wave that would break upon the whole world and sweep so much away. It may be a truism, but clearly, computers and the process of digitisation have radically altered everything for ever, and nowhere more so than in the world of music. Nearly all music recorded since the nineties is made in a process involving computers, sequencers and digital editors. House music was not at the genesis of the electronic revolution – *Musique concrète*, John Cage, Kraftwerk, Cabaret Voltaire, even the Human League had all experimented with electronica long before – but house was the point at which it erupted into a popular form that quickly became ubiquitous and global. When affordable music technology and cheap synthetic drugs collided, the effects were irresistible.

Chipping Sodbury festival would cause deep ripples in the pond. From this point onwards, we became increasingly well known, especially in the south-west, and the name DiY became synonymous with free parties and festivals. One reason for this was probably related to the music our DJs were playing. Although hardcore had taken root across the south of England, or certainly harder and harsher techno, we continued to play tracks that reflected our lineage. Our mission became to take the music of the clubs to the fields and the attitude of the fields back to the clubs. As house purists, our records would rarely go above 125 beats per minute. At Chipping Sodbury, through the night we had refused a long line of young local DJs carrying crates of white labels, which were clearly hardcore, access to the decks. Similarly, in Nottingham, most of the community-based DJs we knew, such as SY, D2, Mayhem and Senator, were now playing music that was too fast and brutal for us. Good lads all, but the schism in house music was now irreparable. Our music was slower, melodic, perhaps with a techno edge but also with vocals and the occasional piano. Eventually, this would become known as deep house, but as then it didn't have a name, although I'm proud to say many people just called it 'DiY'.

Back in Nottingham, we had clubs to attend to and the maintenance of our now broken-in and muddy sound system, but within a matter of three weeks, the solstice was upon us and so we prepared for another gruelling trip down south. Again, there would be advance notification of the site, but word came through at some point that week that it was at a place named Longstock, Hampshire. Digging out the old road atlas again, we found it near the bigger town of Stockbridge, again just a random name on a map at that point. Black Box was loaded and dispatched by Friday morning, 21st June, the day of the solstice. At Vickers Street, we had purchased one of the new-fangled answer machines (complete with small audio cassette) and so began the era of leaving directions on the now laughably obsolete machine. Our phone number, 0602 609518, would become infamous as the only way to get directions to parties, and that ancient gadget would fend off tens of thousands of callers in the years to come.

My old mate from the Bolton days, Cookie, had by now purchased a lovely old vehicle, a 1953 Morris Commercial truck, and we were to travel down in this. In fact, I was surprised to discover that he wanted me to drive as he hadn't actually passed his test yet. We would take this beautiful old green truck with proper four-wheel drive and massive, chunky tires on several adventures that year, though I never quite mastered the clanky old gearbox. In the back of the Morris were two opposing benches for passengers, covered by a frame and green tarpaulin but with an open back. As we approached the site, again without the benefit of mobile phones, we had no idea what to expect. Driving along narrow country lanes, I manoeuvred the considerable bulk of the truck around a corner to be met with what looked like something from the Miners' Strike. A large triangle of grass was blocked on either side by rows of riot vans and dozens of police. A few festival-goers were wandering onto the road on the other side, down which the festival obviously lay, but there seemed no way through. I had a fairly foolhardy idea. I continued driving in the direction that the police were frantically waving us to go, found somewhere to pull in and turned to Cookie: 'How about we drive back up there, slow right down as we get to the green and just drive through the middle of it and right down the other side?'

Cookie thought for a moment. 'You think it will damage the truck?'

'Nah, you've seen the size of those tyres, plus the four-wheel drive. Should be alright . . .'

I don't think Cookie was all that keen to risk his beloved vehicle, but he couldn't really say no. We had four passengers in the back, so I gave them a quick shout, did a multiple-point turn, and then set off back up the road. As we approached the triangle of grass again, one of the officers waved at us vehemently to continue past the first road-block. Complying, I slowed right down, then pulled the truck hard left and just drove over the middle of the flat side of the triangle, in between the blocks of police and through into the lane in the mid-dle. Adrenalin was pumping through my veins; Cookie was shouting and screaming. From nowhere, a policeman in riot gear stepped out and took a close-up photo of us, his massive camera topped off with a huge flash unit. I swerved to avoid him, instinct took over and sud-denly we were through, driving down the lane to the festival in the glorious summer sunshine. It was an outrageous thing to have done, and it was made all the more surreal as I glanced at the truck's side mirror to see an arm extending from the back, waving an inflatable duck at the police lines. I never found out where the duck came from, but the memory will stay with me for ever.

Driving into the festival in the big truck with huge tires, we were greeted on all sides by old friends and people who had seen us drive through the roadblock. The festival itself was unusual in that it was not in an open space but along a long, thin track, or drove, which became known as Rat's Run. With only enough room for a few vehicles on either side of the narrow track, we drove along slowly until we saw the pyramid tent and Black Box being loaded into it. Every festival had its own unique feel and flavour; Longstock was much smaller than Chipping Sodbury and suffered from its strange and narrow layout. There was a big free Circus Warp party near Peasedown Saint John in Somerset the same weekend, and due to the very limited space and early roadblocks, it was probably fortunate that larger numbers didn't attend. It was still wild, though, and is particularly notable as being the first time DiY encountered a new sound system from London, Spiral Tribe.

This moment probably marks the point at which the concept of the free party house system, travelling from a home base where parties were organised to free festivals and even abroad, began to really gain irresistible momentum. Until then, along with Sweat and Circus Warp, we had pretty much had festivals to ourselves, but the impetus for crews all across the UK to buy decks and a rig became unstoppable. My first impression of Spiral Tribe was that they were surprisingly together, and embarrassingly so for us as alongside their system they had set up a café with food and hot drinks, something we had never managed in two years. Although the Spirals would go on to adopt the generic look of shaven heads, the black ex-military clothing favoured by Crass a decade before, and huge, black trucks daubed in their trademark spirals, at Longstock they seemed laid-back and amicable. Chatting to Mark, Simone and Debbie, and clocking their small blue Luton van and their little café, I remember thinking that we could all happily coexist.

Their music was very different to ours, being much faster and harder, but as long as we were far enough apart for the systems not to clash, then the whole point of free festivals was that anything goes. Without wanting to upset any of the other myriad of sound systems which would spring up from the summer of 1991 or after, DiY and Spiral Tribe would become probably the two best known, and although some people on the outer fringes of our two clans encouraged a rivalry over the ensuing years, we never had a problem with them.

Our paths would not cross again until the summer of 1992 when the whole scene had erupted exponentially. One particularly striking DJ who was playing with the Spirals introduced himself as Charlie Hall. After some vetting of his record box, we were happy for him to play on Black Box. He would go on to form the Drum Club with Lol Hammond, and we formed a friendship that would outlast the rave years. Almost comically, considering what would occur later, the Spiral Tribe's driver, it might have been Mark, sought us out on the Monday morning and politely asked if we could give their Luton a tow-start due to a flat battery. Dutifully we dragged their blue van around the site a few times until it started, flattening our own battery in the process and condemning us to becoming stuck and lost on some random Hampshire backroad until Wednesday morning.

# 14

The twelve months following the summer of 1991 would prove crucial in terms of the wider free party dynamic. Many new sound systems would appear, and many big festivals would take place, where the presence of massively amplified dance music and the consequent multitude of ravers began to effectively replace the old formula of travellers and live bands. Profound changes had happened within this nascent scene, although we would shortly find out to what extent. However, it was around this time that we began to become slightly wary of large festivals. They seemed to be growing so fast, with an ever-burgeoning number of hardcore techno rigs and attracting ever-increasing interest from the police, media and state, that we turned our attention to organising much smaller, more intimate, more loved-up outdoor parties with the same rapturous formula but, crucially, with an initial lack of interest from the authorities. There was a formula for successfully getting away with a party, directly proportional to its size and highly influenced by geographical location.

Our affiliated traveller friends had by now long moved on from the outskirts of Nottingham, via a small site party at Stathern in rural Leicestershire to the bucolic yet rugged delights of Derbyshire. It would be here, in the quarries, fields and ancient byways of that beautiful county, that DiY would really find its true party groove. Ringed by the market towns of Matlock, Bakewell and Buxton, and containing the legendary stone circles of Nine Ladies and Arbor Low, this rural enclave would provide all the natural party venues one could possibly desire; over the next few years they became a giant weekend playground for the party heads of Nottingham, Derby, Lincoln and Sheffield. A new site was found on a long drove near to Biggin (population 120), near to Newhaven in deepest Derbyshire, and quickly populated with various vehicles. As was the way with sites, sometimes someone objected furiously and the travellers would be evicted or harassed away within days or weeks; sometimes there was no reaction and the site lasted for months and, occasionally, for years. The Biggin site would remain intact for months, there would be many parties there, and, unlike the free festival-hardened police forces of the south-west, the local authorities left us relatively in peace.

Looking back at the photos that survive from these halcyon early parties on the Biggin site always makes me chuckle. These really were basic acid house affairs, initially with maybe fifty to a hundred people, dancing through to the dawn and well into the afternoon inside and around a saggy green ex-army canvas tent. I remember driving up to the long track in a Luton with Black Box in the back, arriving around dusk on a Saturday night to be greeted by the weary faces of those who had danced until Tuesday and couldn't believe it was time to go again. One weekend, everyone was away at some festival or other. Cookie and I drove up to Biggin with half of the rig in the back of his truck and proceeded to set the decks up and play to about ten people well into Sunday afternoon. At the end of the day, it matters not about the size of a party, it is the vibe that is all-important. Much like some of the parties in woods and tiny sites over the winter of 1990 and spring of 1991, small is beautiful. And, of course, this was all new to the denizens of the East Midlands and South Yorkshire. Young, enthusiastic party people heard about these events, attended from Matlock and the local towns, from the big cities which lay within fifty miles, and Nottingham, of course, and from much further afield. Soon they brought their mates, the word spread, more travellers moved up from the south and the parties began to grow. Starved of anywhere to dance after 2am, among the serious ravers the free party ethic took root and began to blossom across the middle and north of England. Down south, particularly around Oxford, the scene was not only blossoming but starting to explode as weekly parties erupted, which would become huge over the course of the next year. DJs such as Easygroove would become big names on this splinter scene. However, there was again deep division between the versions of house music which we respectively played.

In the midst of this idyllic but hectic time where we relentlessly threw small parties, promoted our flagship club night at Venus and across England, and still managed to load the system into and DJ every Tuesday at the Cookie Club, another big festival hoved into view. Three weeks after the solstice festival at Longstock, over the weekend of 12th to 14th July, across the Mersey from Liverpool on the Wirral, a free festival would occur that seismically changed the face of the whole atmosphere and culture of the festival world. The Moreton Lighthouse event would prove to be the single most infamous, lawless and deranged event that I have ever attended, or that DiY were involved in.

As mentioned earlier, we had attended a small festival on the lighthouse site in the summer of 1990, only a few weeks after the seminal Glastonbury of that year. Situated on a long strip of land adjoining the Mersey, the area around Moreton Lighthouse, which still stood, painted but disused, has long been contested as common land. The locals are convinced it is, but the council decree otherwise. This friction underlay the madness that would happen there over those sunny days in July. It was booked into the traveller fraternity's summer calendar, and so was unusual on three fronts: it had a pre-arranged location; it was so near to a big city; and lastly, the city in question, the Independent Republic of Liverpool, was in the north of England. All these elements would become significant.

As we had a precise location, Cookie and I merrily set off again in his vintage Morris. We spent a couple of days hanging out with our multitude of friends in Liverpool, centred around the property at Bold Place where Barbara had previously lived and where several of our mates still lived. Still smarting from Spiral Tribe's ability to organise a café at their first free festival, I had decided to organise our own. After much-heated debate, especially with our militant vegan and accomplished chef Dave Mooring, we settled on a menu of veggie burgers and veggie chilli. We had a small generator in the back of the truck, a freezer full of ingredients and Rick's 1970s family tent as a structure. The name of the café was to be 'Sledger's Café', in honour of a northern slang word for the effects of an ecstasy tablet that failed to make the ingester dance and whoop but instead lie down and dribble, albeit in a pleasant way. In the back of the truck were some of the same individuals as during the roadblock incident, little aware that this would be an even bumpier ride. We left Liverpool on the Friday lunchtime in glorious sunshine, knowing that the mass of travellers were driving up from the south-west from the new site in Derbyshire and meeting on the M53 to travel in convoy up to Moreton.

Steering the old truck through the Mersey Tunnel, with Cookie whingeing as ever at my misuse of the gearbox, we arrived on the long, suburban road which led to the site. As casually as you can in a large, vintage truck with fuck-off tyres and a love cabbage in the window where the tax disc should be, we drove along the coastal road to reconnoitre the potential festival site. Although the entrance to the site was blocked with large rocks, the kerb was only standard height and would allow access. However, and to our grave concern, a long line of white police Range Rovers were parked along the edge of the fields, blocking access. As we drove past them and the assembled coppers, looks were exchanged before we nonchalantly turned the corner and parked up. Pulling into a small car park, we exchanged some strong words of shock that the site was so heavily obstructed. Without the benefit of mobile phones, we couldn't warn the large numbers of vehicles that we hoped were by now somewhere on the M53 heading our way. And so we waited. And waited. Well past the point at which I thought we had perhaps imagined the whole thing, I heard a revving of engines and looked down the long straight road to see the most outlandish, outrageous and downright welcome convoy of vehicles I have ever seen. Looking utterly incongruous in this quiet suburb of the Wirral, the vehicles stretched back hundreds of yards; dozens of trucks, buses, double-deckers, fire engines, towed caravans, battered taxis and ex-military vans were all lined up in the sunshine.

Recognising many familiar vehicles and faces, we allowed the first five or so to pass our turning before pulling into the convoy, much relieved. In procession, we approached the strip of land where we had intended to pull on and were met by a solid line of police, one with a raised hand, clearly demonstrating no entry. The drivers of the first few vehicles alighted and went to remonstrate with the cops, being joined by many more from vehicles to the rear. Negotiations were clearly not going well, and as we climbed down from the cab to go and listen, a dreadlocked fellow walked rapidly down the line, whispering to each driver that we were all just going to go for it. And so we did.

In the most egregious display of anarchic intent I ever participated in, the lead vehicles started their engines and drove slowly along the strip of land, accelerating en masse as we climbed the kerb and smashed the line of police Range Rovers out of the way before driving at some speed onto the grass. With the line now breached, the whole convoy, for all the world like the cartoon 'Wacky Races', pulled through the gap and onto the site as we sped across the field, four or five vehicles abreast, before slowing down and forming into a good old-fashioned wagon circle. As I drove the Morris, bumping and chugging across the grass, to the right I could see Chilly Phil in the cab of his bus, resplendent in flying hat and goggles, whooping. Cookie and I were delirious with exhilaration, delight and downright terror. Unbelievably, I caught a glance at the side mirror and saw the same duck as had appeared during the dodgy manoeuvre at Longstock being waved by the same arm, which I think belonged to Little Lee. Clearly left in the Morris after the solstice, that duck sure had some tales to tell.

However, as we disembarked from our respective vehicles, jubilation quickly turned to a somewhat icy fear as we realised what we had done: we had destroyed several very expensive police vehicles and massively taken the piss. It was a surreal moment as about two hundred travellers with kids and dogs, wagons circled in the midday suburban Merseyside sun, wondered what would happen next. It turned out to be the arrival of several vans full of riot police, no doubt summoned from Liverpool and therefore probably not messing around, which pulled up on a large green on the other side of the road around two hundred yards away, before dozens of officers climbed out and began to strap on their riot gear. And then, the strangest thing happened. Dozens of locals appeared from the estate behind where the police were tooling up, casually wandered over, introduced themselves and declared their support for our actions. They wanted a festival here due to their ongoing conflict with the council over the land's disputed common status. They were not technically Scousers, as that epithet only applies to those born across the water, but they certainly looked and sounded like Scousers. The situation quickly became surreal as old ladies, kids and people pushing buggies began to climb into the vehicles to have a look, with several of the older men asking if we had a 'bit of draw' or 'a spare joint'. It felt more like a village fete than a situation where a large contingent of crazed travellers had just smashed their way onto a free festival site.

As a Merseyside veteran of many years standing, I was not overly surprised by the locals' reaction, but the travellers, who were so accustomed to the hostile responses of the citizens of Wiltshire, Hampshire or Somerset, were wide-eyed in disbelief. As if the whole scenario couldn't get any more strange, someone then spotted a police delegation heading across the grass; three officers were fully uniformed in the baking heat. Taking the lead, and obviously the senior officer present, a small and ruddy-faced cop marched towards our bizarre gathering, half crusty and half tracksuit, and announced:

'I would just like to say that, from a police perspective, we consider this to be an illegal gathering. However, you are now on this site. I could be prepared to ignore the willful damage to police property, but I cannot allow to pass the serious injury to one of my officers who was hit by one of your vehicles and is now on his way to hospital. I now intend to find the culprit and arrest them.'

This was news to us. We genuinely had no idea that a policeman had been injured, although one driver obviously did and was hiding somewhere. Worried looks were exchanged; this had just escalated into a new league. In the distance, the riot police were now fully kitted up, clearly ready for action.

'What did the driver look like?' someone shouted.

'He had dreadlocks,' came the reply.

Wrong answer. The whole assembly erupted in laughter – travellers, locals and all.

'Good luck with that, mate,' a local wit shouted, and the laughter amplified.

I almost felt sorry for this ranking officer. He was clearly losing any control of the situation and had never faced such a peculiar alliance. I'm convinced to this day that if it hadn't been for the local support and the suburban setting, we would have taken a serious kicking. It just got better as the three officers climbed into a small caravan, which rocked as they were looking around it, before emerging to announce, 'Well, he's not in there . . .'

This time the laughter doubled in response; it was just so ridiculous, worthy of Monty Python. Knowing that he was beaten and facing utter humiliation, the small senior cop went bright red, turned heel and marched off back to where he had emerged, followed by two very sheepish looking constables. After waiting about an hour, the culprit who had knocked down the policeman emerged from the chest freezer in the back of Cookie's truck, somewhat worried and having hacked off his own dreadlocks with one of my kitchen knives.

And so the authorities were pretty much forced to allow the festival to happen; their options were severely limited by the sheer numbers who had now arrived, as was so often the case. To our amazement, the police and the riot vans withdrew, although a police helicopter soon arrived, buzzing overhead the entire weekend. Scores more vehicles soon arrived with hundreds of occupants and would arrive continuously over the weekend. Phil and friends erected the pyramid as Dave and the Free Party People contingent arrived, including Moffball, and set about turning our area into a full-on party environment with arctic tank nettings and backdrops, flags and banners streaming in the estuary wind. Generators were filled; crazy lightshows were installed.

Appropriately, we had Tonka DJs guesting at Bounce on the Friday night back in Nottingham, and so Black Box would not be arriving until Saturday. Enlisting some helpers, we set up Sledger's Café, complete with a small generator, fridge and chest freezer. I suspected that Rick's family tent had not seen daylight since the seventies, but we got her up, resplendent in electric blue and bright orange colours. We chalked up a menu, started to mix the burgers, prepare the chilli and set out the DiY tapes that we had brought to sell. We had been selling DJ mixtapes for a few months now, quietly ignoring the blatant copyright infringement. They had begun to shift in amazingly large quantities, especially in the now DiY stronghold of the south-west, partly due to the heroic efforts of Jo, our tape manager. Suspecting that the festival would become a giant rave, and with it being in the DiY stronghold of the north-west, we had invited Sasha and John Kelly to play alongside our own DJs and local hero Vertigo. Rick also knocked up some flyers, which arrived the next day and were distributed in Liverpool city centre, no doubt further contributing to what happened next: absolute, unmitigated chaos.

Waking up in the back of the Morris on Saturday morning, I opened the back flap and looked out. Not only had the festival grown exponentially overnight, with dozens more vehicles pushing the festival boundaries many fields further in every direction, but the scallies had arrived. For those not familiar with Liverpudlian vernacular, 'scally' is short for 'scallywag' (Scousers abbreviate everything) and is a derogatory word meaning criminally dodgy youths, often to be found wearing knock-off sportswear and purveying poor quality drugs. As I jumped down from the truck, a kid with a heavy Scouse accent who looked about twelve tried to sell me some acid, following that up by trying to sell me a stolen Ford Fiesta which his mates had nicked. All before breakfast. By the time our crew arrived in the afternoon in another overloaded Luton van with the system, decks, mixer and records, the scene was set. By Saturday evening, thousands had arrived, swelled throughout the night as clubs closed, word and flyers flew around and, most of all, because it was featured on the local news. There can be few more surreal experiences than sitting on a traveller's bus, watching a small television as a news helicopter transmits outraged video footage from above the very vehicle in which one is sitting.

I would wager that more drugs were consumed at the ensuing festival, per head, than any other event in British history. On Saturday night, all-night, through Sunday and on into Monday morning, Black Box rocked the pyramid. Two distinct groupings, the travellers and the scouse ravers merged, both beloved of extreme intoxication and revelry, and amicably at first. More sound systems arrived; Circus Normal set up their enormous rig on the other side of the still-expanding site. And still they came. Barbara arrived in her Renault 4, overladen with Rob's lightshow. Jack, Pezz and Simon played, John Kelly arrived and went on to a rapturous reaction. Sasha never made it, but it was truly his loss. All our mates from Liverpool rolled in, too numerous to list, as did the Manchester crew, friends from Hull, Bristol, Sheffield, the ever-keen Nottingham massive and many, many more. Conversely, more stolen vehicles were arriving, some driven onto the dance floor, which had expanded onto the grass outside, way beyond the pyramid. Truly wild, truly unique, truly mental. Daylight broke over the estuary, which is when the photo on the cover of this book was taken. On another gloriously sunny day by the Mersey, thousands of people danced through the dawn, through lunchtime and on into the night.

And slowly, things started to get weird; firstly with those of us running things behind the scenes, and eventually a general descent into outright madness. Muggings were being reported, and heavy-duty local gangsters were heard to be taxing travellers. Rumours spread, exaggerated but believed within a large gathering who hadn't slept for way too long. Someone set fire to a car on the dancefloor; other stolen vehicles were being driven around the site recklessly by fourteen-year-olds on acid. A vintage bus caught fire and, as we rushed round to try and help, we found it was too late; the beautiful wooden body was completely ablaze. Back in Sledger's Café, we were valiantly still selling food, fending off very hard Scouse lads demanding to know what the fuck a veggie burger was and asking, 'Where's the bevvies?'. Several times I looked round to see that cagoule-covered arms had appeared under the side of the tent and were helping themselves to mixtapes. Our perennial source of party funding, the ubiquitous bucket, was having cash stolen from it instead of added, and all the while helicopters buzzed the site overhead. Most party-goers were probably unaware of the bad feeling that was growing behind the scenes as the endless hypnotic rhythms of house music drove the party onwards. It was in many ways a truly fabulous night, driven by huge quantities of pink ecstasy tablets that many thought to be the best they had ever taken. But for every up, there is a down.

What happened was that two very different sets of people collided: the travellers and the scally gangs of Liverpool. Both considered this to be their patch, and in a way they were both correct. Moreton Lighthouse 1991 was a free festival organised by travellers, the site taken by travellers, and the infrastructure and the party created by travellers and associated friends. It was, however, on Merseyside, and so it was geographically within the remit of the Liverpool firms. For the whole of Sunday, the festival rocked on, a riotous, debauched arena of mayhem. Most local people went home on Sunday, no doubt exhausted yet happy, but that was not an option for the travellers. They would eventually leave and end up on a site in Deeside where, allegedly, some of the Liverpool gang came looking for the travellers to settle some scores and five young lads would die in a car crash.

As for DiY, we were exhausted. I packed up Sledger's Café and counted my profits, which miraculously came to over four hundred quid. I decided to re-invest the moiney in those little pink things and managed to get them back to Nottingham intact. As we drove out late on Monday night, we were pulled over at a police roadblock and I thought we were doomed. About eight people were sleeping in the back as one officer signalled for us to climb down from the cab, looked at me and Cookie and said, brusquely: 'If you, or any of your scummy mates, ever come back here for any reason, ever, we will break all your fucking legs. Is that clear?'

Pretty clear, yes. Then Cookie pipes up: 'It's ok officer, we're just diesel enthusiasts.'

Again, as would happen so frequently over these years, I glanced across at Cookie and really hoped he wouldn't speak again.

'Fucking smartarse, eh?' said the copper. 'So, where's your MOT?'

'Doesn't need one, classic vehicle, pre-MOT.'

The officer looked up at the yellow love cabbage where the tax disc should be. 'And the tax disc?'

'Exempt.'

He looked at us with a mixture of disbelief and contempt, and just growled, 'Fuck off. Now.'

And so we did, delirious that we hadn't been arrested or worse. I drove us home without further incident, except for my falling asleep at dawn on the M6 and veering across all three lanes of a fortunately empty motorway in a large military-green truck, waking up moments before impact into the central reservation. Having dropped everyone off, I finally arrived back at Vickers Street, exhausted, with only enough energy to scrawl 'THINK PINK' on the brick wall outside before going to bed, hoping to sleep for at least 48 hours. Fate, as ever, had other ideas.

Our phone rang, which I let the answer machine handle, before Rick's voice, sounding somewhat distressed, kicked in. Picking up the phone, Rick blurted out that they had been pulled in the Luton van, which had been reported stolen, then arrested, were now in a police station somewhere in Birkenhead, and that I needed to get down to the van hire company in Nottingham and pay them some money. At this juncture, I should probably explain our policy towards hiring vehicles in those days. Although by the end of the year we would buy our own truck, with electric tail lift, until then we had been forced to hire Luton vans. Apart from being inherently unstable and highly inappropriate vehicles to move several tonnes of sound equipment in, they were also expensive to hire. And so we had established the rather short-sighted strategy of only hiring the van for one day and then just keeping it for three or four before dropping it off at night. We had no credit cards and only worked with cash in those days, but even so, it was a highly risky approach and had now completely backfired. Clearly, the van had been reported stolen and had been pulled after leaving the festival. Simon had been driving, with Rick, Pete, Dave, Julie and several others in the back. To make matters worse, a single ecstasy tablet had been discovered in a size eleven shoe, and although only one person in that vehicle had feet that big, they were never prosecuted.

Jumping into the Triumph Dolomite that I had recently inherited from my grandma, I went to the hire company and, having pleaded complete ignorance and incredulity, paid for an additional three days' hire that would release the vehicle and its passengers from custody. All except one. Simon, never the luckiest of individuals, had appeared on a national police database when arrested and had been taken away in handcuffs. It turned out that he had given his real name and address to the police in Salisbury when questioned about the last Pepperbox Hill party a year before. As it correlated with his driving licence, he was now, after three gruelling days at a particularly exhausting festival, heading to Salisbury in the back of a police car wearing handcuffs. As the other occupants of the now un-stolen van arrived back in Nottingham, Simon would be held in the cells for days before being bailed to reappear at Salisbury Crown Court, charged with organising unlicensed entertainment in the form of an acid house party. I drove Simon and Nikki down to the ancient wooden court in Salisbury for his trial a few months later, where his barrister did a great job, Simon was found not guilty and I carved 'DiY are Innocent' on a bench in the public gallery, which as far as I know may well still be there.

# 15

Unsurprisingly, the fallout from the Moreton Lighthouse festival was both immediate and far-reaching. Many of the traveller families who were connected to DiY were essentially marooned in the north-west, plus many more, with their vehicles, finances and minds all impacted by the effects of such a loopy and unhinged event. Slowly, the contingent who had been living at the drove near Biggin returned, as did many new arrivals, looking for a place to lick their wounds and repair vehicles before the long trek south. Many more individuals who had been loosely affiliated to the central core of the party travellers were now parked up in Derbyshire. They liked what they saw and would stay for some time in the rolling hills of the Peak District, hidden from the intense scrutiny of the authorities.

Jointly, we began scouring the area for potential party sites. Phil and I spent many happy hours driving my Triumph Dolomite around the locale, finding many suitable spots, including a perfect piece of hard-standing concrete on a disused airfield near Ashbourne. Although there had been many parties at the Biggin site, it was not a great location for a party, being long and thin with parking limited and chaotic, plus there were now many more people living there, including children. Better to take a temporary site for a night and day than attract unwanted attention to a living space.

And so, on 10th August 1991 we threw Derbyshire's first proper hit-and-run free party. With Phil's bus parked across the old airfield, tarps strung from it, Black Box and decks assembled on the grassy concrete, this was truly an acid house party. Rick threw a flyer together:

'DiY SAY GET IN 2 THE GROOVE: THIS PARTY IS ALL-NIGHT, OUTDOOR AND FREE'

We distributed the flyers in Nottingham and Derby and, by golly, they worked. From the dozens of revellers who had made it to the small Biggin parties, we suddenly had hundreds. This level of lawlessness, with no charge, no fences, no security and no end time, was entirely new to most of them – and they loved it. The music went on until sometime on Sunday afternoon; the police arrived at some point with only a couple of cars, but they didn't seem particularly bothered. At the end of the day, why should they be? Does anyone really need to get hostile with a group of happy young people dancing in the sun? However, some hostility did emanate from the local paper, whose headline ran 'Shock Disco Invasion Shatters Night Peace'. We, of course, loved that, later naming a track 'Shock Disco Invasion' in its honour.

Much has been written and debated over the years about why the concept of a 'free' party was so important. Much more than simply the absence of an entrance cost, the 'free' prefix alluded to the whole history of alternative philosophies, a summary of events stretching back to prehistory where the constraints of a modern, regulated society did not apply. Resuscitated in the age of hippiedom, 'free festivals' indicated liberation and temporary elusion from the binds of convention and commercialism. A 'free party' became so much more than simply a rave without a ticket price. It lay outside the legal reach of the police or the local authorities and allowed individuals to trade for no profit and permitted them to interact in a radical collectivist way, wandering through fields at dawn with time to really talk. In the many debates over what constituted the first real free party, some have suggested that conventional club nights or events for which no payment was demanded were first, but I think this perhaps misses the point; such an event may be free of charge, but it still fits within the infrastructure of four walls, security, licensing laws and a two o'clock finish.

However one defines a free party, we were definitely now doing them regularly and had all the ingredients necessary to continue, which we did with relish. For the remainder of the summer of 1991, we were aware of free festivals happening across the south of England but decided we preferred to party in Derbyshire – we few, we happy few, we band of brothers and sisters. On reflection, Moreton Lighthouse had spiralled so out of control and freaked so many people out that big festivals began to feel more like growing collective madness where there was a strong possibility of either getting mugged or arrested, where vehicles and sound systems might get trashed or impounded, and, worst of all, the party might not happen. Over the next few months, free festivals occurred in Bala (Happy Daze), Cornwall (White Goddess), Hampshire (Torpedo Town) and big free parties mushroomed across London, mostly featuring Spiral Tribe and Bedlam, the two best known of the emerging techno free party rigs. DiY, however, were locked into our own growing scene. It felt incredibly special and fresh, getting away with parties every weekend and relieved not to have to book another Luton van and head south with all our kit into unknown madness. Driving through police roadblocks had undeniably been fun, but I'd rather not have had to do it every weekend. That was until we took a call from Dangerous Dave, informing us that the Free Party People had discovered a choice site near Wedmore in Somerset and asking whether we would like to bring Black Box and DJs down over the bank holiday weekend. Well, yes, of course we would.

Held over the long weekend of the last Saturday in August 1991, the Wedmore party was probably the most archetypal and classic free party we ever did. As ever, the FPP had done a fabulous job on the infrastructure. A perfect marquee was in place when my carload arrived on Saturday evening, again with tank nettings, backdrops and endless banners flying in the glorious Somerset sun. A truly amazing lightshow was in place thanks to Dave and Moffball; Rob would bring more, and there may even have been a laser. There was still a real innocence to free parties at this point; it all seemed so full of possibility and beauty, and, as with all innovative scenes, it truly felt like this would go on for ever. Who could not love this synthesis of house music, ecstasy and the timeless wonder of the English countryside? As I recall, Jack and Simon had arrived ready to DJ. I watched in awe as Dave wrestled a malfunctioning generator, in flames, to the floor before it kicked itself out of his grip and jumped insanely across the grass, for all the world like a petrol-driven bronco spitting fire, which explained clearly to me how he had earned the sobriquet 'Dangerous'. In those golden days, we always seemed to have the gods, the old ones, behind us, and soon another generator was found. Everything was ready for the perfect rave except one thing. The Luton van, driven by Rick and containing our somewhat essential sound system, was nowhere to be seen.

Again, we had no way of knowing what had happened, and so we waited. By now we really should have learnt to avoid Luton vans. Rick had taken a bend way too quickly somewhere on the A50 and turned the hire van over, rolling some distance before coming to a halt on its side. In the back were not only a couple of tonnes of speaker cabs, amps and decks but also several human beings. I think in the end, mercifully, only Phil and Rob were in the back, and they emerged shaken and mostly unharmed. The really lucky thing was that our friend Tamsin and her young daughter, Jelly, had also been planning to sit in the rear box but cancelled at the last minute. Thank the Lord. Incredibly, the AA sent a tow truck which managed to pull the van back onto four wheels, they all climbed in again, and Rick drove the van onto the party, arriving to a hero's welcome. Now that's dedication to the cause. I also made a mental note that we really needed to get our own truck.

With the last element in place, the party commenced and rocked on until Sunday evening with no interference from the police. Perhaps the miracle of the PA truck had given everyone an extra spiritual lift and parties always seemed wilder in the sun, but this was a truly glorious night and day. People had climbed onto every available space – the speakers, buses, lighting platforms, anywhere – to dance. And how we danced, devoid of ennui or the exhausted cynicism that inevitably affects movements like this eventually; we danced like untamed pagans, which is pretty much what we were. This was also the zenith of what became known as 'high tunes': joyous, anthemic tracks that were perfect for days like this. I have an abiding memory of Simon dropping 'Everybody's Free' by Rozalla, with its huge opening strings, elegiac vocals and big, dirty rhythms at some point on Sunday morning and the place erupting. At parties such as these, we were collectively so high, in every way possible, and so blissfully, almost religiously rapturous, that I think once you experienced it, once you had undergone this almost holy communion, life could never be the same again. People hugged endlessly, hugged friends, hugged strangers, hugged trees and sometimes tried to hug the police. With the benefit of age and hindsight, it may have been somewhat naïve and chemically artificial, but by God it felt good at the time.

Our dancefloors were the ultimate in egalitarian democracy, a communal space where all were equal, where women could dance without inhibitions and without getting groped or propositioned by predatory men. Dancing created a space within which you could succumb to the music's sensuality and rhythm and just do your thing, no matter how strange it might be considered to be by mainstream society. I had grown up endlessly going to gigs, usually to spend an hour or so watching some people, nearly always male, play instruments onstage while drinking warm lager from a plastic cup. At many of these gigs, people, again mostly male, would mosh at the front, which is a euphemistic word for drunken and inherently macho pushing and fighting.

For us, gigs now looked archaic and obsolete, the old bands like dinosaurs. Our parties would go on for a minimum of twelve hours, often days. 'Seventy-two hour party people', to quote a sympathetic journalist. There were no stars, no hero worship; the DJs were usually invisible and dancers faced in all directions. The parties were free, they drew eclectic and energised crowds that would never have mixed socially or geographically before, and we danced together beneath the stars in our church, our temple; a movable temple with no walls and no barriers. Life, it is said, is not a search for happiness but a search for belonging, and so deeply did we feel this brave new belonging that, three decades later, people are still avidly discussing those parties and festivals. This sense of wonder at what we achieved provided the motivation to write this book. It was a compelling story, life-enhancing for the participants but utterly unseen by the media at the time.

And we lived like this throughout those years, from party to party, utterly committed to the groove and relentlessly organising the next one, never stopping for a moment to draw breath or question what we were doing. People had love cabbages shaved into their hair, people went on the road, people became DJs or sound engineers or producers or promoters as they began to do it themselves. Our posse grew exponentially as more and more people underwent this baptism of love and became equally committed to the dance and to the party. Although we still DJed at clubs and free parties across England, over the autumn and winter of 1991 we further retreated to our underground party zone in Derbyshire and continued to look for suitable venues. Our phone at Vickers Street rang off the hook all week, with all sorts of party offers being thrown at us and endless queries as to where the party would be that weekend. By now, DiY's reputation was expanding, and we began receiving interview requests from national magazines such as *Mixmag*, *DJ Mag* and *The Face*. They could never understand the concept of a collective, always asking for photos of one or two individuals, requests which we always refused. A couple of years later, *Jockey Slut* magazine offered to put DiY on the cover, so long as we only chose a couple of faces. Again we refused, sending them photos Tash had taken in a Nottingham park, with twenty of us all holding identical records over our faces, anonymously. They put us on page eleven.

Soon after the Wedmore party, I drove out to the site at Biggin, hearing that someone had discovered a disused quarry near Ashover, north-east of Matlock, as a potential party venue. Picking up Phil, we excitedly went to have a look, drove through the unlocked gate and round into a stunning stone quarry, overgrown on the top and sides but with amazing vertical cliff faces and a big flat area for vehicles and dancing. It was probably the most perfect venue for a party I had ever seen. This natural amphitheatre was called Butts Quarry and would be added to the roll call of party places that would achieve mythical status among our tribe. And so on one wet Saturday evening in September, we rendezvoused with several travellers and their vehicles, and our lighting guys and several hundred party-heads danced the night and day away undisturbed in the drizzling rain in a quarry in deepest Derbyshire.

It often struck me that our parties, being held in England and through all the seasons, often occurred under grey skies, beneath howling winds and sheeting rain, even snow, and yet no one ever complained, or went home early, or failed to dance. There was just some indefinable, electric communion binding these early parties together, a perfect synergy of mood, moment and music. Our comrade from the early days, Rory, the original love gangster, had by now relocated to his beloved Merseyside but travelled with intrepid enthusiasm, and his constant presence at these parties, and more particularly what he brought with him, in bulk, no doubt also helped us brave the elements and dance through until dawn. A particularly enthusiastic crew from Matlock – Blandy, Miffy, Dave, Jellybaby and Parksy – became regular fixtures at DiY events for years to come.

Two weeks later, we were ready to do another party in this magical location, lying as it did on our doorstep, only around twenty-five miles north of Nottingham. This time the gods of weather were with us and again we assembled within the stone walls and proceeded to create a truly epic happening. Word had clearly spread across the towns and cities triangulated between Sheffield, Manchester and Nottingham; this was probably the biggest party we threw during our Derbyshire era, with getting on for a thousand people in attendance. Rob and Moffball had really gone to town, building a lighting tower and, alongside their now mind-blowing lightshow, they also projected wild visuals onto the quarry walls all night. Black Box sounded devastatingly crisp and clear within the confined stone theatre, which also acted as a buffer to the sound travelling through the night. Constellations of stars twinkled overhead, a fire was lit, all our DJs played during the night and next day, and the people danced as if possessed. It was possible to walk around the top of the quarry and look down at the shamanic ritual below: a magical, exhilarating spectacle.

And then, as if couldn't get any more cosmic, Rob, ever the techo-hippy, set up his latest gadget in a cave in the quarry wall. It was a bio-energiser, which for the uninitiated is a battery-powered device pioneered by Dr Georges Lakhovsky and Nikolai Tesla in the early twentieth century. Believing that all cells are essentially electrical in nature, they created this device which generates frequencies characteristic of living organisms, simultaneously emitting waves between 750 kHz to 3 MHz and, in theory, resonating fundamentally with human cells to create internal physical and spiritual harmony. Anyway, it seemed to work. Throughout the night and the next day, many party-goers climbed into the cave and afterwards excitedly reported various profound experiences.

And so the sun rose on Sunday morning, evaporating the dawn mists and finally breaking over the brow of the quarry and splashing golden rays on the still-dancing troupe of revellers below. Again, the party was untroubled by the police; we were left alone until well into the Sunday. As I wandered from the quarry and between the buses and trucks of the travellers who had actually moved there to live, I was waved onto a crazily painted bus. I sat as someone proceeded to chop out some lines of a white powder, which it has to be said was not uncommon in such situations. I assumed it was MDMA, although there seemed to be some extra anticipation from those gathered on the bus. The substance was, it turned out, a brand-new drug on the scene, known as ketamine, a substance unheard of in the autumn of 1991 but which would soon become infamous across the planet. It has to be remembered that, at this point in time, we had very little knowledge even of what ecstasy actually was, with there being no internet to search out its history or chemical composition, and no books on the subject in which to search for facts.

I had actually taken ketamine a few weeks before at the incongruous setting of the Serve Chilled night at the Cookie Club. Again, a certain lighting technician had brought this substance to Nottingham (he would do the same a couple of years later with DMT) and with it some instructions on 'set and setting', the advice given by Timothy Leary to trainee psychonauts some decades previously. It was recommended to be ingested via intramuscular injection, preferably while listening to recordings of New Age psychochemical guru Terrence McKenna, sitting on some cushions in a darkened room lit by candles. I ignored all this advice, especially that of not eating the powder, and just necked it and washed down with lager in a packed nightclub while Simon played music downstairs.

Within ten or fifteen minutes, I just knew that this would be a qualitatively different experience from any drug I had ever taken. This was utter submersion, a dimensional implosion, crossing into some other parallel realm where concepts such as up or down could no longer be taken for granted. I remember leaning over to my good friend Dave and quietly informing him that very soon I would be unable to stand up or speak and could he please take over my life for a while. I'm guessing this was the first time ketamine had ever been taken in Nottingham, if not the whole Midlands, and I had no idea what was happening or how long it would last. We discovered much later that ketamine was a 'dissociative anaesthetic', first synthesised in 1962, that it was unique among anaesthetics as it didn't repress the respiratory system, and that it formed the chemical backdrop to the film *Altered State*, which portrayed the daily ketamine use and immersion in a floatation tank of celebrated sixties counterculture icon Dr John Lilly. There would also be an unparalleled storm of misinformation about this new drug, with it labelled forever, wrongly, as a horse tranquiliser, or worse.

Either way, it was definitely not for the faint-hearted. Although it had just freaked me out slightly back at the Cookie Club, on that golden morning at Butts Quarry I had the most revelatory and viscerally enlightening experience I had ever had, LSD included. The very surreality of this out-of-body journey was awesome in the truest sense of the word. I was able to climb out of my body and float above the proceedings, looking down at the figures sitting on the bus before being catapulted into the pure vitality of being. Instantly, I understood the inherent nature of all physical things, of energy, of existence. Talking was implausible, standing impossible, and at the risk of sounding like a proper dick, it felt like talking to God.

This crazy new hallucinatory drug was certainly not for everyone. Many people were genuinely disturbed by its effects and vowed never to take it again. Some unfortunate youngsters (says me, being twenty-four at this time) had been sold pills in busy nightclubs containing ketamine, and that is really neither the set nor the setting in which to undergo this spiritually and physically demanding experience. Much of this book is directly linked to drugs; there is really no escaping the fact that without the emergence of ecstasy, acid house or raving would never have happened. It has always been the E in the room and has always been a difficult, double-edged and paradoxical subject. By the mid-nineties, I reckon that within British society, certainly among its youth, more illicit drugs were being consumed per head than by any society before or since. Some estimates at the time place the number of people taking ecstasy regularly at over three million.

I don't think anyone involved in our scene would have loudly proclaimed that drug-taking was good for the body or the mind long-term. They certainly wouldn't encourage the use of life-destroying drugs such as heroin or crack, and wouldn't deny that there were many casualties, but I think we would mostly say that through the vehicle of intoxication and music, we achieved a genuinely loving and caring fellowship, made real connections and friendships that would endure for decades. Certainly, compared to alcohol and the myriad of social ills it causes, the use of ecstasy now seems relatively innocent. Plus, of course, we didn't give a shit. We weren't trying to present a manual for practical living; we were trying to subvert the very foundations of the conformist and pleasure-averse society into which we had been born.

Having set new parameters on how wild and lawless a free party could be, we naturally began to plan for another party at Butts Quarry. What happened next was one of the salutary lessons that occasionally reminded us that we lived within a framework of laws and law-enforcers and that we couldn't actually do whatever the fuck we wanted. I returned home one Friday afternoon, climbing the three flights of stairs to our flat at Vickers Street. Walking into the front room, I saw an unfamiliar personage, wearing a duffle coat, sitting and playing on my new Roland JD800 synthesiser. Rick was hovering, showing the guy how the keyboard's knobs and sliders worked. I thought nothing of it until Rick shuffled me into the kitchen and whispered, 'He's a copper.'

'A copper? Like a policeman copper? Then why is he wearing a duffel coat and why the fuck is he playing my keyboard?'

'He's plainclothes, CID. He said he makes music himself, liked the look of the JD800, so I let him have a go. He's brought an injunction ordering us not to have another party at Butts Quarry.'

'Great, can you now tell him to get off my keyboard and then politely to fuck off. Where's this injunction?'

The detective did leave, praising my keyboard, and I was able to study the injunction. It was real, signed by a judge, naming DiY and actually legally banning us from organising any future events at Butts Quarry. Cunningly, we had put our phone number on several thousand mixtapes that we had been selling. The police had bought one and traced the number to our address. The officer had also revealed to Rick that they had been tracking DiY for the last couple of years and had several folders of intelligence concerning our activities.

We, of course, just went and found another quarry, but I never loved that keyboard in quite the same way again. Over the remainder of 1991, we threw some great parties at places like Two Dales, Matlock and Langar Airfield, the last distinguishing itself as the wettest party we ever did. DiY and others would return to Butts Quarry years later, but this season of parties from the end of summer 1991 through autumn and winter and into 1992 were truly magical and, even at the time, we intuitively knew they were special. We had finally managed to buy a truck, a seven and a half tonne yellow Dodge from a family of three who had, implausibly, been living in it. It featured an electric tailgate, no less, so no more shady hirings of Luton vans. 'The Dodgy' proved a sound investment and it would ferry us on many years of adventures to come, even going on to appear not only on the national news but even a short guest spot on *The Cook Report*

For New Year's Eve 1991, we organised the first of what would become a series of outrageous foreign trips. We had met some Dutch guys that ran a clothes shop in Amsterdam, and they invited us over to DJ at a party in the Jaap Edenhal, a huge ice-skating rink on the Herengracht on the outskirts of the city. We took a coachload of fifty-three over, including a full DJ complement, plus Steve Cobby and David McSherry from Fila Brazillia to do a live set following their superb live appearance within the sweaty confines of Serve Chilled. Compared to later foreign jaunts, the behaviour was fairly acceptable, and, without any arrests, injuries or hospitalisations, we arrived back en masse on the Forest recreation ground, Nottingham, two days into 1992. Unbeknown to us, the coming year would expose our previously surreptitious activities to a national, even global, audience and propel DiY into uncharted waters.

# 16

At the start of 1992, we realised that we needed to make some money. As our activities and profile had grown, so had our responsibilities and overheads. Monthly payments for Black Box plus maintenance and storage, insurance, MOT and diesel costs for a large truck, generator money, a massive phone bill at our Vickers Street flat, records, decks and so on were mounting heavily. Obviously, proper jobs were out of the question; we were way too busy and having too much fun for that. Although Rick did have a short and disastrous spell as a taxi driver, running out of petrol twice in the middle of nowhere at three in the morning and nearly getting a kicking. We had left dealing behind a while ago, a record label was a year in the future, and so the only way was to find a new club where we would get a better door deal and make some proper money. We found a club, the Dance Factory, a small three-storey place in Nottingham's Lace Market. It was owned by the Bailey brothers, heads of one of the hardest firms in Nottingham. We ran it for a year, charged only a fiver, had on occasion 220 people on the guest list for a 350-capacity venue and failed to make any money whatsoever. But what we did do was bear witness to some of the wildest nights I have ever seen within the confines of a nightclub.

Commencing on Friday 21st February 1992 and running until 19th February 1993, our Bounce nights at the Dance Factory were plain mental. Every two weeks on a Friday (Saturday obviously being reserved for free parties), the club was mobbed, forcing us to start a ticket system via local records shops and a clothes shop named

'Bizarre', run by the remarkable and legendarily eccentric Clifford Sherriff. Those who did get in were mostly new to the whole scene, converted by the eclectic and fevered clientele, the huge sound created by us putting all of Black Box on the dancefloor to treble the volume, and the ubiquitous availability of cheap ecstasy tablets. Also provided was top quality music, including notable guest DJs such as Andy Weatherall, Stuart MacMillan, Justin Robertson, Charlie Hall, Laurent Garnier, Steve Vertigo and Paul Daley.

New DJs began appearing from among our own number: Cookie, Little Lee, Dick, Jules, Dan Stroud, Callum, Adam, Stoney and, most influentially, Emma, our first and much-needed female DJ. From sound systems to promoters to DJs, the whole scene had long been a male-dominated world, which we felt keenly and regretted, and so we were only too happy to welcome Emma into the fold. She had, of course, been there since the earliest of days at the first Pepperbox events, living onsite at all the major parties, and now she had decided to DJ – and she was good, very good. Bounce became a kind of incubation for people to start playing records in public, usually upstairs, where it was slightly less intense. It is a nerve-racking experience for anyone trying to mix in a dark, hot, sweaty environment where everyone is dancing and off their faces, so hats off to all who braved it and stuck with it.

Fascinated by our lawless approach, Richard Bailey, the owner, literally collared me and Pete one night. He and his brothers were the real deal: shellsuits, gym fanatics, steroid users, nutters. We met many gangsters along our fabulous and crazy path and these boys were up there with the Scousers and the Mancs. Pete and I would usually count the money with them near the end of the night, but as I walked round to the office, Richard had picked Pete up around the neck with one hand and was just holding him there, legs dangling. He wasn't angry, just inquisitive. Heading into his office, the three of us sat down, and he said, 'You lot don't give a fuck, do you?'

Pete, rubbing his neck, replied that no, we didn't really.

'Do you pay any tax?' he asked, huge and menacing behind his seemingly tiny desk.

Again, we replied that we generally tried to avoid it.

'So, how do you make money? Must be the drugs? Tell you what, boys, the next time you do one of these "free parties", me and a couple of my lads will come up and tax the dealers and we'll split the money 50/50. Deal?'

As ever, Pete and I shot a glance at each other before politely declining. Tempting, though.

Richard continued: 'I don't fucking understand you lot, but I like you. If anyone in Nottingham gives you any bother, you can use my name if they don't fuck off. I usually charge ten grand for that.'

Pete and I thanked him for the honour and quietly slipped away into the sweaty club, wide-eyed. At the Dance Factory, a younger element of the Nottingham crowd started attending. Mostly around seventeen, well dressed and bored of the hardcore scene at crappy townie clubs, a crew of these younger lads started attending and never really left. Joe, Danny Bennett, Twigger, Pez, Danny Keaton, Jamie, Danny Wilcoxson, Robin, Kaylie and Lauren and others were in many ways a breath of fresh air. In other ways they were a pain in the arse, but golly, they were funny and full of life. Developing an unspoken contract, we showed them good music and how to take drugs properly. In return, they mocked our clothes mercilessly, which seemed to work all around. They understood collectivism intuitively; they were natural anarchists. This younger end, the 'Ponies', became firm friends and could always be relied upon to help out lugging the PA, putting up backdrops or jumping in a car to Exeter with five minutes' notice. Another great advantage of having this beautifully unhinged club, never out of the top ten in the dance music magazines, was that people from further and further afield began to attend. Carloads from near and far began to drive up regularly and stay somewhere or other until the free party on Saturday before limping home late on the Sunday night or even the Monday.

In this way, we met a vast array of new contacts and friends: Neil Macey, Gordon, Pat, Martin and crew from Birmingham, Danny Townsend and Henry from Leicester; Jane and Noel, who were now living with an old Liverpool contact Jo and her partner Nick in Sheffield; Bliss and Beige from the Pork Recordings stable in Hull; and big groups from Peterborough, Northampton, Matlock, Derby, Leeds, Bristol, Bath, Cannock and London. Over the course of 1992, Bounce would be exported to all of these cities and beyond as the DiY sound, groove and attitude became hugely in demand. Bounce combined with Voodoo in Liverpool, and at the PSV club in Manchester with local boys Strat, Loxley and the Carney brothers. Soon our DJs would be playing at Back to Basics and Cream as we continued to uniquely straddle the crusty–trendy divide. To the south, we had by now been doing joint parties with Oz and the tVC crew in Kent, monthly nights at Plymouth's Cultural Vibes with Dave Green, and at Volts in Exeter, promoted by our old comrade Mark Darby and his partner Jess from the Mighty Force record shop. It was on a Wednesday night, which in itself is a sign of those times, being such a long drive that we often wouldn't get back to Nottingham until Friday. Often we would walk out of there with some quite serious money, rarely spent wisely. Once, on a Thursday morning, having been up all night and somewhat worse for wear, Cookie and I bought a giant modelling kit of Leatherface from *Texas Chainsaw Massacre*, although I'm still not entirely sure why.

On one of these nights, arriving late from a long drive, Cookie and I had to stand in for the cloakroom attendant. Making the best of it, I left Cookie mismanaging some coats and raffle tickets to grab a couple of pints from the bar. Re-entering the cloakroom, Cookie was sitting on the floor with a striking-looking guy who was trying to sell him a job lot of 'Stussy gear'. He looked like a cross between

Jim Morrison and Jesus, and boy could he talk. His name turned out to be Jon Kosecki: half-Irish, half-Polish and one of the most extraordinary characters in this entire story. Jon looked at me, piercing eyes below a hooded brow and set above geometrically impossible cheekbones, clearly sizing me up.

'I was just telling your mate here, I can get a lovely job lot of Stussy gear, genuine, at a shit-hot price and . . .'

I cut him off there. 'Look mate, me and Cookie are both from Bolton, halfway between Liverpool and Manchester. If we wanted to buy dodgy rave clobber, we wouldn't buy it from a carrot-cruncher. So, drop the bullshit and buy us some beers . . .'

'So, you're the cunt. I knew there had to be a cunt behind DiY and all that fluffy bollocks. My name's Jon. Whatcha drinking? Couple of shots to start us off?'

And with that honest exchange of views, he and I and the rest of DiY became great friends for many years to come. Always larger than life, and with a ferocious appetite for intoxication that even shocked us on occasion, Jon was the frontman for a crew in Bath who were just forming as Deep Peace. With the brilliant organisational brain of Steve Bryant, the musical talent of Steve Wilson, aka Mr Mullatto, and Jon's unique charisma, they began to organise parties, most notably at the Swamp Club in Bath. This last night was an absolute belter, probably coming the closest of any of our sister clubs in recreating the atmosphere of Bounce at the Dance Factory. And on it went, The Thekla and then Lakota in Bristol, nights in Torquay with Jan and the Alpha people, then regular appearances in Kent with Oz and the tVC crew, via Brighton with Felix, Darius and Debbie and the Slack gang, with whom we organised an epic free party up in the hills above Plumpton, later recorded for posterity in C.J. Stone's book *Fierce Dancing*.

There were nights out in Glasgow, Edinburgh and Cardiff, with wild parties at the Hippo Club and Ivor Bach, sweat dripping from the walls, and where a young Sid Thomas raved hard with his big brother and friends, occasionally overdoing it and needing to lie down. Our paths would cross again, some decades later. One night Simon DK and I set off for Coventry in Damian's new BMW, Simon having been booked to play at the Eclipse club. Damian was driving at his customary 110mph while continually fiddling with his ridiculously over-spec graphic equaliser when the engine caught fire. The three of us sat in the car on the hard shoulder for a while, looking at the flames in the dark before deciding it might be a good idea to get out. As the car continued to burn and the flames engulfed the bonnet, it was not looking hopeful for Simon's gig until a van pulled up behind us, the driver recognising the three of us. Sliding open the side door, we jumped in with Simon's records; the driver happily changed course and drove us to the Eclipse. The burning BMW was abandoned and Damian never saw it again. It was like that, then.

There was the night at The Institute in Birmingham where we were hanging out in the VIP area overlooking the dancefloor. Spotting the club's owner, Duran Duran's Roger Taylor, I approached him, looked up into his pretty face and informed him that I thought the video to 'Wild Boys' was 'truly remarkable'. He didn't look very impressed. Another surreal situation developed at the Room club in Hull. As mentioned, we had made contact with Porky and Fila Brazillia in 1990 as they began to take off label-wise, and we had met the rest of the Hull crew, notably Bliss and Bobby, aka Beige, who had been behind the big Opik track 'Free Yourself'. Heading up there to DJ one night, we noticed a couple of the lads had started a new dance which involved making a two-part shovelling action in time to the music. When in Hull, as they say, so we enthusiastically joined in. When we returned a month later, we were staggered to see that the whole club was simultaneously performing this motion; you haven't really lived until you've seen three hundred normally fairly downbeat Humberside boys and girls all acting out digging motions to a driving house track.

By this time, a new pirate radio station had started in Nottingham with the wonderful name Rave FM. Other pirates had sprung up around inner-city Nottingham previously, but these guys were much more professional. Transmitting on a certain frequency, they had one serious transmitter, which was hidden and linked to a much less costly mobile transmitter, which could be moved from location to location very quickly, and, if seized by the authorities, could be replaced easily. This was a genuine multi-racial project. Most of the city's DJs gained a slot playing everything from garage to hardcore to a newly emerging genre known as jungle. Needless to say, we blagged our way right in and ended up with something like twelve different weekly slots. In addition to Simon, Jack, Pezz and Emma with house sets, Boysie did a reggae show, Little Lee and I did a chaotic Saturday morning (Special Brew) Breakfast show and, most brilliantly, Digs and Woosh did a Sunday night Serve Chilled show which quickly became legendary.

At the tail end of another exhausting weekend, they would spin the most ridiculously eclectic music ever heard on pirate radio, jumping from freeform jazz to Funkadelic to movie soundtracks to opera to dub to Kate Bush to the recorded noises of steam trains. Over the top, or rather under the bottom, Digs would provide an ultra-stoned sporadic commentary in a husky, low baritone which was utterly incomprehensible but seemed to fit. Listening absent-mindedly to Rave FM through the day, you could occasionally catch hilarious on-air drug deals, as the DJ gave a shout-out that 'Stevie K message to Admiral – he doesn't want three anymore, just the two, yeah. Still meet at Jolly Higglers car park at seven.' Most of our old spars from the Marcus Garvey days had shows – D2, Mayhem, Senator and Sy – and the pirate ran for a couple of years until their transmission frequency interfered with that of planes landing at nearby East Midlands airport, nearly causing a serious aviation disaster, and were finally shut down by the understandably irate authorities.

Simon, Jack, Digs and Woosh, and Pezz played every weekend somewhere. Often our paths would cross at four in the morning at yet another strung-out service station. We were all out four or five nights a week, every week, if not clubbing or driving somewhere, then looking for free party sites or out flying and flyposting. Free parties were still continuing apace, although the travellers had by now moved south from the Matlock area and were currently at a site near Breedon on the Hill, a few miles north of Ashby-de-la-Zouch, south of Derby. As the festival season of 1992 drew nearer, with its pivotal start date at the end of May, our thoughts began to turn to what would happen this year. We hadn't taken our system to a big festival since Moreton Lighthouse the previous July, instead preferring to organise those stupendous small parties in the hidden depths of Derbyshire. By now, in the spring of 1992, the authorities in Derbyshire had wised up to the presence of these travellers from the south in their midst. They had certainly noticed their alliance with city-based sound systems to the extent that they were communicating with the Nottingham police force and serving joint warrants. Farmers had begun to block off any open entrances with large rocks or similar; gates were locked.

Meanwhile, the country's attention had turned national after a General Election in April. Not that we any longer had much interest in conventional politics, but when John Major and his sleaze-ridden Tories won, prolonging thirteen long years of one-party rule, it definitely felt like a challenge. It seemed as though we should ignore the sham democracy and protest to show that radical alternative lifestyles were still being lived. About this time, the road protests had begun, particularly against the proposed M11 extension in east London. Crusty politics seemed to be hitting the mainstream. There was also something in the air that winter and spring, the feeling that people had gone to hibernate in their own communities, maybe to start their own sound systems or to build new rigs, to do some small parties and gather a crew. DiY were taken completely by surprise when over the first bank holiday in early May, a large festival spontaneously erupted at Lechlade, Gloucestershire, with Spiral Tribe, Circus Warp and Bedlam in full effect. That weekend we were doing a party on the Breedon site, but we were distinctly unimpressed and somewhat disbelieving that we hadn't known about Lechlade in advance.

Avon Free Festival weekend was three weeks away and we decided to go back into battle. The build-up was intense. In those days without mobiles, we had multiple contacts in the Avon/ Gloucestershire area phoning us from phone boxes near sites with the latest updates. Only three or four days before the bank holiday, a site was discussed, perhaps one of the old classics such as Ingleston Common, but the various police forces had other ideas and the mass of assembled travellers' vehicles were shunted over the county line onto a huge common just inside the county of Worcestershire. Late on Thursday 19th May 1992, we received a prophetic phone call. Over a crackly line from a layby phone box somewhere deep in the rolling Malvern Hills, we were relayed the new venue and, as we reached for the well-worn A-Z, wondered where Castlemorton Common might be. A question which, within a week, the whole world would know the answer.

# 17

For anyone reading this book who's unaware of what took place on Castlemorton Common, deep in the bucolic and verdant countryside of south-west England over the bank holiday weekend and beyond in late May 1992, we probably need some facts before this tale is told.

Occupying roughly six square miles of common land, just one mile away from the Gloucestershire border, with multiple entry and exit points and crisscrossed by small tracks and roads, this beautiful and normally tranquil space became the focus of the largest free festival ever to occur in the UK, certainly since the vast Stonehenge festivals of the early eighties and almost certainly larger than will ever happen again. What marked this festival out to such a degree, and made it so epoch-defining, was that it provided the culmination of the free festival and rave crossover that had begun two summers before at Glastonbury 1990.

With hindsight, this was the zenith of the movement, a moment when the antics of sound systems like DiY, Spiral Tribe and others leapt from outraged articles in the local rag to national and international media prominence. As seven or eight loud rigs drove the huge assembly of sleepless dancers into an ecstatic trance and the local residents into meltdown, the event was chaotic and outrageous in its execution and immense in terms of aftershock and legal response.

Beneath five days of uncharacteristically glorious spring sun, and in front of the world's media, an unholy alliance of tens of thousands of travellers, punks, old hippies, ravers, townies and city-dwellers, students, drug dealers and enthusiastic drug-consumers paraded their debauched and bohemian excesses for all to see; our movement would never be the same again. In direct response, a sclerotic right-wing government would attempt to criminalise our way of life and, unbelievably, codify the very word 'rave' into British law. Oh, and someone tried to shoot down a police helicopter.

To return back to a quieter era before Castlemorton (before Wednesday), we knew this event was going to be big; you could feel it in the air. There had been parties erupting everywhere: in London squats, huge free parties around Oxford, on small sites, woodlands and warehouses across the south of England. Lechlade had happened a few weeks before and gave a very clear indication that this scene had grown exponentially, that a myriad of new sound systems had been built and that our troops were ready. As research for this book, I read a copy of West Mercia Police's forty-four-page report, written shortly after the event, entitled 'Castlemorton Common: Invasion by Travellers'. It makes fascinating reading.

During Castlemorton, which actually lasted until 29th May when even Spiral Tribe ran out of energy and petrol, and especially afterwards, the police came in for a lot of stick about their inability to prevent or disperse the unlicensed gathering. There have been various conspiracy theories since. Some claimed that the police deliberately allowed the festival to happen so that the government would give the much-harried forces of Avon and Somerset, Gloucestershire, Wiltshire and Hampshire the legal teeth they had so long demanded to deal with the traveller issue.

The authorities had effectively crushed this movement in the summer of 1985, since when it had shrunk and faded away, but it was now erupting again, reinvigorated by a generation of ravers used to ignoring the law. Hilariously, I remember one local resident demanding to know why the police hadn't been aware of the location when even the Samaritans had erected their pink sanctuary gazebo by Friday night while the police were still scratching their collective heads.

What becomes clear from reading the report is how overwhelmed the police were. There has been much made of the general contempt that the neighbouring force, Gloucestershire, had for their Worcestershire colleagues. The police forces in the UK are still organised along ancient county lines, and in those days before effective digital communication, the landline was often the only method of relaying a developing situation to the next force along. Whether the Avon and Somerset Police allied with their Gloucestershire associates and deliberately suggested Castlemorton Common as a viable site just over the county line will never be known.

What is described in great detail in the report is that, at 15.35 on Friday 22nd May, the first phone call of complaint from a Castlemorton resident was logged by the police switchboard, estimating that between thirty and forty vehicles had driven onto the common. At 15.40, the ranking officer, an inspector, was informed that fifty-three travellers' vehicles were approaching the common from the direction of Coleford along the A4136. By 16.57, multiple reports were starting to flood in of vehicles moving from the A40, the A417, the B4215 and the B4208, with two hundred more vehicles coming down the A38 and, comically, more and more 'hippy-type individuals' asking at petrol stations where 'Castlemorton' was.

And on it goes until, by 6pm, it was on the national BBC and ITV television news, and by around 7pm we were there, driving in unchallenged. By 8pm the police had launched their helicopter and estimated that over five hundred vehicles and three thousand people were on site. Impressive work by the traveller shock troops, not so by the police. The report then discusses a hastily convened meeting between the assistant chief constable and the local superintendent. They jointly decided that they simply didn't have the manpower to set up roadblocks and deal with the undoubtedly chaotic consequences, and so were officially pursuing a policy of 'containment'. In other words, there was such a force of numbers that they lost control, much like they had at the Poll Tax riot in London two years before. Appearing live on national television, senior police officers appealed to the nation's youth not to head towards Castlemorton Common that weekend. With a bank holiday weekend of predicted fantastic weather, this combination was without doubt the most effective way imaginable to encourage them. Never before or since has an unlicensed event of such lawless magnitude been the lead item on the national news, and it is very hard to imagine a more perfect way to drive tens of thousands of people into their cars and towards that common.

We quickly set up Black Box, backdrops, tank netting and lights in the lovely white marquee already set up for us by local legend Rob Pike. Seasoned veterans at this game, three years on from our first parties, we were up and running within an hour. Proudly draping our enormous black and white 'DiY' banner over the side of the Dodge truck and wildly greeting dozens of friends and acquaintances as they rolled in, Pete and I headed up a hill to get a better view. As far as the eye could see, a town was being assembled: it was a town unlike any other, a town with sound systems instead of monuments, a town almost exclusively under thirty years old, a town where it seemed one hundred per cent of the residents were ready to party, and, unfortunately, a town without toilets. Crews began to roll in, Spiral Tribe being the most conspicuous in their massive black military trucks. They had certainly changed since our last encounter at Longstock the summer before. The Spirals had become a real tribe, bonded through their newfound infamy, their uniform look of black ex-military clothes and shaven heads, and their frenetic love of extreme techno beats. I remember heading over to their tentless, open-air space at some point on the Saturday, walking around until I spotted Mark, the guy we had spoken to at Longstock and whose blue Luton van we had tow-started. I went inside his truck, shook hands and chatted, as I suppose representatives of the two infamous sound systems should, before discovering that, bizarrely, we were both called Mark Harrison. In Matthew Collin's seminal book *Altered State*, the other Mark Harrison is quoted many times. Having recommended the book to family and friends, I think many thought I had seriously changed when they read: 'Techno is the new folk music.'

Over Friday night, more and more systems rolled in, set up, kicked off. Some of them we knew (Bedlam, Circus Normal), while others, such as Adrenalin and LSDiesel, we did not. Uniformly that week-end, they all played their characteristic fast techno, or 'nosebleed' as we called it (they called our music 'fluffy'). In our marquee, right on the edge of the already huge gathering, we played house, club music, deep house and garage. On the Saturday and Sunday after-noons, we slowed it down and played an eclectic mix of downtempo beats, soul, funk, hip-hop and even jazz, and we were undoubtedly the only people to play John Coltrane on Castlemorton Common. Many, many people have told us since that, musically, we saved their lives. They came to our tent and never left. Hopefully, however, they missed Simon's set on Sunday afternoon. By that time, he had been up for so long and had so over-indulged that two of us had to prop him up from behind. As he attempted to DJ, he kept placing the turntable needle onto a slip-mat instead of a record.

On Saturday night there were by now so many people that the crowds around different sound systems merged into one enormous dancefloor. Our music at Castlemorton was probably the most effec-tive PR we ever did. Tens of thousands of people passed through our tent and liked what they heard. As dawn broke on Saturday morn-ing, with hundreds of people dancing outside the marquee, we were surprised to see dozens of outside broadcast vans at the bottom of the slope, cameras and microphones pointed our way. Japan, New Zealand, America and Italy were all represented as they beamed the sights and sounds of DiY in full effect back to their respective nations. What we hadn't really considered was that the police were probably studying the same images, including our incredibly prominent ninety-six foot square banner with the letters' DiY' in six-foot monochrome splendour. That backdrop would feature on many news bulletins and shocking documentaries on the moral outrage of drug availability at raves.

For me, as we walked around the still-expanding site on Saturday afternoon, the atmosphere was less of a drug-crazed dystopia and more of a village fete. For once, the sun shone benignly throughout the bank holiday weekend and beyond. It was balmy and warm at night, and raving is so much more pleasant in those conditions. Laughter rang out, old acquaintances were renewed and fresh ones forged. Kids ran around and their parents lazed in the sun. Late to the game, we heard amazing stories of the quarry pool only five minutes' walk up the main drag. Hurrying there, we witnessed the wonderful spectacle of hundreds of festival-goers, half of them naked, swimming in a beautiful, deep natural pool surrounded by ancient quarry walls. This was turning into some kind of English Shangri-La. The sheer diversity of the crowd was striking. Porsches, family saloons and Land Rovers rubbed bumpers with ambulances and ancient double-deckers. The old school festival crew were still there. This was, after all, supposed to be the Avon Free Festival, but they were just swamped. It was no longer a festival; it was a great big fucking massive party. There were mutterings among the old crowd about 'cheesy quavers' and people not burying their shit (a legitimate concern). Effectively, the free festival movement was laid to rest that weekend; the frantic and ravenous synthetic hydra of acid house had buried it.

Again, I was able to surreally watch images on the news on a battered old telly on a mate's bus, as video footage of us below was beamed to the wider world. A day later, someone turned up with the Sunday papers and we realised, with a deep gulp, that we were the nation's news. Being the mouthpiece of the landed classes who really own and run the country, *The Sunday Telegraph* had dedicated almost the whole front page to the events in which we were immersed, below the immortal headline 'Hippies Fire Flares at Helicopter'. God's honest truth, when someone announced the headline, I thought for a second that someone had propelled some wide, seventies-style trousers at the police until I saw the picture; someone had genuinely tried to bring down the police helicopter with a powerful distress flare.

And so the festival continued, on into the week, becoming infamous as the biggest rave anywhere, ever. Our system ran from Friday evening until Tuesday morning, by which time our thoughts turned to getting it out intact. Not only had we been one of the most prominent rigs, but we also had a distinctive large yellow truck that had displayed our name on its side in huge letters. But, as is so often the case, the sheer bravery and daring of the travellers saved the day and a friend, Alix, sneaked our rig out in her horsebox in the middle of the night. The police waved down our Dodge truck with a confident look, only to find it empty apart from a few tank nettings and a lot of empty beer cans. Thank you, Alix, again and forever. Spiral Tribe went through until the next weekend, refusing to stop. They were perhaps less crafty, as confrontation was in their DNA. Thirteen of their number were arrested and their system impounded. They were collectively charged with organising the festival, which they hadn't, and were finally acquitted in Crown Court following what was one of the most expensive prosecutions in English legal history.

A couple of days after returning to Nottingham, Matthew Collin contacted me. He asked me to write an article for *i-D* about how it had felt to have actually been at Castlemorton and what I thought the effects might be. I wrote then,

'No information was printed, it was all word of mouth. All these young people were able to group in one place, set up their own city, a police no-go zone. For a government whose reason for being is to control people, here was a very frightening example of people saying, "We can and will do whatever we like."'

But in many ways, the game was now up. This had been the most blatant and seditious event imaginable, a landowner's darkest nightmare, provoking a howl of media outrage and poking all the demons of Middle England, many of whose offspring had been in there with the rest of us. That venerable institution, the Conservative Party, duly took note, and at their party conference in October 1993, shadow home secretary Michael Howard announced details of the Criminal Justice and Public Order Bill, which, amid a ragbag of Tory populist causes, proposed to make unlicensed 'raves' a crime.

# 18

Returning to Nottingham and a few days' recovery, I was comically asked by one of many new friends, Dickie, for whom Castlemorton had been his first free event, 'Are they all like that?'. I could only reply in the negative; I think we intuitively knew that they never would be like that again. So many random factors had collided to make Castlemorton such a mythical, legendary event, from which the aftershocks would reverberate in so many directions for years and decades to come, that the comparison with Woodstock is valid. Castlemorton signified not the genesis of a new movement but its denouement, a climax that would never be repeated. Even the weather was unrepeatable.

As if to prove this, the next big festival was over the solstice weekend of 19th to 22nd June, near Laxton, Northamptonshire. This time the police were ready and in no mood to compromise. On nowhere near the scale of Castlemorton, it was an ill-tempered, wet and manic event surrounded by a ridiculous number of police. Roadblocking the festival effectively, the authorities ensured no one could get in or out of the site by the Friday evening; trying to party when you're surrounded, lacking numbers and people have been arrested was never much fun. Site paranoia was rampant, always quick to emerge from its dark recesses when things got ugly. Muggings were reported, bad drugs were sold, long-established couples fought physically. Our gang still had fun; we always did whatever the circumstances, but the wider festival was not a great example of its genre.

Although we didn't know it, that was the beginning of an end, both for the free festival movement and for DiY attending the dwindling number of festivals occurring after this point. There were events later that summer at Torpedo Town, Happy Daze and others, but we decided that festivals had become too much hassle; if we wanted to get away with a party, we were much better off doing it closer to home, or on our own, rather than squaring up to the massed ranks of tooled-up police or spending days under siege. By the summer of 1993, free festivals were effectively dead, and the debate about whether rave killed them or breathed new life into an antiquated idea would rage on. From 1992, we began to follow other paths. We desperately wanted to start making our own music. Perhaps we could apply our collectivist principles to establishing a recording studio and a record label? And we wanted to travel, to export this precious vibe that we had created to the global centres of hedonism: to Ibiza and Amsterdam, New York and San Francisco, Thailand and Sydney.

From this point onwards, our paths diverged from that of Spiral Tribe and the rest of the big systems. They were just getting going; the Spirals would bounce back from their mass arrest following Castlemorton and head straight into the heart of the beast with an attempted party at Canary Wharf, right in the Docklands zone of central London so closely associated with Margaret Thatcher. Maybe because we had been doing parties longer, or perhaps because we lived up north, but this approach of directly taking on the authorities did not appeal to us anymore. We had been arrested and beaten by the police. We had our equipment seized so many times that we knew you could never win in a direct confrontation with the state's armed wing. But fair play to them for trying. Eventually, Spiral Tribe and most of their associated systems, tired of the restrictive and culturally blinkered island on which we lived, loaded up their wagons and headed to the wide-open spaces of Europe.

One event that did happen every summer on the Forest recreation ground, the large park in inner-city Nottingham, was Rock and Reggae. Organised by Paul Kilbride, brother of Noel, who lived with the superhosts Jane Bromley, Jo Rhodes and Nick Jevons at the rambunctious Hale Street warehouse space in Sheffield, Rock and Reggae was not the most earth-shattering of events but had always been a laugh. As the name implies, the idea was to feature the best of two of the multicultural sides of Nottingham's musical heritage. That year, in the late summer of 1992, we had been invited to participate. We happily agreed, although raising a collective eyebrow at the finishing time of 10pm. That was always the problem with licences: they might allow you to hold an event that would then not end in arrest and mayhem, but you had to agree to the licensor's terms, usually the local authority.

It was a sunny day in the Forest. We set up Black Box in a marquee and proceeded to play our music, all very polite and tame, although it wasn't the worst way to spend a Sunday afternoon. Our crew watched in awe as the local West Indian guys pulled up, one by one, and began to assemble their systems. They were huge affairs with ten, twelve, sixteen bass bins which, when switched on using power from the central generator, shook the very earth. And so the day progressed, with our battered Black Box system now suddenly seeming a bit puny in comparison. But then we had an idea. Roger whispered to me that he had the generator from the site and maybe we should get naughty after the 10pm cut-off point. This I liked, and so at ten on the dot the big main generator was turned off and the Rasta crews began the task of unplugging and winding cables. We kicked off our veteran 4kW genny, swapped power cables and off we went, in complete darkness. Suddenly we were the only system onsite and had a full-scale rave on our hands, which being in the pitch-black only enhanced the feeling of lawlessness. Instantly the whole site ran into our tent and began dancing, wildly, properly.

I'll always remember James Baillie, of Venus fame, climbing onto a speaker and yelling in his unmistakable Scottish accent at Simon to play 'Bassheads! Bassheads!', which he duly did. For those who aren't familiar with this rave classic, it features a huge guitar riff sampled from The Osmonds' 'Crazy Horses' and it's immense. The place erupted. Seconds later, someone plugged something into something, the lights came back on, and it erupted again.

Within minutes, the organisers came over to ask us to stop, but we refused, at last having a party on our hands. Soon the police were onsite and were not impressed, but we were long past caring what the police thought. Someone came over and said they'd been talking to the police, who really insisted that we stop. I replied, shouting, 'Tell them that DiY doesn't stop parties, we just start them.' We held them all off until about 4 or 5am on the Monday morning when we finally had to wind it down. The front page of the *Nottingham Evening Post* carried the story the next day, adding that there had been 329 complaints, the most the police had ever received from a single incident. I know we should have held our heads in shame, but we were quietly proud. And, for me, the sweetest moment was when a Rasta I knew came over and declared that their system had been louder, to which I agreed, adding that it was a shame they didn't have a generator.

There can be no doubt that Castlemorton catapulted DiY into a whole new level of fame, or rather infamy. People began to offer us record contracts, remixes and front-page interviews in the music magazines. Our clubs were even more rammed and we began to get serious offers to play at large pay raves. Of these, the best was undoubtedly Universe, which was the closest thing you could get to a big free party but with a licence and a ticket cost. In September of that year, they offered us our own marquee at their event near Bath named 'Mind, Body and Soul'. The idea was that we would run a whole tent all night with our own sound system, lights and

DJs. It was a great party, as good as a pay rave could probably be, and the atmosphere in our tent was almost as wild as a free party. The main problem came in the morning when Pete and I were given the nod to go to get paid in cash as agreed. Casually climbing into the static caravan which formed the temporary office, we were faced with two money men, both of whom looked like they had definitely not been up all night as we had, one of them having a metal briefcase chained to his wrist. For the umpteenth time over the years, Pete and I shot a glance at each and instantly realised we were very, very high. More than high, we were absolutely off our tits, but we tried to sit down to discuss the four thousand pounds in cash that these gentlemen were counting out for us. Asking if we wanted to count it, I declined, figuring they were probably far more accurate than Pete or I could be at that moment. And then Pete, saucer-eyed and clumsy as ever, dropped the whole lot, thousands of pounds in used tens and twenties cascading everywhere, across the floor and under the table like confetti. Looking at us in disbelief, the money men looked even more shocked when both of us burst out laughing. We couldn't stop, the floodgates were open, and as we both crawled around on the floor, even having to get under the table where they were sitting to grab some more notes, we were in hysterics. Pete then stood up too soon and banged his head on the underside of the table and we were off again. Although the accountants were frozen in disapproval, we eventually gathered the cash together. We just about managed to run out of the caravan, still giggling, and went to pay the crew.

Throughout the remainder of 1992, we continued to DJ and organise parties wherever and whenever we could, in between our fledgling foreign jaunts. These were both licensed and unlicensed events back in our spiritual homeland around Nottinghamshire and Derbyshire. Of the former, one memorable series of all-nighters called Sponge were in Leicester. Originally approached by a dodgy looking lad named Danny, who'd grown up in that city, we were intrigued to discover that he was the son of Sue Townsend, author of the wildly successful Adrian Mole books. Theirs was truly a crazy family story, Sue having raised her kids alone on a very rough council estate in Leicester with no money, and then suddenly becoming the second best-selling author in the UK and subsequently moving into a large detached house in the nice end of town. Sue was a lovely, warm woman and gave us a signed copy of her latest book: 'To DiY, may you party on forever, love Sue x'.

Danny, however, and I don't think he'd mind me saying this, was still a rough diamond and had done a bit of time due to bad boy behaviour. Anyway, he and his mate Henry, himself a very hard-looking but chilled boxer, had an all-night venue, Starlight 2000, which, much like the Marcus Garvey Centre in Nottingham, used its community status to get a 6am licence. We went over to the Townsend family home one night to discuss a potential party and Danny was sporting a black eye, inflicted, he informed us, by Ian Dury punching him the night before in the garden following his appearance in the stage play of *The Queen and I*.

Having argued long and hard about a name, as ever, we finally agreed on 'Sponge', and this series of four events over six months were notable in many ways. We used ridiculous amounts of PA, hiring ESS, the guys we had bought Black Box from, and then ASS (Acoustic Sound Specialists), who provided, at no small cost, probably the crispest, cleanest and downright loudest system we'd ever heard. Guest DJs were special too: Darren Emerson, Paul Daley, Stuart McMillan and the mighty Andrew Weatherall rocked the house as we dropped thousands of cheap sponges from a net into the crowd. Clearly, our post-Castlemorton popularity had soared. The first and subsequent events were absolutely mobbed with ticketless groups trying to smash through the front doors and break in through the toilet windows. What also sadly marred these events was the first incidents of violence at our parties. This may have been connected to the intense rivalry between the football firms of Nottingham and Leicester, but during the night punches, and then fire-extinguishers, were thrown. The only other night of violence we ever had at a DiY event was at Space City in Bolton, where a full-on brawl erupted and chairs and bottles were thrown, which says a lot about Bolton. Back at Sponge one night, the radiators were all stuck on full blast, and as Danny and I finally tracked down the owner in the back room, he explained that he liked to keep the temperature high to keep his visiting strippers warm. I think that was the final straw.

Another event which is etched into my memory (and is featured in Mark Johnson's wonderful book *Wasted*) was probably the poshest place we would ever throw a party, a twelfth-century abbey owned by a famous financier and associate of Margaret Thatcher. With a helicopter. I won't name the young lady in question as I suspect that, even thirty years later, she is still in trouble with the folks. She was a Bounce regular and mentioned one night that her parents had an 'amazing place' out in Leicestershire. They were going on holiday for a while, so would we be up for doing her twenty-first birthday party in the 'grounds' in October? Well, that was a quick decision. I don't think we'd even been to see it when we rolled in on the Saturday afternoon with full rig – lights, generators, decks and mixer – to go in the rather classy marquee she had arranged.

I drove the battered old Dodge truck through some huge gates and down a long gravel drive, thinking we must have the wrong place. Rounding the fishing lake, we crunched up on the gravel and stared in silence. Originally built in the twelfth century, the abbey before us had clearly been added to over the centuries and was vast, ivy-covered and simply stunning. A couple of the lads in the truck had grown up on council estates in Driffield and they swore slowly in disbelief. The daughter came out to meet us, replete with several Labradors, and we hugged.

'So, where do you want the party – are there many locals to annoy?'

'Not really,' she replied, 'it's an 800-acre estate.'

Well, I have to say, we still managed it. It was a fabulous party, with hundreds arriving from Nottingham and beyond, parking their vehicles on the huge gravel car park and emerging disbelievingly from their vehicles. It properly rocked in the marquee: the music was sublime, the lights and projections were brilliant as ever and, best of all, we didn't have pissed off travellers, locals or landowners threatening to stop us, at least until the morning. As Mark Johnson reveals in his book, as dawn rose over the exquisite estate, one reckless partygoer (I have to admit at this stage it was me) had started a tractor and drove it merrily through the marquee, revellers simply parting, continuing to dance like it was the most normal thing in the world before moving back together. Mark continues:

'When the sun comes up, the light changes and the atmosphere is different. The pace slows and there is a new melody to the music. All the notes are separated. Everyone here is like me. Young and beautiful, our faces shining with life. Girls' clothes fold around them with a special, easy grace. They dance wildly or fluidly or slowly but never awkwardly. They are travellers, punks, hippies and many of them would be complete freaks anywhere else but here their wildness is right and lovely.'

One special ingredient that drove this party into particularly cosmic spaces was the appearance of some very special acid. Small blotters stamped with a dancing test-tube logo, these trips were beginning to be manufactured on a global scale to commemorate the fiftieth anniversary of LSD creator Albert Hofmann's first ever trip, when he accidentally ingested a huge dose through his fingertips while experimenting with it in 1943, completely tripping out on his bike ride home. (During 1993 we would take forty-odd people to stay in San Francisco for a month during the LSD fiftieth anniversary celebrations, but more of that later.) It was easily the cleanest and most pleasurable acid we have ever taken, and when our hostess allowed a select few of us into the abbey, we wandered through the wings of the ancient house in wide-eyed wonder. Medieval stonework led into corridors of Tudor wood panelling. Endless doors opened into endless rooms and bedrooms, many with ornate four-poster beds and original mullioned windows with wonky glass. We came to a halt in one huge room to stare at and get lost in an age-old tapestry depicting scenes from the Middle Ages. There were so many stairs we all got lost, separated; I opened a door and descended some ancient stone steps, only to emerge in the entrance hall. I glanced at a framed photo of an unknown man shaking hands with Margaret Thatcher. Next to it, a solid silver platter proclaimed that the named man had won the Le Mans 24 Hour Motor Race in 1963. Jesus, who was this guy?

And then my reverie was interrupted by Pete saying, 'Come and check this out.' It turned out to be another section of the huge house as we descended some more stairs to find a full-sized snooker room and then, bingo, the wine cellar. We were no experts but the bottles we selected were, I'm sure, not available in Tesco. Now we needed to find the kitchen somehow to get a corkscrew, which took us forever, and all the gang were in there wide-eyed. Angus popped his head around the door and stated, 'I've found a helicopter.' We wobbled out into the dawn mists and opened the door of a long, single-storey barn to be greeted by a line of vintage racing cars and, at the end, a shiny blue helicopter. Naturally, Angus and I climbed into the chopper and, looking at each other in disbelief, noticed that the keys were in the ignition.

And yes, we tried to start the thing, peaking on the most fabulous LSD we had ever taken, but thank God we couldn't, as the unfurled rotor arms would have smashed to pieces on the old stone walls and we would have died. We stayed in the abbey until Monday to recover, which happened to be Little Lee's birthday, so as a breakfast treat, we chopped some lines of MDMA powder into a twenty-three shape on the silver Le Mans victory platter and served it to him in his four-poster bed, although it took a while to find him. Somehow, we had still managed to annoy some neighbours. On Sunday morning, the police had shown up but didn't dare come onto the land, standing deferentially outside the gates. With a few words from the landowner's daughter, they quickly left. That is as succinct a summary of how power works in feudal England as you will ever encounter.

# 19

That year had been one of remarkable escapades and adventures, and it would draw to a close with, in my opinion, the best party we ever did. New Year's Eve was always a special night, for obvious reasons, and we always felt great pressure to come up with something extra special. In 1991, and again in 1994, we took mass numbers to Amsterdam, and years later we would take a coachload to Paris. In 1992, our now close comrades Deep Peace from Bath contacted us and said they had a great venue for a big free party. Biscombe Farm would become another of those quaint sounding English names which would pass into legend. It looked exactly like it sounds: charming, with an old farmhouse made from the exquisite Bath stone so prevalent in the area. The farm had plenty of firm land, good access from the A46 and a slightly nervous farmer. Having offered him a substantial amount of money, the Deep Peace boys set to work.

With freezing fog and terrible visibility, the night of 31st December arrived wreathed in spectral mist. Driving the faithful Dodge truck down from Nottingham, as we arrived we were astounded to see groups of willing helpers, all wearing high-visibility tabards and enthusiastically escorting us to the marquee, already erected. In the Dodge, with its handy crew cab were me, Cookie, Jules and several of the new PA team. By this stage Jules had a small army of helpers including Little Gary and Nick, and the Stroudies such as Dan, Rob, Pete and Nige. We looked on in disbelief as the traffic marshals proceeded to direct arriving vehicles to park in neat rows. 'It's not right,' muttered Cookie with a shake of his head. But recognising the administrative genius of Steve Bryant, I sought him out and congratulated him on being more organised than we had ever been.

This level of traffic logistics had been part of the farmer's deal, as Steve explained. It would be a long night and day for the poor farmer. So we set up Black Box and the decks. Moffball showed up and proceeded to again install his amazing light show with his partner Nancy and a new assistant, Sammy. Interestingly, there was a big Fantazia party around ten miles down the road, more of which later. As we were soundchecking, Spencer from the local crew Eze Love casually wandered into the marquee and asked if we'd be up for throwing his rig next to ours. Absolutely, we replied, only to discover that he had a hugely impressive JBL 10K system, which, when wired in with Black Box, produced the most fantastic sound I ever heard at a free party. There was something in the air that night, a visceral feeling that this was going to be big and it was going to be wild. As the fog descended, more and more cars and vehicles drove in through the gates. It was so cold that everyone was in the marquee, which looked stunning in the hazy darkness and even had proper matting on the floor, and the sound was perfect. More party-heads arrived, and then more. In the end, there must have been around two thousand people at that party – and it was righteous.

Jules and Dan played, followed by Steve Mullatto and on into Digs and Woosh, Simon, possibly Pezz and Emma, and, finally, Jack and Iain Lazy House, and they tore the roof off. I think it was probably the best atmosphere I've ever experienced, anywhere; it was the very definition of what made free parties so special. Another added ingredient was all the freezing and bedraggled ravers turning up from Fantazia down the road, for which they had shelled out twenty-five pounds and uniformly described as shit, there being no real atmosphere to keep the cold at bay. Eventually, the field was so full of cars that people began parking in the traditional way, that being wherever the fuck they wanted, and soon they managed to block the road. I repeatedly had to get on the mic and request that people move their cars, first quite pleasantly and then not so pleasantly, my hoarse Boltonian insults recorded for posterity on the mixtapes that were sold of the night (MC Harry added on the cover by some joker). Somewhere out in that mist was a lost Liverpool contingent who never did find the party, but intead found somewhere nice to break out the supplies and chat through the night, among them a young lady named Dilys, who I was destined to miss again at a debauched party near Bordeaux a couple of years afterwards and would meet again when destiny decreed some fifteen years later.

Then news came through that the police had contacted the farmer and threatened to withdraw his restaurant licence if he didn't stop the rave. Steve Bryant and Jon Kosecki were trying to talk him round in his kitchen for hours, and boy were those two the men for the job. I offered Steve whatever extra cash he needed to bribe the poor sod and this policy worked at about five hundred pounds per hour until finally he broke sometime around lunchtime on New Year's Day 1993, and we had no alternative but to stop. Jack was playing, the atmosphere was electric in that marquee, and we had to break it to him that this would be his last tune, one of the most painful perils of organising raves with no set end time. For his last record, Jack made the truly inspired choice of Public Enemy's anti-authoritarian anthem 'Fight the Power' and the place went absolutely berserk. Of all the years, indeed the decades, of clubs and parties and raves across the world, this was the moment that will stay with me forever as the apogee, the zenith, of that free party spirit. These moments truly showed just what is possible when we escape the shackles of the tame celebrations produced by our often joyless society and truly connect with our wild, shamanic roots. Fight the Power, indeed.

Aside from a quantum leap in DiY's profile, 1992 also brought us a whole range of fresh opportunities and external developments.

New contacts established through the emotional white-heat of parties near and far would suddenly open up new possibilities, especially those of travel and making our own music. And, blessedly for us, as we moved inexorably and exhaustedly away from being just a free party organisation, new and hungry sound systems and party crews began to emerge. From the time of Castlemorton, the number of systems exploded as people across the country formed their own outfits, bought or built rigs and began throwing parties. From North Wales to Kent, from Edinburgh to Cornwall, small local collectives emerged, often inviting us to play at their events. Nowhere did this happen more prevalently than in the East Midlands and South Yorkshire, our traditional stomping ground. From Sheffield and Lincoln, Derby and Nottingham itself, suddenly everyone was DJing and organising.

First and foremost among them were Smokescreen, to whom we would come to owe a deep debt of gratitude, appearing when they did and saving our skins in the process. As documented later, by this stage we were running several club nights in Nottingham alone, a record label and studio, numerous Bounce nights across the country and all our DJs, now probably numbering twelve or thirteen, were playing out all over the UK every Saturday night. Our ability to throw free parties began to suffer and Smokescreen stepped into the breach with a relentless zeal, at a time when we were flagging and getting harassed by eager party-heads every weekend.

Originally a live PA featuring Rodney and Alan Dawson, Smokescreen soon gathered momentum with the addition of John Mead and Laurence Ritchie as DJs, plus the fearsome organisational skills of Laurence's sister, Vicki. Our first encounter with them was at a party at Ringinglow, near Sheffield. This was a classic messy, muddy northern free party. It had rained heavily; cars got stuck and the party ended up as a messy stomp, but for the first time ever, we didn't have to wait around until the bitter end to break down the sound system. The Smokeys were, and remain, a great bunch: dry, solid and a good laugh. They were probably influenced by DiY musically but would find their own sound and quickly attract more DJs and a large, devoted following across the Midlands and north of England. Over time, Fran, Little Steve, Rob, Gav, Andy Riley and many others would make free parties of their own. Often we came together to do joint parties, such as at the return to Butts Quarry, and all was good.

Other systems would emerge and create a unique vibe in the Nottingham/Sheffield/Derby area. Breeze, Quadrant, Babble, Rogue, Pulse, Spoof and others would carry the free party torch for years to come. Conversely, around this time, the concept of the 'superclub' was born, making a fortune out of superstar DJs, high door prices and relentless merchandising, led by the likes of Cream, Gatecrasher and Renaissance.

A myriad of new club nights sprung up in Nottingham and beyond. Balearic nights with tongue-in-cheek names like 'Ask Yer Dad' and 'Back to Basics' in Leeds. One day a young lad from Salford dropped by Vickers Street and asked if we would be offended if he started a club in Nottingham. Surprised by his consideration, we replied that we had no problem. His name was Noel Bowden, aka Bod, and along with his mates and his partner Sally Morris, went on to run Trouble in Mind in Nottingham city centre, even employing our latest female DJ, Pip, as a resident before emigrating to Australia to continue the party in the Antipodes.

Meanwhile, we were off to Ibiza. One day a kindred spirit from Sheffield dropped by the Vickers Street flat where Rick, Pete, Barbara, Rachel and I still lived and announced that he was the 'DiY European Agent', with a business card to prove it. It was the first we'd heard of it, but we had to admire his cheek, so we broke bread together and talked. Jonny Lee was from Sheffield and was a friend of Callum's (a tall, sardonic DJ from Sheffield who we had encountered and was one of the many people who had become obsessed with

Simon and his unique style of music). Jonny had contacts in Shef-field, but then so did we. What we didn't have were contacts in Ibiza.

The story of the White Island and its role in nurturing the acid house phenomenon is legendary and compelling. Everyone knew the orthodox tale of London DJs Nicky Holloway, Danny Ramp-ling, Paul Oakenfold and Jonny Walker holidaying in Ibiza during the summer of 1987, discovering the delights of Balearic house music, fabulous clubs full of fabulous people and ecstasy before bringing those ingredients home to London and inventing acid house. To a northerner, that story has always rankled slightly but there can be no question that Ibiza was still the mythical, sun-drenched home of house and was spoken of in hushed terms of glamour and excess. Jonny Lee's parents had been living there for years, and he wanted to take our DJs over to meet people and play. We were understandably enthusiastic.

Another individual who appeared from nowhere with catalysing fervour was a tall, wiry chap named Steve Grey. Steve never stood still, Barbara nicknaming him 'Ants in your Pants', but as an agency of connection and synchronicity he was amazing. Apart from bring-ing us the impetus to record our first record, he was also an old acquaintance of the Tonka crew, most of whose younger end had relocated to San Francisco and started a party collective very sim-ilar to DiY called 'Wicked'. Over our kitchen table, he regaled us with tales of California, of swimming in the Pacific Ocean, parties in Golden Gate Park, of incredible, wild clubs and international grade drugs. Again, we didn't need much persuading. Steve offered to pay for two DiY personnel to fly to San Francisco to meet our spiritual cousins, and we decided that Rick and Pete would go to America while Simon and I would head to Ibiza.

Simon was to fly out first with his records, then I would fly out to meet them. As always, it didn't quite work out like that. The first night, we ended up outside a random villa and got our heads down on sleeping bags, only to be greeted at dawn by a very large and irate German friend of Jonny's, bare-chested and wearing leather trousers, shouting loudly that this 'wasn't a fucking youth hostel' before throwing us out. Then Simon set fire to his rented motorbike by cunningly using a lighter to see in the dark when pouring petrol from a plastic bottle into the empty tank. Things definitely improved after that, though, when we found somewhere to stay and were taken to the legendary Café del Mar, where we met the equally legendary Jose Padilla, Simon DJing there several times that week and the two of them hitting it off famously. There can be no doubt that Simon was the only DJ to play at both Castlemorton and the Café del Mar that summer, and that kind of explains our mission in a nutshell. We always had a fanatical aversion to being pigeonholed. As we made more connections, we got to see the real Ibiza, the one the tourists and ravers don't get to see. Simon and I hung out with Sid at the Milk Bar in the ancient streets of Ibiza Town; we were whisked to parties in the hills where everyone had moved from a different country and all seemed to wear white; we were guests at Ku, Pacha and Space and swam at the hidden rock pool called Atlantis.

In the spring of 1993, I would return alone to plan some DiY parties for the summer, staying at Jose's place for a week and visiting all the clubs on my rented scooter, a thick file of DiY press cuttings in my bag. We returned en masse in the summer of 1993, the trip advertised as 'DiY '93: Be Careful On Scooters', which we weren't. Over forty of our crew would make it over, all staying in badly ventilated apartments in San Antonio; we would take over the Café del Mar and a club called Summum and everywhere in-between in a riot of Balearic excess. As ever, we came through it all, just, although many people missed flights back and several encountered the uncompromising Guardia Civil, the semi-military police force left over from the Franco days. A friend from Bath was arrested for physically protecting his girlfriend from these thugs, slung in jail for three days and given bleach to drink instead of water, ending with his hospitalisation from where the doctors quietly let him go. In future years, as we cemented our bond with Jose, he would come to the UK over the winter, playing for us often, and in return, he would sort us out a series of lovely villas where eight, ten, even fifteen of us would stay, people rotating as their flights arrived and left.

Up in the hills, the first of these villas in 1994 was fabulous after the chaos of San Antonio the previous years. Andrew Weatherall shared the villa with us at first, then Justin Robertson and partner. All of them, I think, were slightly taken aback by DiY's tendency to always do everything as a large group. People we didn't even know turned up to sta,y such as the awesome Molly Ward, a pattern to be endlessly repeated during the years, unsure at first if they were allowed to stay then becoming instant friends when they realised we didn't give a shit. Jose did turn up and let rip in his feisty Spanish way at how many people we had staying in his villa, but, well, we were a collective and it was more fun that way. As we lounged by the pool one day, I mentioned to Pete that I was feeling slightly guilty up here in the hills of Ibiza with our own exclusive villa and hire cars, not exactly manning the barricades at the anarchist revolution. 'Look at it like this, H,' replied Pete. 'It's payback for all those fucking Sunday nights and Monday mornings lugging bass bins across a wet site'. That worked for me.

In 1995 the villa got better and we had a record number arriving in shifts from the airport. Loads of wondrous women stayed, heading off for the beach every morning: Barbara, Jane, Lucy, Nancy, Becca, Beccy, Molly and Nikki Lee all providing some glamour on wheels as we rocked and rolled our way around the island. Our last big collective year in Ibiza was sponsored by the Ministry of Sound, which shows how far we had infiltrated into the commercial scene by 1996. Simon and Digs and Woosh were booked to play at Space, a club whose outdoor terrace was simply one of the greatest clubbing experiences in the world. The Ministry of Sound team had provided us with the most luxurious villa yet, very spacious on split levels and with a beautiful pool. We even persuaded the Ministry people to pay for several flights. One was for Pete Kenny, who I think surprised them by announcing he had never been abroad before and repeatedly asking why all the houses were white. Our night, or rather morning, at Space was phenomenal. All the disparate friends who had travelled over or were actually living in Ibiza by now were there. It was wild, it was debauched, it was fun, at least until I got thrown out and was assaulted by a naked man wielding a watermelon in the car park. It was definitely our most rock star year on the Balearic island. However, I have to admit we were simply outclassed by Dave Beer from Back to Basics, who disappeared from a bar we were all at, leaving his drink and reappearing ten minutes later water-skiing around the headland, totally off his face and laughing hysterically.

Meanwhile, Rick and Pete had been in San Francisco. Along with Steve Grey, they travelled with the mighty Sharon Storer, a Nottingham girl who had lived on site for many years and had been involved with free parties and DiY since the very early days at Glastonbury 1990. She was seeing Steve at this point and, as her wingman, she took along Kate, a traveller mate, equally as cool and no-nonsense, and who sported an fine mane of blond dreadlocks. When we reunited back at Vickers Street, they were full of crazy tales of the city, connections made, parties attended, substances consumed. They had made full contact with the Wicked people, or some of their main players anyway: Alan, Trish, Jeno, Markie, Garth, Malachy and Emma Brown and more, including the Hardkiss boys Gavin, Robbie and Scott. It transpired that all these people had been in the Glastonbury free field back in 1990. Naturally, Simon and I were now eager to check out San Francisco while Rick and Pete were raring to get to Ibiza, as were the rest of the DJs and our wider mob.

# 20

Steve Grey also brought the offer from a then-unknown group called Alabama 3 to remix their prototype house cover of the Bob Dylan classic 'I Shall Be Released'. To be honest, in those pre-internet days, I thought it had been written by Nina Simone, the version that Steve's friend Rob Spragg brought us contained sampled female vocals and various sequences saved onto disc. This was how remixes were done in those days. Later digital technology would advance to the much simpler manipulation of whole songs via high-capacity digital editing software, but back then we were given some sequences on disc to load into a desktop computer running Cubase sequencing software and some samples which we could load into an Akai S1000. Copyright infringement never crossed our mind, but I'm pretty sure Bob Dylan didn't notice. And so we booked the main studio at Squaredance Studios, a recording complex five minutes' walk from our house, on a side street off Mansfield Road. Run by Tim Andrews and John Crossley, the SquareCentre, containing Squaredance Studios, was perfectly situated for us, halfway between home and Nottingham city centre; it was a beautiful space full of technology, white walls, creative musicians and half a dozen pubs within five hundred yards. Damian yet again bankrolled our first collective foray into a proper studio. Charles Webster was booked as the engineer and, nervously, Simon, Rick, Pete and I, plus Damian and Charles, started working on the track one day in 1992.

Rob, a founder member of Alabama 3, had already been up to re-record his version of the track, which he got done despite mysteriously disappearing to the toilets for long intervals during the recording. Alabama 3 would go on to become massive; their album, *Exile on Coldharbour Lane*, defined an era, and they would record the theme tune for the epic HBO series *The Sopranos*. To be honest, I think Rob later disowned what was their first recording, as he was not in good shape at the time. Later we would discover exactly what he had been doing in the toilets of the recording studio, but later he found help and, to my knowledge, has been clean for decades.

Our first session in the studio was fairly rancorous. There were too many of us in the studio, even one as big as Studio 1 at Squaredance. We all had different concepts and no idea what most of the technology did. Thank the Lord that Charles did, however, and we came out of the studio the next day with a working digital recording of what became the 'DiY Love Cabbage Mix' and our first ever track, replete with samples of distorted didgeridoos and African bush rituals. We loved it. It sounded amazing on the huge wall-mounted monitors in the studio, with the problem being that everything did. Charles advised us to record a copy onto an audio cassette, take it home and see if it still sounded so epic.

As we arrived back at Vickers Street, I'll never forget bumping into Cookie's partner Mitch who lived below us, piling into her flat, sticking it on her tape deck and seeing what she thought of it. Not a lot, it semed, although after a couple of listens I think she added that it was 'OK'. Anyway, it was too late to worry about the track; we needed to do another mix to complete the B side of our first twelve-inch single. So we went back in and, unwisely this time, decided that doing lots of drugs would assist us in making a better track. After some heated discussion around samples and sequences, several grams of MDMA powder were racked out and, for the actual mix-down, the DiY contingent were absolutely off their faces, not emerging from the studio for about twenty-four hours, costing Damian a small fortune when the hire cost was one hundred pound per hour.

Fortunately, Charles did not partake and masterfully steered us on course, ignoring the drugged-up bickering, and we emerged sometime the next day with another mix. There was no doubt that this one was a belter: a minimal slow builder, no vocals, very dubby to the point of being almost tribal. It was christened the 'DiY Dub Mix', and now we had enough tracks to get a record cut. When the test pressings arrived a few weeks later, it was genuinely one of the most emotional moments of our lives. We couldn't believe that we had created a real record, taking our vinyl baby out of the paper sleeve repeatedly, tilting it around to look at the black PVC from all angles, like little kids at Christmas but with more swearing. As they say, you never forget your first time. The 'Love Cabbage Mix' was never a club track, although it was played many times at free parties over the years, but the 'DiY Dub Mix' was a dancefloor success and would directly lead to one of our most notable achievements, producing first a twelve-inch and then an album for our old associates Warp Records.

Still based in Sheffield, Warp had by now become one of the most influential electronic record labels in the world, with their idiosyncratic purple record sleeves dominating the techno market and becoming home to such luminaries as Aphex Twin and Nightmares on Wax. Ultra-northern and ultra-dry, their head honcho Steve Beckett contacted us after hearing the 'DiY Dub Mix', and asked if we wanted to record for his label. DiY were still riding high on post-Castlemorton publicity and Warp, always ahead of the curve with sharp business brains, had clearly calculated that we could shift some units. Trying to keep our cool, we casually agreed while celebrating deliriously behind the scenes. The DiY Dub would become 'Hothead', a name chosen after more tortuous discussion because there is a vocal sample in the track that sounds like that word. It needed three more mixes to fill a twelve-inch. Simon would do one solo, which became the 'Halfamix' (a pun on the popular festival cry of half a mix for a pipe or chillum), Digs and Woosh would produce another (the ten-minute long epic 'Insignificance Mix', leaving us a choice of remixer for the other track.

We consulted Warp to see if they had any preferences, but they replied that it was up to us. And then Simon had one of his moments of pure genius. Having heard that DJ Pierre was staying in London, maybe we could use our contacts to ask if he would be interested in remixing for us? This was a truly audacious plan. For those who are unfamiliar with Pierre, he was, and remains, a titan of the house music world. Chicago born, as 'Phuture' he had pretty much invented acid house, musically at least, with the truly ground-breaking EP 'Acid Trax' in 1987, a record which had stunned the musical underground across the globe with its utterly alien synthesis of huge kick drum and infinite, squidgy meanderings somehow wrestled from a Roland TB 303.

Pierre had gone on to create the Wild Pitch sound in the nineties, epitomised by a Simon DK favourite, 'Rise From Your Grave', a massive, layered track with builds and builds into a huge, overwhelming opus with sinuous acid lines and other-worldly vocal samples. Anyway, to cut a long story short, he agreed, so myself and Damian Stanley, our new engineer, drove to London, picked him up, got him to Nottingham and gave him £750 in cash to do a remix for us in a day. Which he did, with many people commenting later that it was the best mix on the record. Rick and graphic designer Steve Ingram at Iconography (always Fontman to us) got to work on the sleeve, the front featuring a distorted photo of Tash's from Bounce and the back some classic images of free parties. Also on the back of the record sleeve, proudly next to the Warp logo, was our own logo, created a short while before by Rick and consisting of a circle containing a dancer and spelling the letters 'diy'. In the middle, we wrote an unforgettable list of 'Random Respect and Thanks To', which I have recreated below; it makes me laugh and is instructive of where we were at. (NB: it also turned out to be a romantic kiss of death, with nearly all the couples mentioned separating within a year.)

Random Respect and Thanks to:

Darius, Felix, Ollie and Sugarlump; Terry Power; Karen and the Cyberstore; Ollie and Eric; Jean East-West; Loud and Clear; Pepperbox Hill; Sugarhill; Coldcut; John, Steve and Steve and all at the Swamp; Grinners Westy, Phil, Mandy, Chris, Vertigo, Debbie, Andrea, Suzie, Anette, Mo and Emma La'; Quadrant Park; the man with the eyes; 3 Beat Records; Tod Terry; Lisa, Mandy and Platty; Eastern Bloc; Mark, Jess Morwenna and all at Mighty Force; Kraftwerk; the Haçienda; Squaredance Studios and Time Records; Charlie Hall, Lol, Kizzie and the Drum Club; Tony Marcus; Ishabel; Pat Software City; Castlemorton Common; Damien Stanley; Martin and Christine: Barton Stacey Airfield; Deli G; Blaack Box (Italy); Black Box (across the UK); Circus Warp; Lazy House; Smokescreen and Sound Systems all over; Patrick Cowley; Aleister Crowley; Akai; Roland Instruments; John Strypey; Alabama 3; Warp Records; Tanya and the White Van posse; Chilly Phil, Boysie, Emma, Pip, Helen, Slob, Demo, Jo and Jay, Chloe, Max and Kizzie, Martin, Gareth, Jo, Tamsin, Jelly, Sharon, Alex and Gwin, Kate, Molly, Soma, Mote and Jeannie, Barney, Chris, Gavin, Vegeburger Lee, the two Blahs; CRi; Eric; Sister Sledge; Strictly Rhythm; Rhythm Collision; Clifford; Nicki and Merri; Helen and Bizarre; Gerard, Jean, Ollie n Sam; Tribble; Bex; Matthew; Anwar; Quacks to Matthew, Steph, Sonny, Sonny and Nicki; iD Magazine; Johnny Lee; Jose and the Café del Mar; Summum; Martin the Poet; Alfredo; Andrew Weatherall; Darren Emerson; Stuart MacMillan and Slam; Venus; Andy, Levi and the Love Revolution; Beefy Henry and Danny; the M62; Paul, Strat,

H, Loxley and the Funhouse; all DiY DJs; Bolton; Fila Brazillia
and Porky: Opik; Bliss and Lisa; Grimsby Nick; Allister White-
haed; Viz Magazine; Helen Pop; Matt, Ali and the Marquee; Sasha
at Shelleys 28.1.91; Tribe of One; Soul Survival; Lakota; Willie
Wee; Henry and Jill; Rob and Paul Universe; Damian 'Flash'
O'Grady; Ege Bam Yasi; Rob Pike; Pete One-Dread; Charlie
Wagstaff and the Spiritual Home; Testubes; Overall; Mix Junkie;
Digby Johnson; Big Daddy Kane; the Bounce Massive; Moffball;
Dangerous Dave; Pod and Daisy; Nettie; Jay, John and the Lincoln
Mob; Prince Peter Kropotkin; Leo, Angus and the Fire-Breath-
ers; Zac; Paul Babbington; Foxhall Road Fatties; Stroudos, Pete,
Phin, Rich and Rob, Project Love; Enda and Moggy; DJ Sy;
Pinko; that Man from Kent; Dan, Nick and Twins; Jonathon;
Arcade and Selectadisc; Paul Wain; John Kelly; Trev, Gaynor
and Siobhan; Stoney and Damian; Doug and Sarah; Dave, Jules
and Jim the dog; Tina and Jo; John Uzi; Paul and Mart at Wild,
Amsterdam; Ming, Sheen and the Happy Valley, Sydney; Markie,
Jeno and the Wicked people; Royski; San Francisco; Ken Kesey;
Dr Rob and Kay; Ian, Trish and the Garage/Kool Kat; Mixmaster
Morris; Graham Massey; Charles Webster; Rory and Lorraine;
Tommy; Biffo and Nicola; Most Excellent; Lees – both Big and
Little; Dick; Tim, Max and Mozz; Bubbly Becca; Angus 'Chis-
el-Face' Finlayson; Pete Kenny; Cookie, Mitch and Sensi; Joy
Division: Deeelite; Ean, Sheilagh, Shermo and Donday; Coffee
Shop 222; DJ; Touch FM; Eric B and Rakim; Pharoah Saunders;
the Teardrop Explodes; Echo and the Bunnymen; Hannah and
Hamish; Ashbourne Airflield; Matt, Bob and Rupert; Adam and
Tag; Fontman; Helvetica 85 Heavy; Cookie Club; Gallery Café;
Eleanor, Rob, Pete and Richard; Barb and Rachel; Pezz; Jack;
Neil Macey and Gordon; DJ Pierre; TB 303; Michelle Lanaway
and Bev; Steve 'Silk' Hurley; Darren and Suzanne; Amber; Barry;
Digs + Woosh; DK; big burners; Sledger's Café; Parksy; Jan Alpha;

Roger and the Decker; Pat Centresound; Splosh; KLF; ALF; TR
808; Hunt Saboteurs Association; Happy Mondays; Max and
Flying Records; Michael Bentine; Pinko; Simon 'Sasha' Dorey;
Alvaro; John Coltrane; Jerry- the Minister of Noise; Fela Kuti;
Steve Haplern; Forest Fields; On-U Sound; Feva in Manc; Lib
and Rach; Peter Pan and Lottie; Clare and Big Sam; ADAM and
Mary Jane; Dizzy; Hardkiss; JD 800; Butts Quarry; Nature Pro-
grammes; Dodge Trucks; the Dolly; Whitey, Dave and old friends;
Tash; Produce International; Sons of Arqa; Frank Worthington;
William Blake; the Factory; Sarah-Jane and Lucy; James Baldwin;
Laurent Garnier; Bod, Stig and Torch; Decoy Records; George
Clinton; Pete Dog; Butthole Surfers; Bigger Sam; Matt; Gary
Marsden; Sarah and Sally; Glug; Jamie and Scooter; Miles; the
Puppy Posse; Brett and Nikki; Hiziki and Rita's Café; Richard
Harkness and Sam; Criccieth; North and South; Julian and Mel;
Jah Scouse; Michael Clark; Ali; Grub and Jules; Matt Kent; Vicki;
ESS and ASS and Free Party People everywhere...

At this time, in early 1993, our spare bedroom office at Vickers
Street had become unmanageable, with not enough space or computers and nowhere to really meet the constant stream of visitors. It was
also a complete mess, with keyboards, drum machines, reams of paper,
plates of half-eaten food, mugs full of fag ends and empty beer cans
competing for space. Rick, Pete and I, plus two partners, were also
going slightly mad working and living together in a small flat. However, Squaredance were building some new office spaces inside their
Squarecentre complex, so we asked about securing one. Upon being
informed that it came with a cleaner, I said to the manager, 'We can't
have a cleaner, we're anarchists.' But the office did come with a cleaner,
a sparky old gal named Eve, who we compromised with by saying she
was welcome in the office but wasn't allowed to clean and could happily have a fag there as we were the only smoking office.

On paper, it made perfect sense: a secure office nearly in town, more space from which to run our fledgling record label Strictly4Groovers, somewhere we could meet music people, and somewhere to run a DJ agency from. As we released the Alabama 3 record, we wanted to follow it up with more. Our idea was that, although we had never made any money from clubs and obviously not from free parties, perhaps we could do so via a record label. Well, we tried in our own anarcho-capitalist, collective way and, unsurprisingly, we never did make much money from the label. However, through many years of hard work, interspersed with some seriously hard play, we kept the good ship DiY afloat for well over a decade in that office.

We employed Ged, Jean's long-term partner, as our label manager and his mate Damian Stanley as our in-house engineer, which worked well for a couple of years before we drove them both to despair with our business methods. Emma would also come on board to run our DJ agency, which was much needed as we were now getting numerous requests from promoters all over the world to play. Whether we should have got an office and attempted to play the capitalist game or should have stayed as idealistic party renegades is a question that has plagued me for years. It's a question I've never really satisfactorily answered in my own head. Someone recently labelled us 'folk heroes', which seemed to make it all worthwhile. A while later, Casey Orr and Chumbawamba would include DiY in their *Portraits of Anarchists* book. It was a proud moment, although again my mum didn't seem too impressed when I showed it to her. I guess one never knows in life what would have happened if different decisions were made. But really, there's no point in thinking like that; you'll just chase your own tail and drive yourself crazy. Suffice to say, DiY were now becoming a corporate entity that would soon be liable to pay tax and register for VAT. Admittedly, a corporation that didn't do Mondays and never paid any tax was unlikely to achieve great commercial success. I think we proved beyond doubt that we were not natural business heads.

Then fate again stepped in, as so often in our journey, when Tim Andrews decided to sell an entire studio. Housed in an outside broadcast caravan inside the gloomy cellar come car park underneath Squardance, it came complete with a sixteen-track mixing desk, two Akai samplers, a MIDI keyboard, various effects units and an Atari computer to sequence the music on. Everything, in other words, all cabled up and ready to go. A slight drawback was that they wanted £14,500 for it. Well, we knew just the man. Yet again, our benefactor stepped in and bought us the studio. I can still recall Tim's face as we sat in his office to sort the deal, he little expecting our friend to extract the cash, in used tens and twenties, from his hippy bag. Tim quickly took the fat wedge of notes, simply saying with raised eyebrows, 'Well, I won't ask where that came from.' Very wise, Tim, very wise.

In a very short space of time, we had an office with multiple computers and phone lines, our own studio, a DJ agency, a record label, and even a brand-new fax machine. What we needed were loads of new artists and tracks to release. The margins on a twelve-inch single were so small that they were really just for DJs and primers for albums, unless they went huge. This was, of course, long before Napster, iTunes or Spotify. In fact, this was still before the internet was generally available at all. All 'product', as the industry called it, had to be manufactured and distributed to actual record shops. Again, cometh the hour, cometh the man, and our buddy from Birmingham, Neil Macey, suggested a deal with the already legendary Network Records, run by Neil Rushton, a pioneer of early American house music in the UK. Following the Alabama 3 release, our second was a joint effort between Simon and Damian Stanley, with the artist dubbed 'Overview' and EP entitled 'Mobile Music' in honour of our new studio. Multiple artists followed: Charles Webster as 'South Central'; Tim and Max, both close friends and DJs since the early days of the Cookie Club, as 'Essa'; London's Crispin Glover as 'House of Labasia'; and 'Crime', a second EP from Overview.

One new artist who approached us at this time was a very young man, who introduced himself as Nail. Hailing from Beeston, Nail, aka Neil Tolliday, persuaded us to let him use our studio during some downtime over a weekend. Emerging on the Monday with four or five completed tracks, we seasoned professionals sniggered. We would spend that long on perfecting the sound of a snare; you couldn't possibly create that many finished tracks so quickly, we said. But he had, and they were sublime. This boy had real talent and quickly we released four of these tracks as the 'Beeston' EP. Nail would later record for us extensively, including an album, *Big D's Lounge*, which we promoted by recreating a Beeston (a suburb of Nottingham) front room with PA atop a drop-sided lorry outside the *Muzik* magazine awards in Birmingham. Nail would go on to some proper success, becoming half of the duo Bent and signing to the Ministry of Sound, followed by many more musical ventures.

Things were progressing well with our label. Although we weren't making any money, we were getting noticed and Warp got back in touch to ask us if we'd like to do a whole album. As with our studio, we were still staunchly collective in our outlook and so invited all our artists to record a track for inclusion. At this point, we must have been hot property as 3 Beat Records in Liverpool also asked us to a meeting to discuss recording an album. They offered us a ten grand advance, which Warp did not, but we just felt more at home with the Sheffield label. When we sat in the 3 Beat office (where, incidentally, Pezz now worked downstairs in the shop), I explained to John, Dave and Phil that we weren't interested in money. We were interested in working with people who understood our mission. For instance, I offered, if we did a pay party for, say, two thousand people at twenty quid a ticket, we could easily do that and make a lot of money, but that wasn't us. I could see the boys, far better businessmen than we ever were, doing the mental maths before wondering aloud why we didn't do that. Well, because we don't. We never avoided making proper money. In fact, we made a lot of money over the years, con-trary to popular opinion, investing it in new studio equipment and running an office. Well, most of it anyway.

Negotiations with Warp took a surreal turn when we employed Jean's old buddy Sarah Stennett, then an up-and-coming music law-yer who would go on to stratospheric success in the business man-aging Rita Ora, Lil Peep and Zayn Malik. We insisted on a clause giving us a right of refusal to any licensing offers, just in case Coca Cola or McDonald's came knocking. Later we would annoy Steve Beckett even further when the Warp press office announced they had lined up eight interviews for us around the album and we refused to do any, declaring that we didn't want to play the music business game, much like our inspirations Crass and New Order had a decade before. The compilation probably suffered from too many hands. We proudly wrote on the sleeve notes that the nine tracks had been:

'Collectively constructed during the late summer/early autumn of 1993 at s4g studios, Nottingham by various combinations of 14 DiY DJs, engineers and personnel'

And it showed. Apart from Charles Webster, we were all still find-ing our way around a studio. Myself, Bliss, Jack, Tim, Max, Simon, Damian, Nail, Rick, Pete, Barney, Roy and Pip all worked hard to meet the production deadline, but the album, with some flashes of great promise, was slightly patchy and lacked unity, although it still sounds good. It got to number three in the Independent Album Charts, sandwiched between Bjork and The Shamen, which was another proud moment. Some years later, at the MIDEM music conference in Cannes, I would ask Steve Beckett if he would give us a follow-up album, to which he dryly replied, 'We only do second albums to people who help us sell records.'

Around that time, we also began to receive offers to remix other people's stuff, including Bliss and I's remix of Afrokid's 'Dubtown Discoteque' for Produce Records, a remix of a Swains track by Simon and Pip, and many others. Emma recorded a track, 'The Duster' for 3 Beat, and we received a request for a track from T:me Recordings, who were based in the adjoining office to us at Squaredance. Written by Simon and Pete, we were struggling for a name until Pete and I had a great idea. We would ingest some chemicals, stay up all night and see how many variations of words we could invent from the letters D, i and Y. We were having a laugh, of course, and between us came up with Dancing in Yugoslavia, Deranged import Youths, Do in Yourself, the wonderful Dipped in Yoghurt and many more. At some point before dawn, Pete suddenly thought of Dreaming in Yellow, which stopped us in our tracks. Joking aside, it really worked, and so the T:me release became 'Excommunicate' by Dreaming in Yellow, Pete and I both agreeing that we should use the moniker again sometime. We never did, and that's why, in Pete's memory, this book is so titled.

In 1993 DiY no longer had the slightly manic and highly pressured need to organise free parties every weekend, but we were certainly still frantically busy. Bounce continued apace, moving from the Dance Factory to Rockaderos, where we renewed our partnership with James Baillie. Our flagship club night would never quite match the hedonistic heights of the Dance Factory – that level of madness is not sustainable forever – but Rockaderos, and later Deluxe, were great fun, still full of fantastic people from all over the country and beyond, still with that unique set of party people spilling wildly out onto the pavement at 3am, all asking each other where to go to continue the party. As our contact list grew, we began to arrange more and more mass outings to other clubs such as the Haçienda, to other party venues such as a remote Scottish island commune and to other countries, the first of these being our intrepid trip to San Francisco, which featured on the front of *Mixmag*, becoming a month of magic of epic proportions and earning a unique place in DiY history.

# 21

As mentioned, during the previous year Steve Grey had taken Rick and Pete, plus Sharon and Kate, on an exploratory trip to San Francisco. Now it was my turn, and in January 1993, Rick, Pete and I flew with Steve to California, my first time in America. Travelling with us would be the inimitable Jon Kosecki, who was raring to hit the States, if they were foolish enough to let him in. In those days, there was no pre-immigration visa check; you just had to fill out a waiver form on the plane. The first question asked if you had ever been complicit in an act of genocide or had been a member of the Nazi Party in Germany before the war. Fairly easy starter. Question two asked if you were, or had been, a member of a proscribed terrorist organisation. Again, pretty straightforward. The third question, however, caused us some consternation: have you ever been convicted of a crime of 'moral turpitude'? Now, both Jon and I had some very minor offences, but were they morally turpitudinous? Probably, so we lied, just in case.

Shuffling down the non-domestic immigration line at an American airport for the first time can be an anxious experience, especially in the company of some slightly dishevelled young men carrying record boxes who clearly haven't slept for far too long and got really drunk on the plane. Anyway, we were allowed into the good old US of A and the adventure began. Two years later, Jon and I were placed under 'air arrest' on a flight to Dallas following the theft of several top0-quality bottles of champagne from first class. but the police at Dallas airport, charmed by Jon and his truly remarkable blagging skills, ended up not only letting us into Texas but escorting us through passport control. He was like that.

Anyway, our week-long stay in San Francisco was relatively well behaved. Rick, Pete, Jon and I spent the first night sleeping on the floor of an apartment belonging to Al and Trish, two of the Wicked crew, and immediately there was a real rapport. As explained previously, most of the Wicked lot were English, having been part of Tonka before moving stateside to set up their own collective. They had involved some other ex-pats over there, notably Malachy, and had really ignited the house scene in the Bay Area. Rick and Pete had already met most of their main players and now introduced them to Jon and I. Over that week, we would encounter Emma Brown and Jeno, Markie, Garth and Thomas, spending much time in Malachy's basement flat on Haight Street as he and Jon hit it off famously. It felt very much like looking into a mirror of DiY, certainly like visiting cousins; they were doing much the same within the somewhat different parameters of California law, where the cops had guns and really didn't take any shit.

San Francisco itself was mind-blowing. I had long been obsessed with American counterculture in the 1960s and '70s. On the Upper Haight stretch of Golden Gate Park, people had gathered in public to partake in psychedelic substances and listen to amplified music for the first time in history. From these events, I could trace a direct lineage and a cultural template for our own activities.

I saw a poster that summed up the city, where supposedly the native inhabitants of the area had avoided living on in prehistory as it was considered crazy ground. The poster simply read: 'San Francisco: 49 square miles surrounded by Reality'. The city, always enjoying the perfect Californian climate of between 60 and 80 degrees Fahrenheit, can't grow. It is hemmed in by the Pacific Ocean on three sides and by the conurbations of Daly City and San Mateo County to the south. Buildings can't go up due to the earthquake potential and were rebuilt after the Great Quake of 1906 using wood due to its ability to withstand tremors. A truly beautiful city with breathtaking topography, it ranges over hills across a stunning bay and has several beaches within its city limits. But we had headed there because it was also a global capital of discos, deviance and debauchery. With a huge gay population and the most liberal citizens in America, San Francisco had long been a haven of tolerance and rampant indulgence, and we wanted some of that.

On our second day, we were whisked up a famous hill known as Twin Peaks, which not only provided the most incredible view of the city laid out below but was also where the Hardkiss family lived. Unlike the Wicked guys, Hardkiss were all-American: very cool, very laid back and the perfect hosts for the remainder of our stay. Gavin, Scott and Robbie, and two of their partners, the captivating Araceli and Katinka, lived in a beautiful seventies villa nestling into the hill, surrounded by trees except for one side, which opened out onto a lovely deck, giving incredible views of the city. I have a photo of Jon on that deck on our first morning, looking for all the world like some New Age guru, gazing disbelievingly over the city below. DJing and recording as Hardkiss, then Hawke, God Within and Little Wing, our hosts would go on to become some of the biggest stars on the American dance music scene.

And so, in many ways, San Francisco already felt like our second home. Anything seemed possible while we were there, as we were taken from club to club, meeting endless fabulous people: all talented, full of vitality and more than a little crazy. Very few of them had grown up in the city but had all been drawn there by the weather, the parties, the freedom, the tolerance and the bohemian lifestyle. We began to hatch a fairly audacious plan to return soon with the whole DiY crew, or at least as many as we could fit into a rented apartment. Someone introduced us to one of the Wicked crowd, an American called Craig, who just happened to be quite a major landlord in the city. On our last day, we had a quick meeting and he agreed to rent us an apartment somewhere in the city for under two thousand dollars a month, adding that we could squeeze as many people in as we wanted, so long as we didn't trash the place. Hastily agreeing to whatever his conditions were, we headed home and began to plan.

Obviously lacking email, I stayed in touch with Craig via transatlantic landline calls. Around the end of February, he informed me that he had a three-bedroom apartment on Divisadero Street that we could have for a month from 1st April for a discounted price of fifteen hundred dollars. And so, without caution or second thought, we began to spread the word among our people, even mentioning it in *Mixmag*. People would have to pay for their own flights, but we would guarantee free accommodation for the month of April, slap bang in the middle of Lower Haight Street. I can see with hindsight that this may have been somewhat foolhardy, but that is how we ended up with forty-three people staying in one flat in San Francisco for a month, including a terrified music journalist and a legendary rock star, and how we ended up taking over that fair city, party by party. The whole wild adventure was reported in *Mixmag* a month later under the front cover banner of 'DiY in San Francisco: a Gathering of the Tribes'.

Rick, Pete, Barbara and I planned to arrive first, flying from Gatwick into Los Angeles and renting a car, but Rick was searched and detained at Gatwick airport for possession of a tiny piece of cannabis found in his pocket. The three of us had no choice but to board our flights or lose them, and so we left a very dejected looking DJ in the customs sin-bin. Riding his inherent luck as ever, Rick was allowed to fly the next day. The airline changed his flight to a direct San Francisco one and we drove up from LA to pick him up. Driving up Route 1, we felt like we had just woken up in a movie. All those symbols of America, of California, were everywhere.

Redwood trees, diners, motels, yellow taxis, the ocean, endless high-ways, cops in shades, all combining to overwhelm the senses. Finally, we arrived in San Francisco after a 380-mile drive and headed to the Mad Dog in the Fog, a legendary Lower Haight watering hole favoured by British ex-pats in the city. We were able to call someone in Nottingham to learn that Rick's flight was landing that afternoon. I then swung by Craig's office, gave him the cash and he handed over the keys to 453 Divisadero Street. The flat was unfurnished except for one couch and some kitchen equipment, which suited us fine. We genuinely had no idea how many people were heading to stay with us as we drove out to pick up Rick and another friend from the airport for the first of many times.

The others began to roll in. Moffball, then Chilly Phil and Slob. The next day Nicki Lee, Cookie, Simon D; the next day, Clifford, Chris, Helen. Then Matt from Kent with three friends we vaguely knew, and then Darren from Birmingham. Emma and Pezz rolled in. Debbie and Brook from Brighton showed up, and room was made. At this point, we did start to get somewhat concerned that perhaps we should have been more subtle about the free accommodation, but it was a bit late now. A young lad named Jason rang the bell, fresh from a Greyhound bus ride from Miami, and though none of us had ever seen him before, we would become firm friends. Pete Kenny rang on the phone I had paid to be connected; he would be arriving tomorrow afternoon. Barbara and I went to pick him up; he had 36 pence on his person. God only knows how he got through immi-gration. In his pocket, he had a scrap of paper with just one word, 'Divisadero', but spelt wrong. Jesus, if Pete could make it, how many more? Well, quite a lot, until there were ten, eleven, twelve bodies to a bedroom, with one rotating lucky person getting the couch. Our numbers peaked at forty-three, with people coming and going as we sorted out DJ gigs in San Jose and Los Angeles. But despite that, we had probably the most magical month of any of our lives. There was no arguing or complaining, just constant mass outings to bars, clubs and parties. All aided by our adoption by a wonderfully eccentric taxi driver named Buzz, who seemed delighted to throw six or seven of us into his yellow cab and drive us around the city for free.

Simon, Dig and Woosh, Jack, Pezz and Emma all played multiple times across the city and beyond. We took over the End-Up, another of the world's great clubs, partying with the manager Gina until she had to lock up at four o'clock the next afternoon. DiY were guests of honour on a Bulletproof boat party, a truly hedonistic event with two hundred and fifty of San Francisco's finest dancing their way around Alcatraz and under the Golden Gate Bridge. We lost all concept of days, or laws, with people merrily swapping the hash they had smuggled over for top-quality acid and ecstasy. We became minor celebrities, with local party-heads such as 'Guru Mike' turning up to check out the 'crazy Brits'. One morning Genesis P. Orridge, of Psychic TV fame, walked into the front room and declared, 'Fuck me, it looks like Brighton in here', before wandering off into the kitchen to chat to an old acquaintance. We lived opposite an obvious crack den over the road and watched as a succession of crazies disappeared into the back, emerging shortly after completely rocked up. One day it was busted as we watched, and for all the world it looked like a TV cop show.

Some of us visited the Church of John Coltrane, set up in the seventies to worship the divinity of the jazz legend. As I mentioned in a previous chapter, we just happened to be in San Francisco when the whole alternative community celebrated the fiftieth anniversary of Albert Hoffman's first ever LSD trip in 1943. Our group enthusiastically attended several events where free test-tube blotters were given away. One morning, arriving back from such an event, Simon, Chris and I were tripping on the flat roof of a church next to the apartment until a window slid up and two cops, with guns, stepped out and accused us of committing two federal violations. Only a few feet away, dozens of bodies were sleeping in our apartment, surrounded by enough obvious signs of drug-taking to get us all sent to jail for a while. Still, we managed to sweet talk them into letting us climb back into our apartment, our English accents working a charm as always.

And perhaps craziest of all, through all this, we had the *Mixmag* journalist Glenn Barden by our sides, looking terrified most of the time, wearing a fedora hat and imagining he was reliving the Merry Pranksters story in Tom Wolfe's *Electric Kool-Aid Acid Test*. The poor lad had blagged *Mixmag* to pay for his flight to write the article, but he was way out of his depth. Debbie invited us to come and check out the pad that her friend 'Earth Girl' was house sitting up in the hills of La Honda, and we asked Glenn to come along too. It turned out to be a multi-million-dollar estate owned by some guru and we ended up staying for days, with a glass bottle full of some of the best liquid acid on the planet. For days we tripped around the estate, staring open-mouthed at the lavish collection of Thai temple figures, huge white couches and vast windows in the house, made entirely from redwood planks. Someone discovered a golf buggy for getting around and we would drive it, erratically, down to the amazing infinity pool with its stunning view over Silicon Valley. In the middle of all this, Damian arrived, his multi-coloured braids down to his arse, quickly falling in willingly with our chemical experimentation. As our behaviour became more and more tripped out, Glenn seemed to become more uncomfortable. He was dealing with some hardcore drug veterans here and he was not partaking. Earth Girl, who was simply the most Californian person ever, had been keeping the liquid acid in a cup and dispensing it with a pipette onto our willing tongues. Glenn, however, didn't know this and, seeing the clear liquid, picked up the cup and necked the lot. We all stared at him for a second. Barbara gulped. After an extended silence, I spoke.

'Glenn. You know how you didn't want to trip? Well, we respect that, it's your choice. However, I have to inform you that you just ingested around ten thousand micrograms of some of the strongest LSD in the world.'

Poor lad. He didn't know which way to look but soon wandered off down the drive. We really were in the middle of nowhere and shouted at him to come back, but he was gone. About six hours later, he returned, looking somewhat strung out, exhausted and mysteriously clutching half a meat pie. So, quite a month. Simultaneously wonderful, transcendental, deranged. They let us all out of the States to return home and, in June, Glenn's piece appeared in *Mixmag*, creating a furore at the time among some of the San Fran veterans with some lazy journalism and many cliches, but hey, at least he got a free holiday. I'm not sure if he ever recovered and we were never to hear from him again.

Almost immediately after returning home, there was general talk on the free party grapevine of celebrating Avon Free Festival and trying to recreate Castlemorton over the May bank holiday. Glastonbury was continuing its policy of no travellers or free field, plus massively increased security, and the whole of the south-west of England was basically a militarised zone the whole summer. As stated above, we didn't see sense in heading down to this battle zone with our system, undoubtedly facing constant harassment, possible seizure and almost certainly no free party or festival. The whole culture had become too big and too hot to handle. At Glastonbury, Michael Eavis knew he would never get a licence again if he allowed the travellers free access and the free fields to erupt. Ironically, in time Eavis would set up a specific dance music marquee to cater for the obvious need, but in 1993 he was still dead set against any raves or dance music ruining his lucrative and admittedly long-fought festival. We decided we were not going to head into the jaws of the lion and instead would pack the kit up and drive to the northern tip of Scotland, load Black

Box onto a boat and have a little party on a tiny hippy commune over the water.

Having been invited up there by some people encountered along our travels, we agreed that the solstice would be the best time. Scoraig was way north, long past Inverness and probably nearer to Norway than Norwich, and so we anticipated that it would not go dark over the longest days of the year. And so it proved. It was a lovely outing with about fifty people making the ten-hour drive. As arranged, we loaded our system and lights onto one boat and the people onto another, setting sail under sunny skies for our party destination. The residents welcomed us to their tiny, crofted community and we set up the rig. Concerns that our people had not prepared properly for poor weather were confirmed when our mate Jane Brierly stepped off the second boat wearing a t-shirt and Mickey Mouse ears, clutching a now-empty bottle of whisky and asking loudly in her broad Manchester accent where the shop was. The weather came in, the rain began to lash, there was no shop. Makeshift benders were constructed, and the locals took us to shelter in some of their houses in sympathy. Due to the absence of a shop, we had a whip-round and sent Brett and Niki Lee back on the boat to buy several hundreds of pounds worth of alcohol. They were duly dispatched, but as the storm really blew in, they were gone for two long, thirsty days before the sun re-emerged and they were spotted coming over the horizon amid much cheering.

1993 proved itself to be a vintage year, and although we didn't even attempt to get to any free festivals that summer, we did organise a massive variety of parties and events on top of feverishly trying to make enough music to keep the label going. DJs would be dispatched with Jonny Lee to play at his new venue in Thailand. Some of our intrepid souls were invited to play at a unique rave in the Gugulethu township in South Africa, then still in the grip of Apartheid. We had that mass trip to Ibiza, of course, and later in the year, one of our longest-held ambitions was realised when we were invited to do our own exclusive Friday night at the Haçienda. Pete and I had long known Angela, the no-nonsense manager of the legendary Manchester club. They had been through a torrid time, with a death in the club, licensing nightmares and issues with the Salford crew who ran the security and were among the hardest men I have ever met. During that time, DiY's public exposure was probably the highest it would ever be. However, we were even surprised that the Haçienda, still owned by New Order and Factory Records, wanted us to do an exclusive weekend night. This really felt like we had made the big time, and Rick, Pete and I got quite dewy-eyed when we saw the flyers.

Gleefully agreeing to their offer, plus a substantial amount of cash, we organised a coach from Nottingham on 17th December and fity-three of our merry band set off for the iconic nightclub full of cheer. A big queue had already formed around the corner of Whitworth Street, so we dived into the City Road Inn opposite the club for a quick drink. Leaving the crew drinking, myself and the DJs, Simon, Digs and Woosh, Tim and Max and a few of the gang went to the front of the now-massive queue. As I climbed the steps, a bouncer looked at me in disgust, and when I began to explain that we were DiY and could we come in with our records to see Angela, he viciously pushed me down the steps into a crash barrier. Colin, one of our gang and an amateur boxing champion, instantly squared up to the bouncer. Not wanting a fight before we'd even got in, we hilariously ended up having to queue for our own night. When we entered, we found Angela and all was smoothed over. The DJs took over the DJ booth, which at the Haçienda was up in the gods, overlooking the dancefloor, and all was well. Pezz arrived from Liverpool, Tim and Max headed down to the 'Gay Traitor', a bar downstairs for more chilled music.

As I stood on the stairs, overlooking the packed dancefloor grooving to Simon's records, I couldn't quite believe that, ten years on from when Pete and I had first frequented this venerable club, our collective was now playing here. As visions of a young New Order at their magnificent best swam in front of my nostalgic eyes, Nikki Lee was dragged past me by two security guards and the dream evaporated. She had skinned up and lit a joint, which was not the smartest idea in a club which was ultra-paranoid about drug use. So I headed to the door to remonstrate with the doormen, only to suddenly find myself yet again being thrown down the stairs into the cold Mancunian night. Next out of the door was Jane Brierly, giving the bouncers her best Manchester insults, followed rapidly by Dickie, her partner. One by one, more and more of our crew were ejected until at least twenty-five of us were assembled on the pavement outside. Then the chants began, 'Fuck the Haçienda, Tony Wilson is a wanker, na-na-na naa…'. Inside, this had all been reported to the owners and Rick, Pete and Simon suffered the ignominy of being personally removed from the decks by our boyhood heroes, Tony Wilson and Peter Hook. Eventually, we were all kicked out, although we got paid, and merrily sang our abusive songs all the way back to Nottingham on the bus.

We were never quite sure whether this episode had been another slice of rock and roll behaviour or just plain embarrassing idiocy though, probably a bit of both. Still, Angela was to ask us back the following year, so we couldn't have upset them that much. Not fancying another crazy mass outing so soon, we quickly turned our thoughts to New Year's Eve, when the pressure to organise a big free party became intense. Someone among our now extensive contacts notified us of a potential site on a farm in Kent, possibly via Austin or the tVC people. A few travellers had been living there and reckoned we could get away with a party, and that was enough for us to pack Black Box up into the Dodge and set off on the three and a half hour drive to Tunbridge Wells. Arriving quite late, we were pleased to see a marquee had been erected in a big field with plenty of parking space and easy access from the road. With tried and tested efficiency, we unloaded the PA, set it up at one end of the marquee and got busy cabling, arranging the decks, mixer and generator, all the while keeping a close eye on the time.

People began to arrive, parking up, wandering over and chatting, when a senior police officer appeared out of the blue. As always, it seemed to be my job to talk to him, so we walked out of the tent into the bracing night and discussed the situation. He seemed quite important, judging by his peaked hat and badges, and really didn't seem overkeen for the party to start, talking about another sound system, about which I had no idea. Clarifying further, the officer explained that someone else had started setting up before the police had visited earlier, he had ordered them not to, and they had desisted. He made it amply clear that he wished for us to desist too. I patiently explained, now with some experience, that we had been invited onto private land to hold a free New Year's Eve event, at which no alcohol would be on sale, and that this was not a crime. If he wished to make a civil prosecution regarding noise pollution, he would have to wait until we started and get the council to make a proper noise level reading, or at a later date, he could fine the landowner for organising unlicensed entertainment. Either way, I continued, we would be starting the music soon before we missed the midnight deadline. He gave me a look before marching away. Just before midnight, I think we even had a countdown, Black Box pumped into action and we went all night and most of the next morning. It was a great party. The police did not return, although they tried to roadblock the event, but there were too many ways in. Yet again, we made the local paper, 'Peace Shattered by New Year Rave', and, rather comically, the council did serve a noise abatement order, which we completely ignored.

For me, the surreal highlight of the party occurred when Cookie and I, very much worse for wear, wandered away from the party, rounding some trees to come face to face with a big, yellow JCB digger. Jumping up to the cab, we were (again) astonished to see the keys sitting in the ignition. A quick glance at each other and I settled in the driver's seat and tried to start it. The starter motor turned over but wouldn't catch. Probably very fortunately, as I was not in the recommended mental state to drive a thirteen-tonne machine. And then we looked up and the digger was surrounded by five or six angry-looking farmhands, dressed in overalls with hands the size of shovels, obviously drawn by the noise. Cookie climbed down to talk to them, but I was going nowhere and just said, copying Cookie years before, 'Sorry lads, we're diesel enthusiasts' and immediately regretting it. One of them just whacked Cookie on the side of the head with a massive, beefy arm, the others then dragging him away. For a moment, I genuinely thought they were going to kill him, but they kept picking him up and punching him again. Cookie's response was to laugh uncontrollably while sort of hopping around, and I think this really confused them. After a bizarre stand-off, one of them threw Cookie into a large bush in disgust. I clambered down from the cab and half-dragged Cookie back to the party, where we returned to the dance floor and threw some shapes to the rising sun amid happy friends, their breath steaming in the brisk January air, hugging and wishing each other a happy new year.

# 22

If 1993 had been the year of DiY becoming a semi-legitimate business, getting an office and studio, making music and travelling, then 1994 would prove to be the year of politics. All our endeavours, going right back to those early house parties, had been based on equality and collectivism, much like a workers' cooperative. Essentially, this was socialism in practice; providing most of our events for free or certainly at low cost, everyone got paid the same and anyone with kids got a twenty pound 'nipper bonus'. We felt as though we had been political throughout, then basically adding some excitement and colour to the mission statement of the old anarcho-punks, plus providing an income for dozens of people. Throughout this book, I have outlined how DiY had two main drivers: politics and hedonism. However, by 1994 we were perhaps guilty of letting the latter overshadow the former. And then, as mentioned above, at the tail end of 1993, Michael Howard, the vapid home secretary and future leader of the Conservative Party, announced the provisions of the Criminal Justice and Public Order Bill, shortened universally to the CJB, proposing to effectively criminalise our lifestyle.

When the White Paper was published, we quite literally could not believe the government was serious; it felt like a Situationist prank. It was Tash, as always, who obtained the White Paper. Tash, aka Alan Lodge, was another unsung hero of the free festival and party movement. Having quit his job as an ambulance driver many years before, Tash had gone on the road for many years before settling in

Nottingham. Unlike the posturing or nihilistic behaviour of many so-called anarchists, this man was the real deal. Scrupulously well organised, both with his huge library of photos documenting the traveller lifestyle and with his political activism, it was always Tash who sent off for various bills, acts and statutes. It was always Tash writing letters and attending demos, and always Tash heading down to Parliament to represent his people at committee meetings that most of us wouldn't even know about.

And now his hour had come: a proposed Act of Parliament which no one could ignore, and so egregious in its provisions that an entire subculture rose up to prevent it becoming law. The CJB itself was a real ragbag of Tory prejudices strung together in a desperate act of mollifying Middle England and holding off the resurgent Labour Party under its shiny new leader, Tony Blair. It was ill-conceived and badly drafted. The Bill would abolish the right to silence on arrest and criminalise trespass, both basic rights going back centuries, privatise prisons and allow for the potential introduction of prison ships, introduce possible life sentences for juveniles, and allow the police to take and retain intimate body samples in preparation for a national DNA database.

But the most outrage was unquestionably aimed at Sections 63-66, which dealt with 'raves'. That the authorities had even used the word 'rave' was astonishing. By 1994 it had already become an outdated word and only used ironically among actual ravers. Coming from the Tories, it sounded risible, the political equivalent of dad-dancing at a wedding. The four sections made it firstly a criminal offence to organise a 'rave', if outdoors and with more than ten people in attendance, or if refusing to leave said 'rave' if directed to do so by the senior police officer present. For the above crimes, the penalty would be up to three months imprisonment and/or a Level 4 fine, that being up to £2,500. Section 64 would allow the police to enter the land on which the 'rave' occurred, Section 65 to arrest any individuals who attempted to get to the 'rave' when directed not to do so. Finally, Section 66 gave the police the powers to seize 'sound equipment' if they felt that the conditions above had been met. Most infamously, Section 63, Subsection 1, Paragraph b contained a legal definition of music so as to include 'sounds wholly or predominantly characterised by the emission of a succession of repetitive beats'. In other words, the civil servants who had written the CJB did not consider what we played at raves to be 'music' and so had attempted to legally codify that word to include the racket that we made. This was madness, both laughable and sinister in equal measure, but we weren't having it and began preparing for a fight. At an initial meeting at the Cookie Club in Nottingham, representatives of all the local sound systems, plus Tash, met to form a plan of war. We would organise demonstrations and benefits, raise money to publicise the evils of the CJB to the wider public, maybe record some tunes of repetitive beats to highlight our feelings of injustice and anger. It was genuinely a powerful moment when we all agreed on a plan of action, with solidarity among the systems. All we needed now was a name, an umbrella organisation and banner to fight beneath, and when someone proposed the name 'All Systems No', there was no discussion.

In London and the south, other groups were quickly formed, the Advance Party and the Freedom Network being the biggest. We travelled down to a community centre in Brixton to one of the Advance Party meetings, recognising many faces from Spiral Tribe and Bedlam and merrily taking the piss out of each other's music. Shortly after, we attended another meeting at the home of Exodus collective near Luton, those guys having established a commune probably nearest in similarity to Crass of anyone in the whole rave movement and really pushing the boundaries of what an ethical house music collective could be. Nothing creates solidarity more solidly than a shared sense of injustice and feeling compelled to fight it, and for the next eight or nine months the different systems came together amazingly. Together we booked our old haunt, the Marcus Garvey Centre, and held a series of fundraisers and all-nighters, with a DJ from each crew playing and all monies going to the anti-CJB fund.

We used the money to print tens of thousands of leaflets, pamphlets and posters, putting them in record shops, cafés and community centres and flyering outside clubs. It felt good to have a common cause and to be reminded of why we started organising in the first place. A first national demonstration to 'Kill the Bill' was organised in London for 1st May and we subsidised four double-deckers to head down. All our buses were in a festive mood and, when stopped at the services, there were thousands of other party-heads heading to the same spot, equally as celebratory. It became clear that not just the ravers had mobilised. Clearly the CJB had also outraged the squatters, road protestors and many more. There were an estimated 20,000 marchers at that first rally, starting in Hyde Park on a glorious, sunny day and winding its way to Trafalgar Square. From Stroud, the bicycle-powered Rinky Dink sound system turned up, raising a great cheer from the assembly as they pedalled their tandem around the park, emitting a series of repetitive beats.

Although nowhere near the size of the Poll Tax march, now some four years before, it was still a big turnout and a clear signal that we were prepared to resist the government. Finally coming to rest in Trafalgar Square, a series of speakers addressed the crowd. At this point, two of our party became so intoxicated with the atmosphere that they decided to strip naked and jump into the fountains, and I have to admit that I followed them. No one seemed to care; it was a warm day and, well, you know. Climbing back out, soaking, I realised that we were supposed to rendezvous with our coaches very soon and so I grabbed the first person I knew, who happened to be Cookie, and jumped into a taxi. As we swept out of Trafalgar Square, past a long row of riot vans, we thought it would be funny to make obscene gestures at them and made blowjob signals out of the back of the cab. How we laughed as we drove round the corner into Pall Mall, not stopping to worry as a riot van caught us up and overtook the taxi. However, when the side door was opened by a large copper and he started to wave the taxi over, we soon stopped laughing. They yanked open the taxi door, two officers grabbing me and dragging me into the van. Cookie put his hands up to signal surrender and they threw him in on top of me. Slamming the door shut again, the ten or so riot police in the van all gave me a boot in the stomach and the legs, laughing. One held me in a half-nelson, arm behind my back and a boot on my head, squashing my face into the floor.

'Where you from, pal?'

'Bolton.'

'Wrong answer, you northern cunt,' and with that kicked me in the face.

'What football team do you support?'

I remember thinking that I better not say Manchester United, so I grunted, 'Bolton Wanderers.'

'Wrong answer.' Another boot in the face.

This continued all the way to the station, where they took a Polaroid of themselves with 'the glum northerners' and threw us into separate cells. They had turned out my pockets at the custody desk, including my driving licence, meaning I couldn't even give a false address. I was still soaked through from the fountain and realised we must have missed the coach. Eventually, they released us and we somehow found our way to our old friend Eleanor Bailey's house. Back in Nottingham, we both received a summons charging us with Section 4 public order offences, that is acting in a way so as to 'cause the fear of unlawful violence', which I thought was a bit rich. I got onto Peter Silver, the barrister who had defended Spiral Tribe after Castlemorton. When Cookie and I had appeared at Bow Street Magistrates Court in ill-fitting suits, he managed to get the charges reduced and we were both fined fifty pound.

With that distraction over, we continued to fight the CJB until the bitter end. Clearly, we stood little chance of preventing the Bill from becoming law, but we certainly tried. We approached our old mates Chumbawamba and they agreed to do a joint anti-CJB song to be released on One Little Indian, which we duly remixed, including some Noam Chomsky samples, adding more money to the kitty. Another bigger march was organised for 24th July and this time I stayed away from the fountains. Both these first two demonstrations passed off peacefully, but things inevitably turned ugly at the last one in October. All Systems No had rented a drop-sided van and, in the middle of the rally in Hyde Park, attempted to get the sound system mounted on the back into the park. As the van's sides were drawn back, the PA roared into life and dozens of demonstrators leapt onto the van as it moved slowly through the traffic. This really kicked the march into life, as suddenly we had a party on our hands, and the police were not impressed. Someone passed me a jerry can to get more petrol, which is a nightmare in central London, but eventually I found a garage. I headed back to the van when a riot van pulled up alongside me and slid open the door. I swore silently to myself, thinking that I knew how this ended. This time, however, they just confiscated the petrol and I headed back empty-handed to Hyde Park, where things were starting to kick off. The police had blocked the van's entry into the park and so the sound system had been forced back along the road. It was getting dark, and missiles began to fly. The police inevitably charged, and so ensued what the media would call 'the Battle of Hyde Park'.

And so finally, despite all the fundraising, the demonstrating and the anger, the Bill received Royal Assent and became an Act on 3rd October 1994. It has to be said that in terms of preventing large unlicensed raves, they were two years too late, but it did signify a symbolic end to the spontaneous and wild free festivals and parties that had come before. Events like Castlemorton did not happen in a cultural void; the conditions for such a huge illegal gathering had been coalescing for years and had now dissipated, with that level of mass lawlessness being unsustainable for long. Post-CJA, some systems did have their rigs impounded and we hit upon the idea of a 'kamikaze rig' that we would buy between us and would be dispensable if seized. But it has to be said that the golden age of free parties and certainly free festivals had passed. As noted, we had turned our attention elsewhere, although we still dragged Black Box out occasionally to a muddy field somewhere.

Aside from the intense political resistance of 1994, we still had many other irons in the fire. That year saw our first DiY trip to Dallas, to where ex-pat Ian Collingwood had relocated and helped set up the brilliant 'Hazy Daze' collective. For several years they would pay for flights for our DJs to fly to Texas, plus me as their 'manager', playing at their fabulous ranch parties and clubs before flying on to San Francisco to continue the party. We would take a coachload of our crew over to France to a party in a circus big-top near Bordeaux, but that never really happened as the organisers hadn't invited anyone, although, with litres of the new drug GHB and mounds of cheap French alcohol, we made our own party. Mandy would demonstrate that a really effective way to neutralise a sniffer dog was to give it a bumper pack of Wotsits, after which it couldn't smell a thing. Rick, Pete, Barbara and I moved into a new house on Premier Road, a lovely detached four-bedroom house in Forest Fields with a garden, becoming the scene of endless after-parties and questionable behaviour, and where we were joined by Pete's new partner Lucy, the owner of a fantastic but somewhat chaotic record shop in Nottingham city centre called Panface.

We were, rather surprisingly, invited back to the Haçienda. Angela provided fity-three guest passes to the VIP room to avoid the security issue, but which our gang duly trashed, leading us to be kicked out of the esteemed club on our own night for a second time. The head of security collared me as the DiY manager and informed me that we were 'worse than the Happy Mondays', which I had to admit to him made me feel strangely proud. This was on the Friday night, and we further compounded our reputation for infamy on the Saturday by robbing two grand's worth of booze from a locked bar at Jonny Lee's weekend party at Baskerville Hall and having to jump en masse out of a first-floor hotel window.

And above all, that year was our legendarily disgraceful second mass trip to Amsterdam for New Year's Eve. Packing ninety-two people onto two coaches, we took over the ferry on the way. Nikki Lee ended up behind the bar pulling pints yet again as families abandoned the entire bar area and left us to it. We had booked the entire wing of the Amsterdam Novotel via the coach company, and, I have to say, we did not treat the hotel entirely with respect, putting endless meals and drinks in fictitious names and room numbers and amassing a joint bill of over fifteen hundred pounds. Unable to pay, we were forced to do the first mass runner by a coach in history. People were still jumping onboard half-dressed as we drove out of the car park in the morning, the hotel staff running after us waving pages of unpaid bills. In Amsterdam itself, the party at a squat in the city centre progressed into all of us getting taxis, trams and buses to the 'Fun Factory', a nightmare Dutch rave where the music was truly awful but it was warm. Pete and I were offered a lift from a promoter in his mate's top-end BMW, and as he drove us through the Amsterdam night in silent luxury, he passed us two big bags, one containing ounces of cocaine and the other top-quality MDMA powder. Pete and I stuck a straw in each one and the other end in our nostrils, fully complying with his offer to 'Ja, help yourselves, really' and arrived at the Fun Factory probably the highest I have ever been, bumping into Joe and gasping, 'I've finally overdone it, Joe, I think I'm going to die.' Jon Kosecki was arrested somewhere; someone was hospitalised. We left two or three people behind and someone got arrested for shoplifting on the ferry back.

Before all that, though, we had our fifth birthday celebration to consider. On 23rd November 1994 it would be five years to the day since our first event as DiY. We booked the Kool Kat on a Wednesday night, charging a pound. We produced a little blue flyer proclaiming '1826 Days of Undiluted Fun' and expected quite a few people to turn out; it was absolutely mobbed, a massive queue snaking round the corner and people trying to climb in through the toilet windows. I guess we must have done something right over those five years. People had grown up with DiY; from wide-eyed, idealistic chancers, we had morphed into battle-hardened, veteran chancers. Most importantly, those of us at the core of DiY had never fallen out – well, not for long; we had stuck together through arrests, deaths, insane trips abroad and deranged days spent in muddy fields.

And indeed, the wider collective had felt empowered; we had, I think, made a real difference. The first five years of our mission had been bookended by the optimism of the dismantling of the Berlin Wall and five years later the pessimism of the Criminal Justice Act. Via our insistent collectivism, we had brought some ethics into dance music, all the while revelling in a hedonistic milieu not seen since the sixties. We had taken on the police, the government and pretty much everyone else in authority. While we were never going to win, we had unquestionably breathed new life into protest and introduced many sections of a new generation into questioning the values of a plastic, consumerist world where profit was king, and maybe made them think about the inherent evils of capitalism and how it was destroying the planet. There are other ways to organise society, according to need and with a genuine communal celebration at its heart, and we had, hopefully, demonstrated this. I suspect we had built the biggest, most wonderful, creative and lawless gang there has ever been, anywhere, ever.

On that cold Wednesday night in November, hundreds of people came out to celebrate and show their love, not only for DiY but for each other and the magical, flawed community they had built over the years. Many things lay in the future: Labour governments, Oasis and Britpop, the Millennium and the massive joint free party where some miserable fucker wouldn't let me play Prince's '1999', which I had been planning for years. Our DJs would go on to global success and have residencies in Barcelona and Paris, DiY Discs would release another 80-odd singles, albums and CDs, plus many others on our Diversions label.

Bounce would celebrate its fifth anniversary. Further crazy trips to Prague, Australia, Ibiza, Atlanta, Canada, New Zealand, Amsterdam and beyond would be organised, and each time, some of our personnel would stay or relocate; many still live in those places to this day, with some having children and putting down new roots. Jeremy Healy's annoying bondage trousers would be clipped to the stairs by us from underneath on a boat party around Sydney Harbour, so that he would fall over when he moved. I would get into an argument with Shaun Ryder backstage at the Fillmore in San Francisco, which would end in a bizarre scuffle outside, half inside his limousine, half on the street. Something called the internet would appear and new friends made such as Drew Hemment, organiser of the then Futuresonic festival, referred to then by Pete, as 'your internet mate', which seems quaintly comical now.

There would be relationship crises, tragedy and treachery on an almost Shakespearian level, and many of us would succumb to the perils of addiction and some onto rehab. Some would have children, some would transition genders, some would inevitably pass on to the great dancefloor in the sky. We would steal the giant wings of the massive goose they use as a symbol of Nottingham's Goose Fair in the middle of the night and ransom them back for future free tickets. At dawn, in a caravan somewhere at a Smokescreen party, I would christen a young DJ and street artist 'Banksy' and advise him solemnly that there was no future in graffiti. We would visit New

York and stand rooted to the spot as Francois Kevorkian dropped the full extended mix of Kraftwerk's 'Tour de France' on the dancefloor at Body and Soul. Remarkably, we would mostly make it to the DiY twentieth, twenty-fifth and even thirtieth-anniversary celebrations fairly intact. We have, I think, left a legacy that it is possible to have wild and hedonistic times and still change the world in a small but important way.

DiY friend Scotty Clarke, poet and documentary filmmaker, would write many years later about his impressions of DiY, and I don't think it can be beaten:

"DiY and the Free Party People did something to Nottingham that I have not witnessed before or since. DiY brought tribes together. Students, townies, inner-city ravers, blow-ins, immigrants, travellers, oddballs, weirdos and revellers. Gay, straight, black, white and those from afar who were paying attention and flocked to the deep house Mecca of the Midlands, to groove together, on its dance floors, fields and houses. The inherent love that united dance floors spilled over into an industrial city in decline. The fact that there were many hundreds of those assembled tribes from Nottingham at Castlemorton festival speaks volumes. Townies who had been working nightshift at pork farms or enduring the poverty of unemployment through their love of music found themselves at the defining event of their generation. That culture clash allowed ideas to permeate into what could have been closed minds. Beyond the love that DiY and the Free Party People brought to the city of Nottingham, they also brought an attitude. An attitude of rebellion. An attitude of defiance, as opposed to an attitude of compliance."

After the Kool Kat DiY fifth birthday night, we organised an after-party at the Staircase club, run by our old mate Denis. As ever, we took the whole place over and dug in, ending up with our indomitable Nikki Lee again running the bar. There was no way our gang was going to bed before dawn. Jon Kosecki had shown up and, as it was my birthday, too, at the ripe old age of twenty-eight, he had harassed me all night about taking more and more drugs, with admittedly little resistance. By around four in the morning, I was attempting to dance on the sticky dancefloor before deciding I just wanted to lie down for a bit. Jon was having none of it and repeatedly hovered above me, blowing cocaine up my nose with a straw. And, as I lay there on the dancefloor, amid these wonderful friends assembled to celebrate the fifth birthday of the collective we had built, having drugs inundated into my brain by this crazed messiah from Bath, those five tumultuous years flashed through my exploding mind and I pondered DiY's existence. Well, I thought, we definitely did it ourselves and, you know what, perhaps we even did it all rather well.

# EPILOGUE

Friday 23rd October 2020. Three weeks earlier, my oldest friend Pete had died following a long battle with an aggressive form of cancer. Only he never wanted to call it a battle; he didn't like that terminology. Eschewing conventional therapy, he had put his faith in medicinal cannabis and clean living, becoming abstinent from all intoxicating or toxic substances. And now, finally, he is gone. In the afternoon, a small group of his closest friends had picked up his body from the undertakers, wrapped in a white shroud and placed on a beautiful bespoke ladder made from birchwood. Slats of oak had been woven through the rungs and rosemary, eucalyptus and lavender wound around to represent remembrance, strength and calmness. A series of gold letters ran down the length of the shroud, spelling out the words 'Love is the Most Important Thing', and it's hard to argue with that because it is true. Lovingly, he was placed in the rear of Dave's battered Mercedes van, where he seemed at home. We drove off slowly down the road, music began, a bottle was popped, Kate lovingly wiggled his little foot, Andrew and Jackie whooped and we all simultaneously burst into tears.

On the morrow, we would bury our comrade, lover, inspiration, legend, friend. Pete may have been small in physical stature but was huge in spirit: a catalyst, a magician, a shaman. We would lay him to rest in a primal ceremony presided over by the extraordinary celebrant Tim Holmes in a beautiful plot in a natural burial ground. We had invited representatives of the many stages of Pete's life, and many of the pivotal figures featured in this book were there. Beneath crazy skies, torrential rain and eventually glorious sunshine, streaming live to an international audience, we celebrated his life. Passion, laughter and deep sorrow were offered to the elements.

On the day of his burial, it felt as though the assembled and watching congregation were not only celebrating the passing of an extraordinary life; we were celebrating the passing of a way of life. Inevitably, scenes from the glory days of DiY flickered through my mind, private showreels of the epic adventures which I have attempted to outline in this book. No doubt a large piece of DiY died with Pete's passing, and yet it is impossible to extinguish a state of mind. Pete exemplified, along with many of our other comrades who fell by the wayside, the flowering and triumph of an attitude, a rejection of the materialist society into which we had been born. An attitude that was always impossible to quantify but something that grew from the idealism and the hedonism of the nineties and blossomed among a hidden nation of believers who worshipped at the same altars, fell in love with each other and danced beneath the stars. Despite the inevitable vicious reactions of the state apparatus, somehow we had triumphed over the dark forces of oppression, if only for a few transient moments.

At the graveside, between glorious readings from close companions and sumptuous pieces of music reflecting Pete's life, I thought and spoke of his words at Castlemorton some twenty-eight years before, wondering if we really had pushed it too far. But as I looked at his resplendent grave through rain and copious tears, festooned with flowers and myriad tokens of love, I could hear him, on the wind, quietly whispering again, 'It's never too far.'

# SPECIAL THANKS TO THOSE WHO PRE-ORDERED THE BOOK

J Alderson, Andrew Allday, Jon Allen, Neil Amison, Dave Anderson, John Anderson, Paul Anderson, Lauren Andrew, Louise Andrews, George Ankrett, Anton Ardakov, Warwick Arthur, Magnus Asberg, Richard Austin, Waq Aziz, Daniel Badder, Damien Bailey, Eleanor Bailey, Esther Bailey, Jason Bailey, James Baillie, Jes Baines, Roger Ballance, Martin Banks, Rebecca Barker-McLean, Alexandra Barnes, Tim Barnett, James Barrett, Kieron Barrett, Adrian Barsby, Beth Barton, Nick Bateman, Deborah Bathurst, Daniel Bayley, Tim Beaver, Philip Beddard, Alan Beddow, Richard Bee, Tony Beech, Gavin Belton, Enrico Benini, Charlie Bennett, Dylan Bennett, Daniel Berman, Jim Bethell, Rachael Bevan, Sarbjit Bharj, Anil Bhoomkar, Paul Binning, Nicola Birch, Helen Black, Keith Blackie, Mark Blagg, Richard Bland, Chris Blore, Jody Boehnert, Jelle Frans Bollen, Claire Bone, Bob Boram, Roly Boughton, Zak Boutell, Stevie Bowerman, Noel Bowden, Rob Bracher, David Bradbury, Nicola Bradshaw, Emma Bramley, Stuart Brealey, Mark Bristow, Jane Bromley, Wendy Brooking, Alix Brooks, David Brooks, Jason Brothwell, Emma Brown, Jo Brown, Neil Brown, Shuggy Brown, Guen Browne, Cami Brunjes, Rob Bryant, Edward Buck, James Buck, John Buckby, Charlie Bucket, Ainsley Burton, Richard Burton, Andrew Butler, Chris Butler, Steven Butters, Enrico Caballero, Rob Calcutt, Martin Callow, Cassius Campbell, James Capewell, Paul Carney, Ed Carpenter, Charles Carr, Philip Carr, Dan Cartel, Jeannie Caton,

Alex Caulder, Peter Chard, Roger Chedgey, Simon Chedzey, Rebecca Cheetham, Timothy Child, Paul Chilton, Tom Churchill, Helen Chuter, Jonathan Clark, Scotty Clark, Adrian Clarke (Spike), Jo Clarke, Phil Clarke-Hill, Ruth Claxton, Pol Clementsmith, Jess Coburn, Thomas Coirie, Allan Cole, Jemma Collis, Simon Columbine, Andrew Compton, Charlie Compton, Heidi Connor, James Cook, Amanda Cooke, Clare Cooke, Paul Cooling, Matt Copley, Sheena Cormack, James Coward, Lee Cox, Grant Craven, Alex Croall, Rob Crook, Sam Crossley, Rupert Cue, Richard Curen, Shirley Curran, James Currington, Andrea Cygler, Osborne Daniel, Iain Danielson, Mark Darby, Simon Darrington, Tony Davey, Terry Dearlove, Tom Davies, Craig Dawson, Ged Day, Matt Dean, Joe DeCambre, Vivienne Deitmers, Stephen Dennis, Vasco de Souza, Patrick Devereux, Simon Devine, Ben de Vos, Stevie Diamond, Nadia Dickinson, Neil 'Orange Peel' Dickinson, Rebekah Dilley, Neil Dilworth, Sarah Dixon, DJD2, Kevin Dobson, Daniel Doherty, Richard Donohue, James Dougill, Aaron (P71) Dowds, Josh 'Jahman' Dowling, Pete Draper, James Drew, Bstorm Ds, Olivier Ducret, Yvonne Duffield, Ben Duncan-Jones, John Ebbs, Tivey Edward, Roz Edwards, Aurelie Elder, Chantal Ellam, Tim Ellaway, Martin Elliott, Marc Ellis, Frankie Eriksson, Matt Eris, Garry Espin, Paul Evans, Simon Evans, Nick Everett, Benjamin Ewins, Nick Eyre, James Fairbairn, Nima Falatoori, Martin Farino, Andy Faulkner, Alex Ferguson, Rachel Fernyhough, Martyn Field, Angus Finlayson, Kruger Fitch, Vita FitzSimons, Steve Flanagan, Lucy Fleming White, Toby Fletcher, Dan Foat, Debbie Forde, Tom Forrest, Tim Forrester, Ali Fox, Richard Fox, Mike Foy, Mark Francs, Franklin Franklin, Matt Freer, Lee French, Patrick French, Matt Frost, Rufus Fry, Mark Fugler, Justin Gage, Julia Gajlikowska, Lee Gardner, Greig Gaskill, Algis Gasperas, Claire George, Tim Gibney, Stephen Gibson, Ben Gill, Simon Gill, James Gillespie, Darren Gillingham, Fiachna Goggins, Chris Goss, Gary Grant, Rob Gray, Jonnie Greaves, David

Green, Fran Green, Glenn Green, Harold Green, Simon Greenhalgh, Jason Gregory, David Griffith, Matt Grimes, Jon Gwinnell, Stuart Hall, Sam Hallam, Ian Halliday, Sarah Halliwell, Miles Halpin, Arfan Hanif, Poppy Hannon & Paul Nokip, Lisa Hancox, George Hannon, Rich Hanrahan, Ky Harcombe, Alison Harkness, James Harmer, Paul Harpham, Mark Harridge, Brenda Harrington, Jonathan Harris, Robert Harris, David Harrison, Judith Harrison, Jean Harry, Lewis Harvey, David Harvie, Ned Hawes, Miles Hawthorn, David Hayes, Sally Hayes, Nikki Hayford, Pete Hayward, Helene Hazell, Max Heath, Paul Heath, Robert Hele, Drew Hemment, Manda Hempstock, Anita Henderson, Yusuf Heusen, Steve Heywood, Thomas Hnatiw, Emma Hobbs, Kim Holden, Kirsty Ellen Holmes, Mark Holmes, Sue Holmes, Tim Holmes, Kate Hopkinson, Jayne Hooton, Rob Horne, Mark Hosken, Jonny Loves House, Lisa Howard, Simon Howat, Jason Harris, Tara Hill, Sharon Hitchen, Asa Hudson, Nick 'Metro' Hudson, John Hughes, Josh Hughey, Gary Humphreys, Anton Hunt, Matthew Huntingford, Ed Hunton, Wolskie Hylander, Mark Ingham, Patrick Irwin, Rochelle Isace, Samir Izri, Jamie & Eve, Paul Jarman, Lee Jenkins, Matt Jenkins, Joanna Jevons, Quentin Johns, Carl Johnson, Ellen Johnson, Mark Johnson, Alex Johnston, Paul Johnston, Dilys Jones, Lee Jones, Lisa Jones, Richard Jones, Tristan Jong, Ravinder Kaur, Alex Keithlow, Simon Kelly, John Kelsey, Si Kemp, Jenny Kenny, Pete Kent, David Kerslake, Rob Keynes, Noel Kilbride, Ian Kimber, Adam King, Emma Kirby, Jodie Kirkham, Simon Knee, Tim Knight, Will Knott, Vilém Kropp, Magda Kuczmik, Ross Laing, Stuart Land, Janet Lang, Solar Langevin, Richard Law, Jamie Lawder, Victoria Leadbeater, Julia Leary, Jonny Lee, Nicola Lee, Mick Leivers, Alexis Le-Tan, Dafydd Lewis, David Lewis, Matt Lewis, Nia Lewis, Ross Lilly, Trevor Lindsay, Tim Locke, Tony Longbone, Alexandra Lort Phillips, Georgia Loryman, Sally Lovejoy, Chris Lovell, Chris Lumb, Aidan Lynch, Barbara Lyons, Molly Macindoe, Ian MacKenzie, David Maclean,

Mufeed Mahmood, Nevine Malek, Jayne Malpas, Judy Manners, Richard Marder, Robin Marsh, Kevin Marsh, Adam Marshall, Alge Marshall, Beki Martin, Kate Martin, Karl Martinez, Paul Mason, Joanna Matson, Steve Maxwell, Dan Mayer, Nicola Mayer, Andy Mcarthur, April Mccabe, Keith McCartney, Ixy McGarvie, Ian McGee, Susan McGrady, Catherine McGrath, Mike McKenzie, Marlon McKetty, Alex McLaren, Steve 'Lightning' McLay, Morgan McLintic, Brian McMillan, Jane McNamara, Alan McQueen, Justin Mead, Michelle Miles, Peter Miller, Ian Mills, Jeremy Mills, Fiona Mitchell, David Money, Alice and Dan Monkman, Dave Mooring, Paul Moran, Bryn Morgan, Dave Morgan, Darren Morris, Gavin Morris, Miles Morris, Paul Moylan, Shona Munro, Nicole Murphy, Tracy Murphy, Philip Neale, Kim Ngo, Tim Nicholl, Alastair Nightingale, Rory Noone, Jackie Norbury, Eric Oakes, Alice O'Grady, Ryan Oldcorn, Ben Oliver, Deboragh Oliver, Ros Justine Oliver, Scott Oliver, Nancy O'Regan, Ben Osborne, Tim Overill, Mel Owen, Valerie Packer, Shumana Palit, Rose Pandzioch, Ian Park, Michael Parker, Nick Parker, Melissa Parkinson, Mack Parnell, Becki Pate, Nicholas Patton, Thomas Paul, Dave Payling, Gaz Peacham, Samuel Pearce, Jenny Peers, Andrew Pegg, Adrian Perry, Jonathan Perry, Beate Peter, Lucy Pettigrew, Gary Pfeffer, Carl Phillips, Paul Phillips, Claire Phipps, Ric Pickering, Ian Pickett, Nick Pighills, John Place, Ed Plumb, Neil Poole, Jemima Pope, Tamsin Pope, Gay Porkolab, Cate Potter, Robert Potter, Richard Powell, Tyler Powloski, Rachel Poznanski, Ben Prole, Alan Prosser, Joe Public, Nicole Puller, Kath Pyer, Andy Pyett, Eloise Queen, Amy Rai, Tom Ralph, Sarah Rand, Tom Raphael, Dani Rastelli, Henry Ratcliffe, Al Read, Louise Redhead, Chris Reed, Nic Reed, Rowena Reeday, Paul Reid, John Richardson, Jonathan Rigby, Andy Riggs, Andrew Riley, Matt Ringrose, Chrissie Ritchie, Tara Rivero, Large Rob, Stephen Robbins, John Robinson, Laura Robinson, Stuart Robinson, Cass Roc, Fay Roe, Rachel Roe, Sarah Romary, Ross and Debs, Jaime

Rosso, Max Rowsell, Petra Roziňáková, Wil Russell & DJ Bong, Graeme Salt, Ed Samuel, Bob Sanderson, Ben Sansum, François Savoureux, Andrew Scanlan, Claire Ccawn, Stephen Scott, Rebecca Seager, Christian Searle, Ginny Sellors, Jes Sewerin, Gil Schalom, David Sharland, Clifford Sherriff, Tom Shillington, Dan Short, Richard Short, Simon Siddle, Paula Simms, Alexia Singh, Tyron Slack, Pablo Smet, David Smith, Giles Martin Smith, Gregory Smith, Hazel Smith, Kate Smith, Mark Smith, Nick Smith, Sharon Smith, Steph Smith, Marion Smylie, Alex Sparrow, Tamsin Speight, Stuart Spring, Claire Stephenson, Georgette Steudlein, Robin Stevens, Tim Stoakes, Ryan Stockton, DJ Stoney, Sharon Storer, Nick Strang, Andrew Stratford, Leigh Strydom, Kay Stuart, Anthony Stubbs, Matthew Summers, Toby Sutton, Martin Swinckels, Ian Taylor, Owen Teers, Duncan Theobald, Dianne Thomas, Mandi Thomas, Rian Thomas, Sid Thomas, Stuart Thomas, James Thomson, Neil Tolliday, Daniel Townsend, Ian Townsend, Guy Tremlett, Emma Treweek, Aaron Trinder, Justin Turford, Paul Twomey, Grub Tyler, James Underhill, Robert Upton, Linzie Vasisht, Anthony Vaughan, Johnny Venables, Sam Vine, Helen Waddingham, Sally Waddingham, Joanne Wain, Paul Wain, Steve Wainwright, Richard Walker, Amber Walls, D Walters, Olly Ward, Robert Wass, Christine Watson, Richard Webb, Barry Welch, Kim Westcott, Simon Westfield, Samantha Wheatley, Andrew White, Tim White, Adam Whitehouse, Mark Wightman, Dan Wilcockson, Helen Wilcockson, Peter Wilcox, Wilbur Wild, Deiniol Williams, Liz McCarthy Williams, Mark Williams, Paul Williams, Paul Williamson, Tom Wilkinson, Adam Wilson, Jared Wilson, David Wiltshire, Aubrey Wood, Jane Wood, Mark Wood, Rob Wood, Emma Woods, Ady Workman, Robert Worm, Jay Wray, Alex Wren, Kaylie Wright, Ben Wyatt, Kevin Yates, Tara Yazigi, Rebecca Young, Jon Young, Toby Young, Alvaro Zaldua, Eric Zampoli, Nathan Zivelonghi

# ALSO ON VELOCITY PRESS

## JOIN THE FUTURE
### BY MATT ANNISS

Since the dawn of the 1990s, British dance music has been in thrall to the seductive power of weighty sub-bass. It is a key ingredient in a string of British-pioneered genres, including hardcore, jungle, drum & bass, dubstep, UK garage and grime. Join The Future traces the roots, origins, development and legacy of the sound that started it all: the first distinctively British form of electronic dance music, bleep techno.

## STATE OF BASS
### BY MARTIN JAMES

As UK government legislation, standardised music and bad drugs forced the euphoria of the rave into the darkness, a new underground movement emerged – jungle/drum & bass. Drawing on interviews with some of the key figures in the early years, State of Bass explores the scene's social, cultural and musical roots via the sonic shifts that charted the journey from deep underground to global phenomenon.

## FLYER & COVER ART
### BY JUNIOR TOMLIN

Showcasing the mastermind behind some of the most iconic rave flyers and record covers of the late eighties and early nineties, Flyer & Cover Art is a comprehensive insight into Junior Tomlin's incredible back catalogue. It is the first time his work has been documented and presented in such a comprehensive, cohesive fashion.

## BEDROOM BEATS & B-SIDES
### BY LAURENT FINTONI

Bedroom Beats & B-sides is the first comprehensive history of the instrumental hip-hop and electronic scenes and a truly global look at a thirty-year period of modern music culture based on a decade of research and travel across Europe, North America, and Japan. Combining social, cultural, and musical history with extensive research and over 100 interviews, the book tells the B-side stories of hip-hop and electronic music from the 1990s to the 2010s.

## BOOK TWO
### BY THE SECRET DJ

In this hilarious, gripping and at times deeply moving follow-up to the smash hit first book, the mysterious insider pulls no punches, wryly lifting the lid on misbehaving stars, what really goes on backstage, how to survive in the DJ game, and where the real power lies in rave. Above all, they chart how capitalism bought and sold the utopian dreams of the Acid House generation - and whether those dreams can still be saved.

## SYNTHESIZER EVOLUTION
### BY OLI FREKE

Synthesizer Evolution celebrates the impact of synths on music and culture by providing a comprehensive and meticulously researched directory of every major synthesizer, drum machine and sampler made between 1963 and 1995. Each instrument is illustrated by hand, and shown alongside its vital statistics and some fascinatingly quirky facts.

## WHO SAY RELOAD
### BY PAUL TERZULLI & EDDIE OTCHERE

Who Say Reload is a knockout oral history of the records that defined jungle/drum & bass straight from the original sources. The likes of Goldie, DJ Hype, Roni Size, Andy C, 4 Hero and many more talk about the influences, environment, equipment, samples, beats and surprises that went into making each classic record.

## LONG RELATIONSHIPS
### BY HAROLD HEATH

Written by former DJ/producer Harold Heath, Long Relationships is a biographical account of a DJ career defined by a deep love of music and a shallow amount of success. From the days of vinyl, when DJs were often also glass-collectors, to the era of megastar stadium EDM, it's a journey of 30 odd years on a low-level, economy-class rollercoaster through the ups and downs of an ever-changing music industry.

## TRIP CITY
### BY TREVOR MILLER

In the summer of 1989, when Trip City was first released with a soundtrack by A Guy Called Gerald, there had been no other British novel like it. This was the down and dirty side of London nightclubs, dance music and the kind of hallucinogenic drug sub-culture that hadn't really been explored since Tom Wolfe's The Electric Kool-Aid Acid Test. Maybe this is why Trip City is still known as "the acid house novel" and an underground literary landmark.

## THE LABEL MACHINE
### BY NICK SADLER

The Label Machine is the ultimate guide to starting, running and growing your independent record label. You will learn all about the music industry business and how to navigate the tricky dos and don'ts.

## DAFT PUNK'S DISCOVERY
### BY BEN CARDEW

Daft Punk's Discovery is a homage to a fascinating, troubled beast of an album that casts a huge shadow over the 21st Century. It's a global view of Discovery as a cultural phenomenon, placing the album at the centre of celebrity culture, fan clubs, video, the music business etc., while also examining its profound musical impact.

## TAPE LEADERS
### BY IAN HELLIWELL

In the form of a richly illustrated compendium, Tape Leaders is an indispensable reference guide for anyone interested in electronic sound and its origins in Great Britain. For the first time a book sets out information on practically everyone active with experimental electronics and tape recording across the country, to reveal the untold stories and hidden history of early British electronic music.

## THE SECRET DJ PRESENTS TALES FROM THE BOOTH

Tales From the Booth raises the BPM, rounding up an all-star cast of Secret DJs to tell their anonymous stories of what it's really like to rock dancefloors for a living. From strange encounters on tour to side-splitting debauchery and afterparty excess to the seamy and even dangerous side of the industry, this is your access-all-areas backstage pass.

## COMING TO BERLIN
### BY PAUL HANFORD

Coming To Berlin reflects, through the lives and music of migrants, settlers and newcomers, how a constantly in flux city with a tumultuous history has evolved into the de facto cultural capital of Europe. And how at the heart of this, electronic music and club culture play a unique role.

## FRENCH CONNECTIONS
### BY MARTIN JAMES

Drawing on a dazzling array of exclusive interviews with the biggest names in French electronic music history, French Connections: From Discotheque to Daft Punk - The Birth Of French Touch explores France's significant contribution to dance music culture that paved the way for the French Touch explosion.

## OUT OF SPACE
### BY JIM OTTEWILL

Out of Space plots a course through the different UK towns and cities club culture has found a home. From Glasgow to Margate via Manchester, Sheffield and unlikely dance music meccas such as Coalville and Todmorden, this book maps where electronic music has thrived, and where it might be headed to next...

# VELOCITYPRESS.UK/BOOKS